Ballads of the Lords of New Spain

THE WILLIAM & BETTYE NOWLIN SERIES
in Art, History, and Culture of the Western Hemisphere

Ballads of the Lords of New Spain

The Codex *Romances de los Señores de la Nueva España*

Transcribed and translated from the Nahuatl by

John Bierhorst

University of Texas Press, Austin

Requests for permission to reproduce material from this work
should be sent to:

Permissions

University of Texas Press

P. O. Box 7819

Austin, TX 78713-7819

www.utexas.edu/utpress/about/bpermision.html

⊗ The paper used in this book meets the minimum requirements
of ANSI/NISO Z39.48-1992 (R1997) (Permanence of Paper).

Library of Congress Cataloging-in-Publication Data

Romances de los señores de la Nueva España. English & Aztec.

   Ballads of the lords of New Spain : the codex Romances de los
señores de la Nueva España / transcribed and translated from the
Nahuatl by John Bierhorst. — 1st ed.

       p.   cm. — (The William and Bettye Nowlin series in art,
history, and culture of the western hemisphere)

   Includes bibliographical references and index.

   ISBN 978-0-292-72345-0

   1. Nahuatl poetry. 2. Nahuatl poetry — Translations into English.
I. Bierhorst, John.   II. Title.

   PM4068.6.R65 2009

   897'.4521008 — dc22

                                              2008025278

Contents

Preface

Comprising thirty-six song-texts apparently dating from the early fourth quarter of the sixteenth century, the so-called *Romances,* or "ballads," stands as one of the two principal sources of Nahuatl song. Unlike its sister compilation, the more voluminous *Cantares Mexicanos,* the *Romances,* whether by design or accident, takes the form of an organized anthology — an Aztec *cancionero* — that may be read with a sense of unity from start to finish.

Although it can be agreed, at least, that Aztec songs are richly figurative and carry an aura of mystery, the underlying question is whether they are inscrutable. Is it profitable to consider them at all? In my view, now as previously, the answer is yes, both for the sake of history and for the sake of art. Yet as early as the 1580s, when the songs were being performed in public, the redoubtable missionary-ethnographer Bernardino de Sahagún seemingly took a stand against translation, warning that "no one knows what [the singers] say except themselves alone," thus hinting at a position still widely, if tacitly, respected. That is, by cautiously steering away from the topic, many Mexicanists have treated Aztec "poetry" as something akin to what the late Franz Boas — the father of American anthropology and an occasional Mexicanist himself — used to call a *Scheinproblem,* or sham problem, to be avoided as insoluble.

A second view, developed by antiquaries and latter-day historians in the early 1600s, takes the songs to be poetic ruminations of old kings stationed in flowery gardens — like shepherds stepped out of the *Eclogues* — interlarded with firsthand reportage from pre-Cortésian battlefields. The method compartmentalizes the two aspects of the genre, the aesthetic and the martial, treating the texts as a mass of fragments to be examined for scraps of history, on one hand, and, on the other, bits of found poetry that seem to touch on classic themes of friendship and mortality. This kind of interpretation, which casts a glow of humanism over Mexico's ancient past, survived through the end of the twentieth century and is not likely to be abandoned.

A third view is suggested by Sahagún's equally sober but provocative observation that the native leaders were "using" the songs "to persuade the people to do their bidding, whether it's war or other business that is not good." My earlier edition of the *Cantares*—*Cantares Mexicanos: Songs of the Aztecs*—explored this third approach, presenting Aztec songs as a mid- to late-sixteenth-century testament of nativism and defiance in the face of colonial authority.

The *Romances de los Señores de la Nueva España,* then, offers another opportunity to consider the matter. More integrated than the *Cantares,* as mentioned above, and not as overtly ethnographic, the *Romances* is surely connected to the social fabric of its time, even if transcending it as a perennially fascinating work of ritualistic art.

I am indebted to the many who commented on the *Cantares* edition in published essays and in private communications. In the work that follows I have addressed the questions they have raised and have accepted various suggestions. I especially thank Louise Burkhart for putting the interpretation of colonial Nahuatl texts on a more secure footing; James Lockhart for a quarter-century's worth of spirited criticism; James Taggart for his reminder that the native term *netotiliztli* is sufficient to designate the genre represented by the songs in the *Cantares* and *Romances* manuscripts; Jane H. Hill and the late Robert E. MacLaury for their analysis of the role of Montezuma in sixteenth-century mythmaking; Elizabeth R. Wright for her reflections on European and Mexican literatures; and John Ceely, Alan Sandstrom, and, again, James Taggart, generally, for their insights and encouragement.

My overall view of the *netotiliztli,* emphasizing the passage of native warriors to and from the other world, corresponds to an observation set forth in the 1964 edition of the *Romances* prepared by Angel M. Garibay K., who may be given credit here. On pages 106–7 of that work, Garibay singles out the *xochicuahuitl,* or "flower tree," of *Romances* songs II, XI, XII, and XXXIII, treating it as a guiding concept:

> [. . .] it puts us on the road of correct investigation. The antecedent of this concept is well documented in the complex of ancient prehispanic codices. For each of the directions of the universe there is a particular tree; and in the center, another. Surrounding the central tree are

the beings who came from this life and will return to it. There exists in the ancient culture, not wholly explored, a doctrine of reversion to the present life (*[…] nos lleva por el camino de la indagación recta. El antecedente de este concepto se halla bien documentado en el conjunto de códices de la antigüedad prehispánica. Para cada dirección del universo hay un árbol especial. En el centro hay otro. En torno de éste se hallan agrupados los seres que vinieron de la vida y regresarán a ella. Hay en la antigua cultura, no del todo explorada, una doctrina de la reversión a la vida presente*).

Although my readings differ from Garibay's in significant ways, it will be seen that I have continued to travel the indicated "road."

I acknowledge, gratefully, the Nettie Lee Benson Collection, University of Texas Libraries, Austin, for access to the *Romances* manuscript; the pioneering edition of the *Romances* published by the late Angel Garibay, as noted, still useful after forty years; the National Endowment for the Arts and the National Endowment for the Humanities for their repeated support; and especially the National Endowment for the Arts Translators Fellowship that enabled me to complete the present work.

A Note on Orthography

In the following pages Nahuatl terms, wherever introduced in isolation from a particular text, are written in a modernized Franciscan orthography descended from the spelling methods of the Franciscan missionary-linguists of the 1500s. This is the Spanish-flavored orthography widely used by present-day writers on Mexican topics, generally disregarding vowel length and the glottal stop. Thus vowels, roughly speaking, have the continental sounds (*ah, eh, ee, oh, oo*), except that *oh* and *oo*, both represented by the letter "o," are not distinguished from each other. Consonants are approximately as in English, except that "x" is pronounced *sh*, "z" has the sound of the "s" in "simple," and the combinations "cu," "hu," and "tl" are similar to English "qu" (in "quick"), "w" (in "water"), and "tl" (in "atlas" whether initial, final, or mid-word, never like the "tl" in "bottle").

A modernized Jesuit system, derived especially from the seventeenth-century Jesuit grammarian Horacio Carochi, differs from the Franciscan in marking long vowels with a macron, or overbar, and in consistently using the letter "h" (except in the combination "hu," see above) to signal the glottal stop. At various points in the present work, terms are respelled in the modernized Jesuit system so that they may be found more easily in modern dictionaries such as Frances Karttunen's *Analytical Dictionary of Nahuatl* and my own *Nahuatl-English Dictionary* (here cited as DICT). For simplicity, macrons are omitted except in a few cases, as needed.

The *Romances* transcription, however, is strictly paleographic (not respelled or repunctuated), and all quotations from the *Romances* are likewise paleographic, regardless of inconsistencies and outright errors (which are clarified, as necessary, in footnotes to the English translation). Similarly, quotations from the Florentine Codex (CF or FC), *Cantares Mexica-*

nos (CM or CMSA), Alonso de Molina's *Vocabulario* (MOL and MOLS), and other old texts are paleographic.

It may be added that all linguists seem to accept Carochi's (oversimplified?) dictum that Classical Nahuatl words are to be stressed on the second-to-last syllable.

Further observations on Franciscan, Jesuit, and paleographic orthographies will be found in CMSA xi–xiii and DICT 8–11.

Using the Online Edition

The University of Texas Libraries, together with the University of Texas Press, has launched a complete online version of the print edition of the *Ballads of the Lords of New Spain* at www.utdigital.org. The website reproduces the Nahuatl text and English translation as printed here, but with "pop-up" excerpts from the Commentary to allow the songs and the explanatory synopses to be read together. Extra features include a normative transcription (searchable), a map showing the "geography" of the *Ballads*, audio of the two-tone drum cadences accompanying two of the songs, and a photographic facsimile of the *Ballads* codex.

In addition—and with a nod to the expanding field of corpus linguistics—the *Ballads* website amplifies the "whole corpus" approach to translating and interpreting both the *Ballads* and the closely related codex *Cantares Mexicanos* by mounting a single-word extract from the *Ballads/Cantares* concordance that demonstrates the unity of the diction. To facilitate the interpretation of the *Ballads*, the website includes the *Cantares Mexicanos: Songs of the Aztecs* and *A Nahuatl-English Dictionary and Concordance to the Cantares Mexicanos*, courtesy of Stanford University Press.

A word of thanks is due E. Casey Kittrell at the University of Texas Press for conceiving the *Ballads* website and guiding it to completion, and to the University of Texas Libraries and its Nettie Lee Benson Latin American Collection for co-sponsoring the project.

Ballads of the Lords of New Spain

Introduction

The *Romances de los señores de la Nueva España,* or *Romances,* as the codex has been called for short, is a hastily penned Nahuatl manuscript of forty-two folios, undated, unsigned, and with a few stray comments in Spanish, jotted even more hastily, by an anonymous glossator. Evidently the work is a transcript of an original now lost, with numerous scribal lapses that betray imperfect copying.

Preserved with the *Relación* of Juan Bautista de Pomar, composed March 9, 1582, as its author states, the *Romances* may have been intended as an adjunct to the *Relación* and therefore compiled about the same time. The extant copy of both *Relación* and *Romances,* however, has been assigned to the 1600s.[1] As for the presumed *Romances* original of ca. 1582, behind it one glimpses no fewer than four urtexts, perhaps workbooks, from which the compiler drew the four *partes* of his compilation. These hypothetical workbooks, containing the texts of *cuicatl* 'songs', subsequently dubbed *romances* 'ballads', were evidently taken from the lips of native singers.

To whom, then, might we owe the workbooks or worksheets? Angel M. Garibay, the first modern editor of the *Romances,* suggested that during the second half of the 1500s, when the initial dictation seems to have taken place, there could have been no one but the tireless and resourceful Bernardino de Sahagún, orchestrator of the encyclopedic Florentine Codex and (very possibly) the unsigned *Cantares Mexicanos,* who might have recorded such material; or at least the method was his, if we assume that Pomar prepared the urtexts; and perhaps Pomar had been a student or follower of Sahagún's.[2] Of Pomar little is actually known aside from his authorship of

---

1. "[…] de letra antigua, como de los primeros años del siglo XVII" (García Icazbalceta 1941, vol. 3, p. vii), a judgment accepted in Gibson and Glass 1975:355–56; and CMSA p. 85.
2. Garibay 1964:x–xi.

the *Relación,* which summarily treats the history, customs, and physical environment of Texcoco, the old seat of Acolhuan kings (thirty kilometers
northeast of the center of Mexico City).[3] As noted evocatively by the early-
seventeenth-century historian Fernando de Alva Ixtlilxóchitl, Pomar was
one of several *infantes de la ciudad de Tetzcuco, hijos y nietos del rey Nezahualpiltzintli de Tetzcuco* 'princes of the city of Texcoco, sons and grandsons of
King Nezahualpiltzintli of Texcoco'.[4]

As for the thirty-six songs of the *Romances* itself, these are not only in
Nahuatl but in oral Nahuatl, as distinguished from the written Nahuatl of
missionaries and acculturated native speakers. The difference is between an
older, economical (or paratactical) diction and a newer manner influenced
by Spanish syntax. A barrier between the two styles is detectable, and in
the case of song diction quite pronounced, since the singers distorted their
utterances with untranslatable vocables. The point is worth making because
Aztec songs were already beginning to be imitated, sometimes deceptively,
by writers using Nahuatl.[5] The songs in the *Romances* are oral productions.

The Terms *Romances,*
Señores, and *Nueva España*

Like the old ballads of England and Scotland, which express a broad range
of human concerns, the *romances,* or ballads, of Spain cannot, or should
not, be characterized in a word. Yet the twentieth-century scholar and collector of Spanish and Latin American folklore, Aurelio Espinosa, undoubtedly expressed a sentiment of long standing in stating repeatedly that the
Spanish *romances* were to be identified first and foremost as "the old historical ballads that sing the praises of the Castilian heroes in their struggles
to reconquer Spain."[6] These Spanish ballads, which began to be collected in
the 1500s, derive from the celebrated *cantares,* or epics, of the eleventh and

3. Pomar's *Relación* has been published in García Icazbalceta 1941, vol. 3; and in Garibay
1964.
4. IXT 2:137. Further notice of Pomar is in TORQ lib. 11, cap. 27, including the information
that Pomar's mother had been born to Nezahualpilli and a slave woman.
5. Apparently the earliest are songs I–XIII in the *Cantares* manuscript, bearing traces of
the newer, more literary manner even though vocables have not been entirely left behind. Various observations are included in the sections labeled "Missionary Nahuatl" and "Remarks" in
CMSA pp. 47, 430–34.
6. Espinosa 1985:77; cf. Espinosa 1972. Discussion of Espinosa is in Smith 1972:8 et seq.

twelfth centuries, notably the *Cantar de mío Cid,* an epic of 3,735 lines, which itself is divided into three parts, or *cantares.*

Comparison, therefore, came easily to the sixteenth-century collectors of the Aztec *cuicatl* 'songs', who found the Nahuatl texts peppered with the vocabulary of war and the names of old kings and dubbed the two principal collections *Cantares mexicanos* and *Romances de los señores de la Nueva España.*

Señores, in sixteenth-century Mexican Spanish usage, are 'lords', meaning rulers of pre-Conquest city states 'in all that is now called New Spain' (*en todo lo que agora se llama nueva españa*), with the term *rey* 'king' reserved for the most important among them. As for Tenochtitlan, its *señores* were 'emperors' (*los señores della fuerõ emperadores*).[7]

The title of our manuscript, then, with its emphasis on "rulers," may be compared with the Nahuatl heading given to songs XX–XLIII of the *Cantares Mexicanos* by its glossator:

> Here begin the so-called plain songs that used to be performed in the palaces of Mexico, Acolhuacan, and the Dry Lands in order to entertain the rulers. *Nican ompehua in motenehua Melahuac cuicatl yn mehuaya tecpan Mexico Acolhuacan tlalhuacpã ynic ymelel quiçaya tlahtoque.* (*Cantares* 16v: 4–6)

Melahuac cuicatl 'plain song' is the term used by missionaries for the heterometric *canto llano* of the church. If the native *cuicatl* of the kind found in the *Cantares* and the *Romances* were heterometric (without regular meter), as seems likely, this could have been a designation applicable to all these songs.[8] The three locations refer to pre-Conquest Mexico and its two Triple Alliance partners, Acolhuacan (or Texcoco) and Tepanecapan (also called *tlalhuacpan* 'dry lands').[9] Thus *romances de los señores de la Nueva España* may be taken as an approximate paraphrase of the heading used for *Cantares* songs XX–XLIII—four of which in fact recur in the *Romances* as songs II (*Cantares* XXV), XIX (*Cantares* XXVIII), XXIII (*Cantares* XLIII), and XXVIII (*Cantares* XL).

7. FC introductory volume, 70.
8. CMSA pp. 44, 82, 93.
9. DICT tlalhuacpan 2.

Relationship to the *Cantares*

In addition to *Romances* songs II, XIX, XXIII, and XXVIII, eight other songs, or parts of songs, have close variants in the *Cantares*. These are *Romances* VI, XI, XIV, XVIII, XX, XXI, XXIV, and XXVII. In all, about thirty-six percent of the *Romances* reappears in the *Cantares*.

Minor differences in wording reveal that the songs were not simply transferred from one compilation to the other, and in some cases there is wholesale rearranging of stanzas. Evidently the texts derive from independent recitations.

The editorial style of the two manuscripts is similar, however. In both compilations the stanza form of the songs is clearly indicated, with each stanza presented as a discrete paragraph; and, in both, occasional drum cadences are given, using the syllables *to, co, ti,* and *qui.*

Like the *Romances,* the *Cantares* is unsigned. Various clues, such as vocabulary items from the *Cantares* that Sahagún utilized in his *Psalmodia christiana* and the stylistic resemblance between *Cantares* folios 60, 60v, and 73 and Sahagún's *Memoriales con escolios,* indicate that the *Cantares* may have been prepared under Sahagún's direction,[10] as suggested above. A link between Sahagún and the *Romances,* also mentioned above, is less clear, though not inconceivable.

The *Romances* as a Unified Work

Like the *Cantares* manuscript, the *Romances* seems to have grown by accretion, adding songs in recognizable groups. Yet its songs taken together have a unity lacking in the *Cantares.* Nearly all have eight stanzas. Only the older rulers are mentioned, none who held office later than the 1520s, and none, even if baptized, who are called in the songs by their baptismal names. Historical events, whether pre-Conquest (i.e., pre-1521) or post-Conquest, are never directly talked about, so that the songs, at least superficially, have a timeless quality even if datable rulers are named.

A natural question is whether the arrangement of songs in the *Romances* reflects the compiler's taste or the order of native performance on (four?) particular occasions.

10. CMSA pp. 11–12.

It may be noted that each of the four parts (except part three) begins with a kind of incipit or invitational phrase: "Friends, let us sing" (part one), "Now let us begin" (part two), "Begin in beauty" (part four). Not lacking are songs that challenge, or at least doubt, the native doctrine of the warrior's passage to and from the other world, the staple precept of the entire repertory. Yet the final song in each of the four parts of the *Romances,* or at least parts one, three, and four, reaffirms this religio-militarist dogma.

By contrast, the *Cantares* is more of a disorganized source book, with short songs and lengthy, rambling songs intermixed; songs with narrative and satiric elements; songs that have Bible stories sandwiched in with native material; and songs that reenact actual battles, including the Conquest of 1521. Far removed, no doubt, from the pre-Conquest mnemonic aids called *cuicaamatl* 'song sheet(s)' or *amoxxotl* 'book(s) more or less',[11] the *Romances* manuscript with its neat division into four parts and its presumed date (1582) calls to mind the Spanish verse anthologies, or *cancioneros,* of the fifteenth and sixteenth centuries, especially the well-known *Flores de baria poesía,* compiled in Mexico City just five years earlier, in 1577, and neatly divided into five parts.[12] With some justification we may therefore refer to the *Romances* as a Nahuatl *cancionero.*

Rulers Named in the *Romances*

In the highly schematized world of the songs all kings and their warriors are *teteuctin, pipiltin* 'lords, princes', interchangeable terms denoting members of the princely class. Warriors are not called by name unless they are the warrior kings themselves, with exceptions made for a few heroic military leaders and high officials of the city-state of Mexico.

In the *Romances* the named rulers may be divided into two major categories, each with three subcategories:

1. Rulers of Triple Alliance cities
   A. Rulers of Mexico
      i. Borough of Tenochtitlan
      ii. Borough of Tlatelolco

---

11. FC bk. 3, app. ch. 8, p. 65 (cf. HG 1, lib. 3, ap. cap. 8, p. 307); FC bk. 10, ch. 29, "Mexica" sec., p. 191.

12. Peña 2004:126.

    B. Rulers of Texcoco (Acolhuacan)
    C. Rulers of Tlacopan (Tepanecapan)
2. Rulers of non–Triple Alliance cities
    A. Rulers of Huexotzincan cities
    B. Rulers of Tlaxcalan cities
    C. Rulers of Chalcan cities

When named in combination within a single stanza, the rulers are always from either category 1 or category 2, never mixed, though representatives of both categories may appear within a single song. As is well known, Huexotzinco, Tlaxcala, and Chalco were the traditional enemies of Mexico and its Triple Alliance partners—and allies of Hernán Cortés in the Conquest of 1521. In a few songs Tepanecapan (category 1C) is represented by the city of Azcapotzalco, the seat of Tepanecapan prior to 1430, when its government was moved to Tlacopan. And while Acolhuacan (category 1B) is generally treated as Mexico's ally, in some songs it emerges as an enemy (as in *Cantares* song 15), since it defected—or a faction defected—to Cortés in the final struggle of 1521.

The Texcoco Connection

The singer or singers responsible for the *Romances* seem to have a particular fondness for songs that name Texcocan rulers. Or else the compiler, if he picked and chose, favored such songs. Number XXIII raises the possibility not merely of selection but of tampering.

Romances XXIII appears also as *Cantares* XLIII (which is the third in a suite of three songs) and again in *Cantares* LXII (as the third part in a three-part song). All versions treat "Cuacuauhtzin," presumably the fourteenth-century Cuacuauhtzin who was king of Tlatelolco. But "Cuacuauhtzin" is also the name of a fifteenth-century ruler of Tepechpan, a small city controlled by Texcoco—according to several sources,[13] including the anonymous *Romances* glossator (who labels song XXIII "of Cuacuauhtzin, lord of Tepechpan") and the Texcocan historian Alva Ixtlilxóchitl. Ixtlilxóchitl relates, colorfully, that King Nezahualcoyotl of Texcoco sent the Tepechpan ruler to his death in battle in order to obtain his beautiful wife for himself;

---

13. Described in León-Portilla 1967:77–87, 1992:99–111.

and before setting off, this "Cuacuauhtzin" gathered his "friends" (*amigos*) and sang for them "some sad songs" (*unos cantos lastimosos*).[14] Did Ixtlilxóchitl use the *Romances* as his source?

The *Cantares* versions do not mention Nezahualcoyotl, while the *Romances* version, differently, has the third-stanza verbs in the second person (rather than the first person), interpolating "you, Yoyontzin [an alternate name for Nezahualcoyotl]." As for the "friends" and the "sad songs," the *Cantares* and *Romances* texts both have *tocnihuan* 'friends', *cuicatl* 'song(s)', *nentlamati* 'grieve', and *choca* 'weep', but these terms are formulaic throughout the two manuscripts. It is conceivable that the *Romances* singer has doctored the song to give it a Texcocan flavor and that Alva Ixtlilxóchitl cooked up the story about the gathering of "friends" and the "sad songs," using the *Romances* text and his own imagination.

The similar case of song XXVI, in which the singer appears to have adapted Mexica material by inserting the name of the Texcocan ruler Cacamatl, is discussed in the Commentary.

The *Romances* Glossator

Both the *Cantares* and the *Romances* manuscripts have their incautious glossators, who evidently understand Nahuatl but, of course, are versed in the new written tradition. Their training in the oral tradition, if any, cannot be verified.

Both commentators are interested in labeling or detecting pre-Cortésian material. The *Cantares* glossator, for instance, has labeled *Cantares* XX–XLIII as songs "that used to be performed in the palaces," as noted above. But since the twenty-four songs in question invoke God, Santa María, and Jesucristo, the description is in need of qualification at the very least. In the same vein the *Romances* commentator constantly glosses the textual *dios* 'God' with the expression *totecoyo*, as he writes it (i.e., *toteucyo* 'our lord'), a useless observation if he means 'our lord' in the Christian sense. However, *toteucyo* is pre-Cortésian usage for addressing or referring to the god Tezcatlipoca.[15] Further, song XVIII as a whole, which addresses the supreme power as father, God, and *ipalnemohua* 'life giver', is glossed *a lo divino gen-*

---

14. IXT 2:117–20 (cap. 43).
15. FC 6:1:18, FC 6:95:10, and FC 6 passim.

tilico 'to the pagan divinity'. The name Ipalnemohua apparently did refer to Tezcatlipoca in pre-Conquest usage, yet in colonial texts it much more frequently meant *dios*.[16] As he looks for the idol behind the altar, brushing aside the contemporary reality, the glossator stands at the head of a persistent and very long tradition.

Other songs are seen as eyewitness accounts of specific historical events, a kind of newspaper archive in which we may read the declarations and responses of the key participants. Thus song V, the glossator believes, reports the agony of Cacamatl (and in his own words) as he faced death at the hands of the Spaniards in 1520. Songs XIX and XXVII are also imagined as reportage (on the events leading up to the Tepanec War, ca. 1430, and on a war between Mexico and Huexotzinco, ca. 1498). The similar case of song XXIII and its connection with the historian Alva Ixtlilxóchitl has been reviewed above. Treated elsewhere is the difficult question as to whether this glossator could have been Ixtlilxóchitl himself.[17]

And it may be asked whether the gloss *de Nezahualcoyotzin* for songs XVII, XIX, XXVIII, and XXXIII means that the glossator considered Nezahualcoyotl the author of at least these four pieces. His preposition *de* 'of' need only mean 'pertaining to', not 'authored by'; but it is well known that Alva Ixtlilxóchitl regarded Nezahualcoyotl as a composer (probably on account of the phrase "I, Nezahualcoyotl" in some of the song texts). The internal evidence of the songs themselves, in context with the formulaic diction of the *Cantares* and *Romances* as a whole, fails to support Ixtlilxóchitl's conjecture. Nor is there native testimony that any pre-Conquest ruler had (or had not) been a composer or even legendarily a composer. Documentary evidence, frequently claimed to exist, has never been produced. The matter is discussed at length elsewhere.[18]

Dating the Songs

Filled with references to *dios*, the songs in their present form could not have been put together earlier than the Conquest period, 1519–21, and more likely after the beginning of Franciscan evangelization in 1523–24.[19] A still later—

---

16. DICT ipalnemohuani.
17. CMSA pp. 85–86, 446; cf. ibid.: 96, 101–5, 112–18, 477.
18. CMSA pp. 97–105. See also the Commentary for songs XIX and XXII, below.
19. Ricard 1966:2, 21.

perhaps much later—date may be required if the subtlety of the Christian allusions in the *Romances* is fully appreciated.

Time may be needed to convert *dios* into *dios ipalnemohua* and to add *espiritu santo* 'Holy Spirit' (1v:15) and *S maria* 'Saint Mary' (10:2). Subtler still are the *huelica tzihuatl* (read *huelic cihuatl*) 'fragrant woman' at 7:12–13 and the *tocuiyc tonatihu* (read *to[te]cuiyo tonatiuh*) 'Our Lord the Sun' at 10:1. These are evidently not syncretic terms for Mary and Jesus, as might seem, but adaptations into Nahuatl of established Old World concepts, in which the mother of Christ is identified with a proverbial garden and Christ himself with the sun.[20]

In song V there is a reference to "God's loved ones," meaning the dead warriors, or "loved ones," of pre-Conquest lore who reside in the house of the sun. But "*God's* loved ones" are the saints of Christianity residing as angels in heaven (see the Commentary for song V).

It might be supposed that Christian touches are irrelevant, since the terms could have been tacked onto old songs at the last minute. Such a possibility is hard to entertain, however, since the same phrases in the same positions (mentioning *dios*) are found in some of the *Romances* and *Cantares* duplicates, or near duplicates, that otherwise vary, indicating separate performances if not separate singers.

Further, stylistic unity throughout the *Romances* and across the *Cantares* argues for a single school of composition, not various schools scattered over centuries or even decades.

Two of the songs in the *Romances*, I and X, make use of historical figures from different time frames. Song I has them separated by a generation, song X by several generations. In both cases the more recent figures, mostly from category 2 (see above), belong to the Conquest of 1521. The older figures, proverbial heroes from category 1, rise out of a more distant past; and, in both cases, category-1 figures are given the last word. It is difficult, therefore, to imagine a date of composition very close to the most recent of these time frames (i.e., 1521), since the named rulers and heroes—with chronological distance—seem to have become mere symbols.

Four songs in the *Cantares*, LV, LVI, LVIII, and LIX, carry the dates 1553,

---

20. Burkhart traces Mary's identification with the biblical *hortus conclusus* to medieval texts as early as the twelfth century (Burkhart 2001:15, 25, 54) and finds that the identification of Christ with the sun was a "liturgical standard" (Burkhart 2001:25, 28, 54, 68; Burkhart 1988).

1550, 1564, and 1536, respectively. The aberrant 1536 is most likely a copyist's error for 1563,[21] and the first and third of the four dates should probably be corrected to 1555 and 1562.[22] Although none of these four songs has a variant in the *Romances*, the dates show that songs using the formulaic diction found in both manuscripts were being composed in the 1550s and 1560s.

A fifth date, 1581, can be proposed as an approximate terminal date. On March 27 of that year don Alonso Axayacatl, *gobernador,* or puppet ruler, of Itztapalapan and nephew of Montezuma II, made his will; presumably he died not long thereafter. Since the songs that carry dates name post-Conquest figures who died shortly before those dates, *Cantares* song XC, which names don Alonso, was probably composed in the early 1580s, if not 1581.[23] No song in the repertory mentions any figure who died later than this.

None of the foregoing is meant to suggest that pre-Conquest songs were not being retrofitted during the years 1550–85, only that these are the dates we have to work with. And in view of the singers' sheer inventiveness, brilliantly displayed in the *Cantares,* it is unnecessary to believe that native people were mindlessly parroting old songs they did not understand. It should be kept in mind that the *Cantares* and the *Romances* are not salvage ethnography, as is the Florentine Codex, but evidence of an active sixteenth-century genre, marked by borrowing back and forth between singers, the reshaping of old material, new composition, and public performances.[24]

The songs repeatedly deal with the problem of reasserting the old native war ethic in the face of Christian values. In *Cantares* song VII a singer openly contrasts the lure of battle "in the old days" with the lure of a Christian heaven, "that world of flowers in the sky." In *Cantares* song LVIII we learn that "through Santa María he came to take his precious incarnation; through his precious death he came to save us, and he gave us everlasting life." The

21. As proposed by Garibay (1953–54 1:156).

22. CMSA p. 107.

23. DICT alonso axayacatzin; CMSA pp. 413–19, 511–14; Gibson 1964:167.

24. Descriptions of public performances in Mexico City during the 1560s are in a document made known by Angel Garibay, the *Anales de Juan Bautista* (see CMSA pp. 68, 98, 461, 466–67, 480, 499, 504, 527). Lockhart 1992:399 mentions that similar (the same?) information, also from the 1560s, can be gleaned from documents in the Archivo Histórico of the Museo Nacional de Antropología e Historia. Less public, perhaps, are the performances deplored by Sahagún in the late 1570s: "This happens most frequently among the [native] merchants when they hold their feasts, entertainments, and banquets" (FC introductory volume, p. 81). Still other performances, sponsored by the native *gobernadores,* are discussed below.

Romances does not include texts as explicit as these. But the ferment is there, as the singers struggle to forge a nativistic doctrine combining old and new elements.[25]

Linguistic hypertrophism may also serve as an age indicator, deceptively perhaps. One jumps to the conclusion that overloaded verbs and compound nouns prove ancientness. But the opposite may be closer to the truth. Florid locutions such as *teoaxochicuauhcocoltica* 'with flood-flower eagle sadness' (*Romances* IV:7–8) or *tiquetzalzacuanxiuhquecholhuihuicomacan* 'let's make troupial-and-turquoise-swan plumes twirl' (*Cantares* 47:24), so unlike the leaner diction in the Florentine Codex, even in the no doubt pre-Cortésian "devil" songs, suggest a combative verbal stance more Aztec than the Aztecs. A sign of nativism in response to stress?[26] Similarly choked compounds, like *mochipahualizichpochaçucenaxochicelticayotzin* 'your pure and maidenly lily-flower freshness' (from a prayer addressed to Saint Mary),[27] rear up in the ambitious Nahuatl of missionaries; and even native writers were sometimes forced into weighty neologisms in order to approximate a European concept—such as 'myth' (*tlamachiliztlatolzazanilli*), literally, 'wisdom-word fable' (CC 75:1). Setting aside the question of who is imitating whom, or whether exhibitionism is at issue, the evidence is for novelty, albeit mingled with tradition.

After the 1590s

Songs of the kind found in the *Romances* were regarded as either benign or potentially dangerous, depending on whether the vantage point was before or after the 1590s. By that decade or a little earlier the songs as we know them from the *Romances* and *Cantares* manuscripts seem to have been dying out.[28]

The two manuscripts, however, were in circulation during the 1600s, along with similar song compilations that have not survived. Charmed by these relics of a presumed distant past, the new writers treated the song texts as (1) fossilized accounts of pre-Conquest doings safely entombed in the amber of history, (2) evidence for the existence of pre-Conquest poet-

---

25. See especially song XXXIV and the corresponding Commentary.
26. The matter is discussed in CMSA pp. 47, 109; GRAM sec. 8.3.
27. Burkhart 2001:56 (translating from the *Santoral en mexicano*).
28. See below (the rest of the Introduction).

kings, (3) echoes of glorious old failures on the battlefield, or (4) luscious imagery waiting to adorn a new polite diction in the service of Christianity. Examples of the four approaches, since these have a bearing on the devolution of Aztec song scholarship, may be summarized here:

(1) *Chimalpahin (1579–1631?).* The historian Chimalpahin, like the *Romances* glossator, used song texts as reportage, sprinkling his — nevertheless invaluable — chronicles with excerpts meant to add immediacy and color. A passage that has come to light recently in an edition by Arthur Anderson and Susan Schroeder includes the phrase *hecamecatlon onmalintoc yn chalco, in Tenuchtitlan a ohuaya ohuaya,* which the editors translate, faultlessly: 'Long discourses lie entwined in Chalco and Tenochtitlan'.[29] Faultlessly, because this is no doubt what Chimalpahin had in mind. In view of the whole corpus of surviving song texts, however, the more probable reading is *he ca mecatlon onmalintoc yn chalco in tenochtitlan a ohuaya ohuaya* 'Hey! for the garlands are whirling in Chalco, in Tenochtitlan! Ah! Ohuaya, ohuaya'. 'Garlands', in the diction of the *Cantares* and the *Romances,* are incoming warriors from the other world; and while the entire song, had it been preserved, would probably recollect a pre-Cortésian struggle between Tenochtitlan and Chalco, it would also echo the Spanish conquest of Tenochtitlan in 1521, in which Chalco played a role.

(2) *Cantares de Nezahualcóyotl (1618).* Purportedly dictated to Alva Ixtlilxóchitl but more likely gleaned by him from earlier manuscripts, these *cantares* include a "lamentation" that begins: *Tlacxoconcaquican hani Nezahualcoyotzin etcétera* (read *Tlaoc xoconcaquican ha niNezahualcoyotzin etcétera*) 'Listen indeed to what I, Nezahualcoyotl, etc.'. No further Nahuatl text is given, but Ixtlilxóchitl offers his Spanish translation of the entire seven stanzas, beginning: 'Listen carefully to the lamentations that I, King Nezahualcoyotl, make regarding the empire [...]. O king [meaning Tezozomoc, chief ruler of the Triple Alliance during Nezahualcoyotl's younger years], [...] when that time comes after your death [...] then the mandate and governance of the empire will not be in your hands but in the hands of Dios the Creator and All Powerful'.[30] Thus Nezahualcoyotl, whom Alva

---

29. ACHIM 2:47–49.

30. IXT 1:26 (the date and other details), 1:546 (composed songs of much morality), 2:132 (songs as though they were prophecies), 2:132 (Nahuatl text), 2:267 (Spanish transla-

Ixtlilxóchitl calls a composer of songs "of much morality" and songs "as though they were prophecies," predicts the Spanish Conquest nearly a century before the event.

(3) *Discursos en mexicano* (*1640s*). A thinly disguised etiquette manual with an agenda of language improvement,[31] the *Discursos* re-creates an antique milieu by drawing upon various Nahuatl manuscripts from the previous century.[32] One passage, showing how a *gobernador* might elegantly reply to a group of singers who have just entertained him, incorporates phraseology from an actual song: *Auh huel ōnonnotlamachtì, huel ic ōnompāc ïnīc ōnichuālcactoca ōanconmēhuilìquè yāōcuīcatl ic pŏyōmicquè Ācōlhuàquè tlaxcallan yāōtĕpānco, ye achi quēxquich cāhuitl in niquelēhuia noconcaquiz*[33] 'Well now, I quite enjoyed myself—I was quite glad to be hearing your good selves sing that war song in which the Acolhuans died gloriously on the battlefield in Tlaxcala; for quite some time now I've wished to hear it!' The translation follows Garibay, who sees *pŏyōmicquè* as 'died a perfumed death' (*poyon-*, the combining form of *poyomatli*, as in *Romances* 1:13), freely 'died gloriously', which is no doubt what the author was thinking. But an idiomatic reading of the song diction requires *pŏyōmicquè* to be translated '[are] drunkards' (i.e., "drunk" on blood lust), turning the *gobernador*'s 'I've

---

tion); CMSA pp. 116–17 (commentary); Gibson and Glass 1975:352–53 (on the *Cantares de Nezahualcóyotl*).

31. Among the influential courtesy books of the sixteenth and seventeenth centuries, beginning with Baldassare Castiglione's *Il libro del cortegiano* (1528), a likely source of inspiration (though not a model) for the *Discursos en mexicano* would appear to be Stefano Guazzo's *La civil conversatione* (1574), especially its book two: 'which holds forth [. . .] on the particulars to be observed in the conversations between young and old, nobles and commoners, officials and citizens [. . .], religious and lay persons [. . .]' (*si discorre [. . .] delle particolari che debbono tenere, conversando insieme, giovani e vecchi, nobili e ignobili, principi e privati [. . .] religiosi e secolari [. . .]*) (Guazzo 1993 1:77). I am indebted to Elizabeth R. Wright for calling my attention to Guazzo.

32. The *Discursos*, then, is a product not of the folk but of the library.

33. "Discursos en mexicano" 12v:27–30; cf. Garibay 1943:104; Karttunen and Lockhart 1987:164–65. The elsewhere unattested *poyomicque* (i.e., *poyonmicque*, better *poyommicque*) may be compared to the homologous *xocomicque* (DICT); see also DICT *poyon, poyomahtli* (and note that *poyomahtli* has the combining form *poyon-*, written *poyo-*, at *Romances* 1:13). The usage *poyo*(*matli*) 'narcotic' is well displayed in *Cantares* song LIV-C (36v:6–22) (CMSA p. 251).

Note also that the unidiomatic and incorrectly written *yāōtĕpānco*, literally, 'enemy boundary place', might be the author's paraphrase of an urtextual *atempan oo* or even *teoatempan oo* 'at the flood's edge, oo!' (i.e., 'on the battlefield'). FC 6:74:4: *teuatenpan* 'battlefield'; cf. DICT *tentli* 6.

wished to hear it!' into an unintended joke.[34] Here again—as in example 1, above—an echo of the Spanish Conquest (in which Cortés was aided by Tlaxcalans, imagined in the song text as trounced by savagely victorious— not "gloriously" defeated—Acolhuans, who would normally be in league with Mexico).

(4) *Laso de la Vega's Guadalupan Legend (1649)*. Like the *Discursos*, the fa- mous "legend" is an exercise in antiquarianism, borrowing freely, in this case, from *Cantares* song I.[35] The poor Indian Juan Diego "as he approached the hill called Tepeyaca, just at dawn, heard music...," and, as the story unfolds, the Virgin (of Guadalupe) appears to him, enables him to gather flowers even though it is the winter season, and leaves an imprint of her image on his *tilma*. Laso's distinctive vocabulary may be compared with *Cantares* folio 1: *tzinitzcan* (1:7, LASSO 26:10/LASSO 62:1); *manoce* (1:7, LASSO 26:23/ LASSO 62:13); *nocuexanco nictemaz* (1:10, LASSO 42:21/LASSO 78:27 has *quicuexanten*); *iuhquin tepetl quinnahnanquilia* (1:13, LASSO 26:8/LASSO 60:28 has *iuhquin quinànanquilia Tepetl*); *coyoltototl* (1:17, LASSO 26:10/ LASSO 62:1); *tonacatlalpan xochitlalpan* (1:28, LASSO 26:16/LASSO 62:6 has *inxochitlalpan intonacatlalpan*); *xixochitetequi* (1v:3, LASSO 42:13/ LASSO 78:20 has *xochitl xictètequi*); *teyol quima* (1v:8, LASSO 26:9/LASSO 60:28 has *teyolquimà*); etc. *Cantares* song I itself is a deritualized literary composition in which the 'flowers' *xochitl* have become tokens of divine grace. Standing behind these acculturated *xochitl* are the *xochitl* of the oral *Cantares* (all ninety-one songs in the manuscript except for I–IV, VI–IX, and XI–XIII), representing a somewhat different worldview. Laso further appropriates the flowers, turning them into *Caxtillan tlaçòxochitl* 'Spanish roses' (LASSO 42:18). With Laso, for whom the old songs were undoubt- edly a source, we encounter the first milestone in the history of *costum- brismo*—the literary manufacture of palatable, nonthreatening folklore.

---

34. *Pŏyōmicquè* is a noun, not a verb; literally, 'they are narcotic dead-ones', comparable to *xocomicque* 'they are fruit[-wine] dead-ones' (i.e., drunkards). DICT poyomahtli, xocomicqui.

35. Laso undoubtedly borrowed at random from other literary sources as well, as suggested by the editors in LASSO p. 8 n1. But it is *Cantares* song I that sets the tone, while the narrative itself follows the outline established in the Spanish-language *Imagen de la Virgen Maria* of 1648 by Miguel Sánchez (relevant excerpts translated in LASSO 131–45). The diction is reworked again in Guadalupan texts from the eighteenth century (Sell, Burkhart, and Poole 2006:60–61, 166–67, 206–7, 214–15).

Observers who knew the songs before the 1590s, however, took a more cautious view.

Before the 1590s

During most of the 1500s Spanish authorities either forbade native song performances or carefully monitored them, making an attempt to distinguish genres.

Conquerors and early colonists had promptly recognized two kinds of songs, those in honor of "devils" and those in praise of "conquests" or, more fully, in praise of "past kings, recounting wars, victories, deeds, and such things." Both were performed with dancing, but of different styles: the former called *macehualiztli* in native usage; the latter, *netotiliztli*.[36] Either could be referred to as song or dance, since singing and dancing were integral to all the performances. Evidently the *Romances* and the *Cantares* are *netotiliztli*, a term that will be adopted here—even though in native-language texts it was occasionally used synonymously with *macehualiztli* and the two terms were sometimes confused or even disregarded by writers of Spanish.[37]

The *macehualiztli* were the more worrisome. It was *macehualiztli* that had precipitated the soon-to-become-legendary Toxcatl massacre of 1520, when 80 (some say 130) of Cortés' men were stationed, uneasily, in Tenochtitlan.[38] Made nervous by the exotic, large-scale performance, the Spaniards had ambushed the dancers, slaughtering several hundred. Retelling the event from the vantage point of the 1550s and 1560s, the academician Francisco Cervantes de Salazar, adding his own emphasis, could write that, although the *cantares* performed on that hair-raising occasion were sacred, *en este trata-*

---

36. Motolinía 1971b:386–87 (parte 2, cap. 27); López de Gómara 1988:104–5 (cap. 70). DICT ihtotia:mo, mahcehua.

37. The source verbs *macehua* 'bailar o dançar' and *itotia.mo* 'bailar o dançar' (identically defined in MOL) are used synonymously in FC 3:21:3. In CM and RSNE the verb is always *itotia* 'to dance' (*mitotia* 'he, she, or it dances'), except at CM 39v:24 (which has *macehua*). Sahagún did not label the song texts he included in his *Historia general* as *macehualiztli* or *netotiliztli*, but at least many if not all of Sahagún's twenty *incuic tlatlacatecolo* 'songs of devils' (FC 2:207–14, Sahagún 1997:128–52) would appear to be *macehualiztli* in the sense that Motolinía defined the term.

38. A source for the "130" is *Procesos de residencia* 1847:36–39, per Padden 1970:292 (n3).

ron la conspiración contra los nuestros 'in this business they plotted conspiracy against our own'.[39]

The chronicler Francisco López de Gómara, the usual source for the Toxcatl massacre, whose description Cervantes borrowed, states explicitly that the Toxcatl performance was *macehualiztli,* not *netotiliztli.* Yet Sahagún's detailed Nahuatl-language account of activities for the feast of Toxcatl mentions *netotiliztli* only and repeatedly; and he indicates the same style of dancing (*netotilo, mitotia*) during the massacre itself.[40]

By Cervantes de Salazar's time the *macehualiztli* had been proscribed at least twice, once by ecclesiastical writ in 1539 and again in the penal code issued in 1546. The latter mandate also outlawed certain other "cantares," apparently *netotiliztli,* unless they were of the kind taught by the friars, on pain of a hundred lashes for each infraction.[41]

Nevertheless, *netotiliztli* of the kind *not* taught by the friars are known to have been performed in public after 1550 and could well have been witnessed by Cervantes de Salazar. Evidently the obscure figurative language made the texts impervious to censorship. According to Sahagún, speaking of the *netotiliztli* in particular, "no one knows what [the singers] say except themselves alone." Cheerfully, Durán heard the same songs and found nothing to reprehend "in general," though he conceded that the texts were so obscure that he could not understand them unless they were "explained" (*conferido*) by the natives.[42]

Exasperated, Sahagún noted in 1576 that the situation had worsened: "[…] they sing when they wish […]. This continues; every day it grows worse […]."[43] And in the only work of Sahagún's published in his lifetime,

39. López de Gómara 1988:147–48 (cap. 104), retold with embellishment in Cervantes de Salazar 1985:463 (lib. 4, cap. 102). Varying accounts of the massacre are compared by Anthony Pagden in Cortés 1986:475–76.

40. FC 2:64–73 (ch. 24), FC 12:53:5–17 (ch. 20).

41. In these mandates the distinction between *macehualiztli* and *netotiliztli* is not entirely clear. Presumably the *fiestas de sus advocaciones in que haya areitos,* banned in 1539, referred to the festival chants in honor of old gods, or "devils," hence *macehualiztli;* and the *areitos de noche* specified in the code of 1546 meant the same thing (cf. Motolinía 1971b:386). For the writ, García Icazbalceta 1947 3:154; for the code, Paso y Troncoso 1953 1:414. As for the kind of songs taught by the friars, these were clearly imitations of *netotiliztli,* many of which were published, finally, in Sahagún 1583 (see CMSA p. 34).

42. Sahagún 1583:[iii]; cf. HG lib. 2, ap. 6, para. 1 and lib. 10, cap. 27, para. 28 or FC introductory volume, pp. 58 and 81; Durán 1967 1:195–96 (*Ritos* cap. 21) or 1971:299–300.

43. FC introductory volume, p. 81 (CF lib. 11, cap. 27).

a psalmody of Christian texts designed to replace the dangerous *netotiliztli*, he inveighed against the native songs in explicit terms, writing in his prefatory remarks that

> they insist on returning to the old songs in their houses and in their tecpas [. . .] and they use other songs to persuade the people to do their bidding, whether it's war or other business that is not good, and they compose songs for this purpose, and they do not wish to give them up. *porfian de boluer à cantares antiguos en sus casas ò en sus tecpas [. . .] y otros cãtares vsan para persuadir al pueblo à lo q̃ ellos quiere, ò de guerra, ò de otros negocios que no son buenos, y tienen cãtares cõpuestos para esto, y no los quieren dexar.*[44]

Yet at what appeared to be the height of its intensity, the native *cantares* movement was apparently losing momentum. Rather, it was about to change. When it resurfaced in the 1600s the oldstyle stanzas had become *coplas* in the Spanish mode, though unreported remnants of the older material, much reduced, may well have survived.[45] A surprisingly late performance of a *michcuicatl* 'fish song', evidently *netotiliztli*, judging by the title, is mentioned in Chimalpahin's *Journal* for the year 1593.[46] The entry is suspect, however, in that the future historian Chimalpahin was only fourteen years old at the time.

Revitalization

What does Sahagún mean when he speaks of tecpas, persuasion, war, and other business that is not good? And why did the situation seem to be "growing worse every day"? Evidently the tecpas (Nahuatl *tecpan* 'palace') are the houses of the native *gobernadores*. Durán, more credulous than Sahagún, speaks defensively of these native lords presiding in their tecpas:

> [. . .] today the chiefs of the towns keep [singers] in the old way. I do not consider this improper since it is all done for a good reason and to prevent the lowering of the authority of their persons. For they too

---

44. Sahagún 1583:[iii].
45. CMSA pp. 88–91.
46. ZCHIM 2:41 or Muñón Chimalpahin Quauhtlehuanitzin 2006: entry for Sept. 5, 1593. Compare the *michcuicatl* 'fish song', *Cantares* song LX.

are sons of kings and great lords in their own way, like those who came before them.[47]

As for the "persuasion" and the "worsening," noted by Sahagún, the prolific (and devoutly Catholic) nineteenth-century documentarian Joaquín García Icazbalceta was able to suggest an answer:

What truth is there in all this? Was Father Sahagún endowed with greater perspicacity than his colleagues or did he see evil where none existed? [...] In the early days of the conversion, people of lower class, who had suffered under their overlords and had borne the enormous burden of human sacrifice, did eagerly embrace Christianity if for no other reason than that it offered a great advantage over their own blood-stained religion. They did not fully understand it, to be sure, and accepted it more out of emotion than conviction. But the native lords and priests, despite civil coercion, were unprepared to give up polygamy, tax collection, and the exercise of authority without a struggle. In fear they bowed their heads. Yet they did no more than that. The common people, from long habit, were so respectful and frightened of the privileged classes that they dared not break with them. The Spaniards, out of political necessity, left in place much of the old hierarchy: the governors and judges, still, were Indians, who abused their authority by forcing the people to keep up the old idolatry. They believed they could best obtain their objective by circulating the prediction that Spanish rule was to last only eighty years. The poor ignorant people, pressed from both sides, did not fail to credit the prophecy, fearing that when the time was up and the Spaniards had gone, the lords and their pagan priests would come down heavily on those who had disobeyed them by denying the false gods. The people wished to accommodate both sides: the padres, by attending their Christian ceremonies; the lords, by covertly keeping up the old idolatry, which steadily increased as the date set for their restoration came around.[48]

47. Durán 1971:299 (*Rites* ch. 21).
48. Translated from the Spanish in García Icazbalceta 1886:302 or 1981:370. The ill-fated prediction that Spanish rule would end after eighty years comes from Martín de León's *Camino del cielo* of 1611, per García Icazbalceta 1981:369.

Icazbalceta's approach to this matter was to be echoed in succeeding generations by writers who would find that "many examples confirm the observations and pessimism of Sahagún" and "few ecclesiastics were so perceptive,
or so outspoken,"[49] while historians in the second half of the twentieth century, nevertheless, became more interested in the mechanics of accultura-
tion than in the politics of resistance.

As for Sahagún's "war or other business that is not good," the songs
themselves provide a few clues. The reader may take a look at *Romances*
XVII and XXX and decide whether either of these pieces might be read as
a call to arms. And note unmistakable allusions to the forbidden topic of
human sacrifice in song XXX (*ytzimiquixochitli* 'flower of knife death'), song
VIII (*tiçâtl a y∎huitl* 'chalk ah! and plumes'), and song XXXVI (*motiçâyo
ye [mi]huiyon* 'your chalk, [your] plumes'), comparing the same terms in
the documentation so scrupulously prepared by Sahagún: *jtzimjqujzxuchitl*
'flower of knife death' (FC 6:171:30) and *ytiçaio yujio* 'his chalk and plumes'
(FC 2:48:7).

Passages in the *netotiliztli* that appear to be exercises in philosophy—
or, as Alva Ixtlilxóchitl might say, moral philosophy—are expressions of
the war ethic and the concept of the warrior as *icnotl* 'bereaved one' resolved in favor of war (not peace) when the *netotiliztli* are considered as a
whole.[50] Moreover, echoes of the Spanish Conquest are heard throughout
the corpus.[51]

These elements, taken together, accord with a minimum definition of
what may be called revitalization. Although it came too late to incite rebellion, the *Cantares* movement, to give it a name, staged a recurring drama of
resistance during the ostensibly pacific third quarter of the sixteenth century, celebrating a war ethic at odds with the newly dominant culture.[52] If it
is understood that in this drama dead warriors are being brought back from
the other world—a subject to be explored in the following essay—it will
be seen that the songs of the *Romances* and the *Cantares*, cryptic though
they may be, exhibit a signal feature of the classic revitalization movement;

49. Ricard 1966 [1933]:274; Gibson 1964:101.
50. TRAN sec. 12.
51. TRAN secs. 6, 17, 20.
52. The emphasis placed by Stephanie Wood (2003:x and passim) on the "diversity in native
responses to the invasion and occupation" and the probable truth in her intimation that a majority of native people were collaborators, either actively or passively, are not being questioned
here.

that is, a movement among at least a segment of a subdued population that appeals to the supernatural when the opportunity for open rebellion has passed.[53]

The Future of Nezahualcoyotl

Out of the ashes of the *Cantares* movement arose two of the potent symbols of modern Mexican consciousness as it began to take shape in the first half of the 1600s. These were the flower world of Juan Diego — Saint Juan Diego as of the year 2002 — crafted by cleric Laso de la Vega in 1649; and the poet-king Nezahualcoyotl — namesake of a modern city and subject of several twentieth-century biographies — created by the historian Alva Ixtlilxóchitl in 1618. Both are traceable to the *netotiliztli:* Juan Diego's literary setting to the *Cantares Mexicanos,* as mentioned above; and the poet-king to the codex *Romances.*

Although the *Cantares* contains songs that have been ascribed to Nezahualcoyotl, attention in this regard centers on the *Romances,* with its suggestive glosses and the pedigree that seems to have been given to it by Pomar and Ixtlilxóchitl. Pomar, who apparently attached the *Romances* to his *Relación,* claimed that the religious views of Nezahualcoyotl were to be found in the "ancient songs" (i.e., the *Romances?*), and Ixtlilxóchitl stated, helpfully, that King Nezahualcoyotl had composed "sixty and some" songs addressed to the Creator (again, the *Romances?*).[54] In fact the *Romances* has thirty-six songs, thirty-seven if XXIX and XXIX-A are counted as two. Yet Pomar considered the "ancient songs" to be in "fragments"; and the modern scholar Garibay, seeing discrete thematic units, divided the *Romances* into sixty songs, several of which he divided further in his commentaries.

Nezahualcoyotl's role in modern nation-building — in any event a phenomenon to be viewed through the lens of mythography rather than history — may be better understood in relation to the parallel case of Peru. Like Mexico, Peru faced an overwhelming native heritage, dangerous but also ripe with opportunity. The challenge, for nation builders, was to demonize native resistance while simultaneously integrating the native past. To construct the necessary story, two figures were required.

---

53. CMSA pp. 60–69.
54. Pomar in García Icazbalceta 1941 3:23–24; Ixtlilxóchitl in IXT 2:125 (cap. 45), but elsewhere Ixtlilxóchitl counts "seventy and some" (IXT 1:546).

For Peru these two were Viracocha Inca, eighth ruler of Cuzco but first of the actual emperors (ruled ca. 1402?–40), and Atahualpa, last of the de facto emperors (ruled 1525–33). From legends that came to light in the 1500s we learn that Viracocha Inca was a proto-monotheist who predicted the Spanish Conquest and, with it, the triumph of Christianity.[55] Atahualpa, on the other hand, had become a figure of shame, who "murdered left and right" and "came to an evil end as punishment for his cruelty and bloodshed."[56]

For Mexico the two corresponding figures ought to have been Montezuma I, fifth ruler of Tenochtitlan but first of the actual emperors (ruled 1439–68), and Montezuma II, last of the de facto emperors (ruled 1502–20). In fact Montezuma II did collect the blame. However, since the mythologizing of a scapegoat had been the first order of business, "Montezuma" was no longer an available name by the time the first notice of the prophet appeared, in 1582 (in Pomar's *Relación*). If for no other reason than to avoid ambiguity, the paradigm shifted sideways, substituting for Montezuma I the only major figure among his contemporaries. This was the ruler of Texcoco, Nezahualcoyotl (ruled 1431–72), staunch ally of Tenochtitlan and relative of Montezuma I — some said his brother.[57]

Montezuma II, demonized in sixteenth-century legend and never rehabilitated in mainstream literary lore, had now become the "weeping," "fainting" coward who had allowed the empire to fall;[58] or, in stronger terms, the arrogant despot "drunk with his own power," addicted to human sacrifice, who ignored warnings issued by the God of Christianity.[59] Nezahualcoyotl, on the other hand, objected to the worship of "devils," practiced a virtually Christian brand of monotheism, and predicted the arrival of the Spaniards precisely to the year — 1 Reed (i.e., 1518).[60]

These paradigmatic figures are not without duplicates and further ramifi-

---

55. Cobo 1979:131; Cobo 1990:23; Garcilaso 1966:304–6 (bk. 5, ch. 27).

56. Sarmiento de Gamboa 1965 cap. 64.

57. Montezuma II and "Yoyontzin" (i.e., Nezahualcoyotl) are both among the "children" of "Itzcoatl" in *Romances* song XXIX.

58. Hill and MacLaury 1995 (an analysis, especially, of passages from bk. 12 of the Florentine Codex, i.e., Sahagún 1950–83).

59. Sixteenth-century tales in which Montezuma II becomes an object of scorn include the legend of the talking stone (Durán 1967 cap. 66, TEZ cap. 102), the story of Montezuma's wound (TEZ cap. 103), and the Papantzin legend (TORQ lib. 2, cap. 91; FC bk. 8, ch. 1).

60. IXT 1:58–72 (items 109 [worships "un solo Dios"], 146 ["un solo Dios Verdadero"], 148 [says idols are "devils"], 218, 260, 261, 263 [predicts Spaniards' arrival in 1 Reed], 265 [repudiates idols]).

cations. The Inca Mayta Capac, for example, rivals Atahualpa as a legendary barbarian. Topiltzin Quetzalcoatl is better known than Nezahualcoyotl as a proto-monotheist. Spaniards in the sixteenth century identified *themselves* with Viracocha Inca and with Topiltzin Quetzalcoatl.

The special virtue of Nezahualcoyotl, the quality that makes him modern even for the twenty-first century, lies in his role as poet and humanist.[61] Alva Ixtlilxóchitl spoke for future generations when he declared that the songs of Nezahualcoyotl contained phrases to rival "the divine Plato and other great philosophers."[62] Equally forward-looking, Ixtlilxóchitl's immediate predecessor, Mexico's first modern historian,[63] Juan de Torquemada, could write:

And [Nezahualcoyotl] ordered his singers to sing a song that he himself had composed, which began thus: *Xochitl mamani in huehuetitlan*, etc., which means: Among the copses and the cypresses there are fresh and fragrant flowers. And continuing on, it says that although for a while they are fresh and attractive, they reach a time when they wither and dry up. It goes on to say that all who are present must end and cannot come rule again, and that all their grandeur must finish and their treasure must be owned by others, and they are not to return and enjoy it once they have left it behind. (TORQ 1:156 [lib. 2, cap. 45])

Thus in one breath Torquemada delivers the pastoral diction of European poetry and a hint of the Old World *carpe diem* theme, features derived from

61. Montezuma, honored in the *netotiliztli* no fewer times than Nezahualcoyotl and even in the phrase *nimoteuczoma* 'I, Montezuma' (CM 20:2), has never been established in popular or scholarly literature as a composer or "poet." The paradigm evidently does not permit it.

62. IXT 1:404–5. As proof, Ixtlilxóchitl gives the phrases: *Ypan yn Chahconauhtla manpan meztica intloque nahuaque ypal nenohuani teyocoyani ic el téotl oquiyócox ynixquex quéxquix mita ynamota* (read *Ipan in chiucnauhtlamanpan mitztica in tloque nahuaque ipalnemohuani teyocoyani icelteotl oquiyocox in ixquich quexquich mitta in amotta*) 'He who dwells above the nine levels [of the other world], the Ever Present, the Ever Near, Life Giver, Creator, Only Spirit, who created all that is seen and is not seen'. The passage is not from the *Cantares* or the *Romances*; it bears the stamp of Christian influence and is possibly from a now-lost literary composition inspired by the *netotiliztli*.

63. Alva Ixtlilxóchitl generously credits Torquemada with being the 'first discoverer of the explanation of the paintings and songs' (*primer descubridor de la declaración de las pinturas y cantos*) (IXT 2:137; cf. CMSA pp. 112–14). By decorating his great *Monarquía indiana* with snippets of supposed precolumbian poetry, Torquemada initiated a tradition that became irresistible to those who followed in his footsteps, including no less a figure than William Prescott and, most recently, the British historian Hugh Thomas.

the Greeks (Theocritus, Epicurus) and conveyed by the Romans (Virgil, Lucretius), conferring the unmistakable badge of humanism.[64] *Xochitl mamani in huehuetitlan* actually means 'flowers stand [as a group, over an area] beside the drum' (cf. *Romances* 13v:3). Torquemada has read *huehuetitlan* 'beside the drum' as *ahuehuetitlan* 'beside the cypresses' and has added Virgilian 'copses' for good measure, 'freshening' the flowers to make room for Lucretius. Never mind, for the moment, what these 'flowers' might mean. Nezahualcoyotl, remade and perdurable, has entered the narrative of the new culture.

64. On pastoral see TRAN sec. 17, below.

On the Translation of Aztec Poetry

Contents

1. Techniques of Ritual

1.1 A glance at the oral literature of Aztec Mexico, preserved in sixteenth- and seventeenth-century manuscripts, will show that the *Romances*, or "ballads," belong to one of the three abundantly attested Aztec genres that may be called ritualistic: the *conjuros*, the *huehuetlatolli*, and the *netotiliztli*.

1.2 Of these three, the most rigidly technical and therefore potentially the most obscure are the *conjuros*, which include agricultural and hunting charms, love charms, sleep charms, spells connected with divination, and incantations calculated to cure specific infirmities. Least obscure, certainly, are the set speeches known as *huehuetlatolli* 'words of the elders', designed to beseech a deity, install a ruler, greet a visiting dignitary, admonish a child, or mark a rite of passage.[1]

1.3 Between these extremes stand the *netotiliztli* 'dance(s)',[2] represented by the songs in the *Romances* and the closely related *Cantares Mexicanos*. The "dance" songs, evidently, are less technical than the *conjuros* and therefore presumably less obscure, though they are by no means as transparent as the *huehuetlatolli*.

1.4 Unlike the *conjuros* and the *huehuetlatolli*, however, the *netotiliztli* have come down to posterity without a contemporary Spanish translation or commentary. Further, even when they were new, the songs began to be deritualized by native and non-native litterateurs who raided them for vocabulary to dress up their own compositions. Sahagún himself published a book of ersatz *netotiliztli;* and several examples, probably written by native or part-native scribes, are preserved in the opening folios of the *Cantares* manuscript — notably *Cantares* song I, which in turn played a part in inspiring the decidedly nonritualistic "legend" of Juan Diego and the Virgin of Guadalupe.[3]

1.5 Helpfully, the presence or absence of ritual technique separates the genuine *netotiliztli* of oral tradition from the written imitations (as does the terse, or paratactical, syntax of the former as opposed to the Europeanized

---

1. The Aztec *conjuros* are in Ruiz de Alarcón 1953, 1982, or 1984. The largest collection of *huehuetlatolli* is FC bk. 6; other *huehuetlatolli* sources are discussed in Sullivan 1974:79–85 and in Karttunen and Lockhart 1987:8–9.

2. Song titles listed in Hernández 1945 libro 2, cap. 6 ("Del nitoteliztli"), link the *Romances* and the *Cantares* with the term *netotiliztli,* as discussed in CMSA p. 92.

3. See "After the 1590s" in the Introduction.

Nahuatl of the latter). And comparison with the *conjuros* and the *huehuetla-tolli* helps to clarify both the method and the means of expression. Accordingly, it will be seen that the *Romances* texts, even if they strike the modern eye as poetry, are essentially ritualistic, not literary.

1.6   The purpose of ritual, it may be granted, is to bring about a desired result, and its language, even if it may be judged beautiful or interesting, is utilitarian — frankly coercive in its stronger forms, as with the *conjuros,* and at least admonitory in the milder, more decorous *huehuetlatolli.*

1.7   Like both the *conjuros* and the *huehuetlatolli,* the *netotiliztli* use imperative verb forms. Yet the declarative mode is more frequent, and, as in the case of the *conjuros* especially, the statements are short and jaculatory and carry a coercive overtone (necessarily, since the action described by the ritualist is beyond the reach of natural observation).[4] As with the *conjuros* the songs make much use of the verbs 'to come', 'to arrive', 'to come forth', as though the words themselves had the power to summon. Appropriately the *conjuros* that are designed to bring about, or summon, a cure have been called by the native term *zantlatoltica tepatiliztli* 'remedies by means of words only'.[5] Note the insistent use of the verbs *huitz* 'come', *huallauh* 'come', *aci* 'arrive', *eco* 'arrive',[6] *moquetza* 'appear', *quizaco* 'come forth', *quixtia* 'bring forth', *temohuia* 'bring down', and *temo* 'descend', in *Romances* songs I, II, III, V, VI, VIII, IX, X, etc.

1.8   Like the *conjuros,* the songs use rhetorical questions with implied yes or no answers, setting forth open-and-shut arguments that favor the needed result.

1.9   Even more so than the *conjuros,* the songs are "dramatic," in the sense that the speaker may assume more than one voice within a single song. Though the texts are monologues, it is often as if two or more speakers are present, their roles played by the same ritualist.[7] (For this reason quotation marks have been added to certain passages in the *Romances* translation to indicate the change in voice.)

---

4. For examples of the "coercive indicative" (as it replaces the imperative in otherwise duplicate passages in the *Cantares*), see GRAM 6.12. See also Andrews and Hassig in Ruiz de Alarcón 1984:259 (item 7).

5. MOLS folio [55].

6. DICT ahci, ehco.

7. The "dramatic" aspect of the *conjuros* has been pointed out by Andrews and Hassig in Ruiz de Alarcón 1984:27; cf. ibid.:102. Dramatic monologues in the *Cantares* are discussed in CMSA pp. 45–46, 509, 525.

1.10   Moreover, in true incantatory style the ritualist addresses figures of power or authority and, often, speaks for them.[8] In the *conjuros* these figures are deities; in the *netotiliztli*, historical kings and military leaders. Thus in the *conjuros* we find the ritualist saying *niquetzalcoatl* 'I am Quetzalcoatl' and *nimictlantecutli* 'I am Mictlanteuctli [lord of the underworld]';[9] in the *Romances* (2:16 and 2v:1), *nitemilotzin* 'I am Temilotzin [a native general during the Conquest]' and *niyoyotzin* 'I [am] Yoyontzin [an alternate name for the fifteenth-century king of Texcoco, Nezahualcoyotl]'.

1.11   In "dramatic" fashion a single song may refer to the same figure in the first person, the second person, and the third person. Thus *Romances* song II has *niyoyotzin* 'I am Yoyontzin'; *titecpiltzinn i necāhualcoyotl tecuitli yoyotzin* 'you, O prince, O Lord Nezahualcoyotl, O Yoyontzin'; and *neçahualcoyotzin* 'it's Nezahualcoyotzin'.

1.12   If the *netotiliztli* is ritual, then, what is its purpose? What function does it serve? If the songs themselves can be taken at their word—

> I have flowers, *Romances* song I
> craving flowers, song II
> pick up your flowers, song III
> flowers are scattering down, song V
> flowers are gold, song VI
> flowers are sprouting, song VII
> flowers descend, song VIII
> he brings them down, these drunken flowers, song IX
> here are your flowers, song X
> let me dress myself in these. These flowers, song XI
> delicious flowers, song XI
> and here they are, your flowers, song XII
> where are the flowers? song XIII
> etc.

—it may be conceded that a major preoccupation of *netotiliztli*, if not the purpose, is the production or acquisition of "flowers." The further question is: What are these flowers?

8. The same technique can be found in the two traditions that the Aztec *conjuros* most closely resemble: the Yucatec Maya medical incantations (Arzápalo Marín 1987 or Roys 1965) and the Cherokee "sacred formulas" (Mooney 1891 and 1932; Kilpatrick and Kilpatrick 1965 and 1967).

9. Ruiz de Alarcón 1982 or 1984, tract 2, ch. 1; tract 5, ch. 1.

2. Companions, Birds, Flowers

2.1 Although the *netotiliztli* have been preserved without elucidation, various other texts, particularly the *huehuetlatolli* and the *conjuros*, help to make sense of the songs—as implied above. Among these other texts is the opening passage of the *huehuetlatolli* spoken by a midwife as she cuts the umbilical cord of the newborn boy:

> Know this, hear this: your home is not here, for you are an eagle, a jaguar; you are a swan, a troupial; a companion and bird of the Ever Present, the Ever Near. This is merely your nest, you are only hatched here, simply arrived, come forth, issued forth here on earth. Here you burgeon, you blossom, you sprout. Here you make a nick [in the shell], break [out of the shell]. [...] You've been sent to the edge of the flood, to the edge of the blaze [i.e., to the battlefield]. Flood and blaze [i.e., war] is your duty, your fate. [...] Your actual home [...] is beyond, the home of the Sun, in the sky: you'll cry out to Him, you'll give pleasure to Him, the Shining One. Perchance your lot, your fate, will be knife death [...]. *Xicmati, xiccaquj: amo njcan muchan, ca tiquauhtli, ca tocelotl, ca tîquechol, ca tîçaquan in tloque, naoaque: ca tiicoauh, ca tiitotouh: çan njcan motapaçoltzin ijeian, çan njcan timotlapanaltia, çan njcan taci, teco, çan njcan titlalticpacqujça, njcan tixotla, ticueponj, titzmolinj, njcan titzicueoa, titlapanj [...] teuatenpan, tlachinoltenpan in tioalioaloc: teuatl, tlachinolli, molhvil, motequjuh [...] in vel muchan [...] vmpa in tonatiuh ichan in jlhvicac, ticoioviz, ticaviltiz in totonametl in manjc: aço mocnopiltzin, aço momâceoaltiz in jtzimjqujztli [...].* (CF lib. 6, cap. 31, fols. 146v–47).

2.2 Compare the song texts:

> *Romances* song VII (8v:4–13): Cacao flowers, popcorn flowers are sprouting in Mexico. They're budding, they're blossoming. Lords, eagles, jaguars [i.e., warriors] are standing as a multitude. They're forming buds, they blossom. And so these shield flowers [i.e., warriors] are to wither [i.e., die] in Anahuac [i.e., on earth], in the [battle]fields. *omn itzmolitimani oohuaye / yn ca cahuaxochitla / yn izquixochitla / y meesico y / mimilihui oo / cueputimania / omvaya ohuaya çâno y maniya yn tecpilotl / yn cuauhtin oçelo / mimilihui oo / cueputimaniya /*

omhuaya ohuaya a ynca yycc ocuetlahuiçôo - çâ chimalixochitli / ya om-
nahuac a yxtlahuaquitecâ.

Romances song II (2v:1–7): "I'm coming, I, Yoyontzin, craving flowers,
hatching [*or* breaking open] flowers here on earth, hatching cacao
flowers, hatching comrade flowers." And they're your flesh, O prince,
O Lord Nezahualcoyotl, O Yoyontzin. *nihualaciz ye nicâ ye niyoyotzin*
yhuiya çâ nixochiyeelehuiya ehuaya nixochitlatlapanaco tlalticq̃ nocoya-
tlapana yn cacahuaxochitli nocôyatlapana ycniuhxochitli ye tehuâ mona-
cāyo titecpiltzinn i necāhualcoyotl tecuitli yoyotzin.

Romances song XXXIII (40v:8): Our good flowers walk abroad [*or*
march along, i.e., of warriors]. *nenenemiya yectli ya toxochihui.*

Cantares song XV (8:3): Where do the flowers go? Where do they go,
they that are called eagles and jaguars? *Canon yeĥ yauh xochit cano ye*
yauh yeh intoca quauhtli ocelotl.

2.3   It may be seen that "flowers" are persons,[10] specifically warriors destined
for the other world, where they will become *coatl* 'companion(s)', or *icniuhtli*
'comrade(s)', of the Sun. The same, evidently, may be said for "birds." And
it is seen that their activities give "pleasure," or "entertain," or "gladden," as
the songs frequently have it.

2.4   Moreover, a theme of *elehuia* 'desire', or *ehelehuia* 'craving', recurs in the
songs. The warrior desires captives (who will be sent to the sun) and desires
that he himself may become a captive (to be sent to the sun):

Cantares song LI (32:3–5): Blaze flowers, war flowers! Who doesn't
want them? Who doesn't crave them, O princes? *tlachinolxochi-*
tla y yaoxochitly acon anquinequi [read aquinequi], acō anquelehuia o
antepilhuan.

Cantares song XVI (9:26): I seem to crave knife death, there! in battle.
O anquin ye oncan yaonahuac noconelehuia in itzimiquiliztli.

2.5   As for the otherworldly location mentioned in the *huehuetlatolli,* this is
known in the *netotiliztli* by a variety of names: some suggesting brilliance

10. As stated unambiguously by Garibay (1953–54 1:101): "Las 'flores que bailan' no son otros
que los guerreros [the flowers that dance are none other than the warriors]" and "'flores que
se ambicionan' son los cautivos que serán inmolados [the flowers that they (i.e., the warriors),
crave are the captives, who will be sacrificed]."

(*xochitonalocalitec* 'in the house of sun flowers', *tlahuizcalli* 'dawn's house'); some suggesting fruitfulness (*xoxopan* 'green places', or *tamoanchan* [see section 18, below]); some with neutral or even somber connotations (*tochan* 'our home [or haven]', *ximohuayan* 'place where all are shorn', *mictlan* 'dead land'); others betraying Christian influence (*ilhuicatlitic* 'heaven'). A few of these names may designate *ixtlahuatl* 'battlefield' or simply 'field', as well as the (celestial) field(s), or world beyond.[11]

2.6   In the blissful realm the dead warrior becomes *yolqui*, defined by Molina as *el resucitado de muerte a vida* 'one who is brought back to life from the dead'. As expressed in the *Cantares* (39:25), *onca ye yolque in teteuctini* 'there the princes are brought back from the dead'.

3. Supreme Power and Its Agents

3.1   In addition to resemblances of style and technique, there are procedural similarities between the *conjuros* and the *netotiliztli*. In both cases absent figures are summoned in order to enact a drama of conflict. Notice that the traveler's *conjuro* against bandits (the third incantation in the great collection compiled by Ruiz de Alarcón) draws upon the power of a supreme deity then summons lesser gods as warrior-agents (and also summons the imagined bandits themselves), setting up a scene of combat between the two sides:

> It is I in person. I am Quetzalcoatl. I am Matl. I indeed am Yaotl; I am Moquehqueloatzin. I consider things as nothing [i.e., I am afraid of nothing *or* I respect nothing]. It will be at this time [i.e., I am ready]. I will give pleasure to my older sisters, my human kinsmen [i.e., I will fight my weak enemies]. In order for me to give pleasure to them, come, Rubber-owners, *Iyauhtli*-owners, you who strike things in their company, you who pound things in their company [i.e., you gods]. Indeed here come my older sisters, my human kinsmen. We will give them pleasure. They come possessing blood; they come possessing color [i.e., they come being vulnerable]. *Nòmatca nèhuatl niquetzalcoatl nimatl ca nèhuatl niyaotl nimoquequeloatzin, àtle ipan nitlamati.*

11. *Romances* 1:4 (*xochitonalocalitec*), 1v:17 (*xoxopã*), 2:10 (*mictlan*), 4:10 (*tocha*), 7v:12 (*ximohuaya*), 8v:12 (*yxtlahuaquitecã*), 39v:5 (*ylhuicatliteco*). DICT tlahuizcalli, xopan, ilhuica-tlihtic, etc. Further synonyms for the other world are listed in CMSA pp. 39–40.

Ye axcā yez; niquinmàahuíltiz nohueltihuan, nitlacaxillohuā, inic niquin-
màahuiltiz tlaxihualhuian ollòque yaoyòque, in īhuan tlahuitequi, in ihuā
tlatzòtzona; canicā huitze nohueltihuan notlacaxillohuā tiquinmàahuil-
tizque, yèhuantiz ezçotihuitze, tlapallòtihuitze.[12]

3.2　In the *netotiliztli* various names are used for the supreme power—
including *yaotzin* 'Enemy' (*Cantares* 61v:11), *moquequeloa* 'Mocker' (*Can-*
tares 13:9), and *xiuhtototl* 'Turquoise Bird [i.e., the Sun]' (*Cantares* 17v:17–
21)[13]—terms that overlap with the names given in the *conjuros* and the
huehuetlatolli, the most frequent of which, at least in the *netotiliztli*, are
ipalnemohuani 'Life Giver' and *dios* 'God'. The supremacy of Life Giver is
acknowledged repeatedly: the flowers are *yxochiuh yn ipalnemoani* 'Life
Giver's flowers' (*Cantares* 18:12), and, as it is said, *quē huel xoconchihua quen*
huel xoconcuili yxochiuh aya ypalnemoani 'You must produce them! You must
get Life Giver's flowers!' (*Cantares* 21:20).

3.3　Just as the lesser gods arrive in order to "strike" and "pound" (in the *con-*
juro quoted above), in the *netotiliztli* Life Giver's agents arrive as historical
kings, bringing "flowers." Thus, as the singer announces, *nechhualihua dios*
nehua nixochhuātzin nehua nitemilotzin 'God sends me here. I have flowers,
I am Temilotzin' (*Romances* 2:14–16). Or, as *nixochhuātzin* might be translated, "I am flower owner" or "I am flower master."

3.4　The kings may well be compared to lesser gods. Note that the *huehue-*
tlatolli ritualist who addresses a newly installed ruler proclaims: *yn axcan*
ca otiteut [...] ca aocmo titotlacapo 'now you are deified [...] no longer are
you human, as are we' (FC 6:52:31–34), and the point is emphasized by the
sixteenth-century chronicler Diego Durán: "the one who commands there
[i.e., Montezuma I of Mexico] [...] is the image of the god Huitzilopochtli"; "Monarchs in this land were adored as gods"; "For the kings were held
to be divine men"; "Motecuhzoma [i.e., Montezuma II of Mexico] called
his palace 'the house of God.'"[14]

3.5　As with the traveler's *conjuro*, again, the *netotiliztli* texts summon both
allied and enemy warriors, as may be seen in *Romances* songs I, X, and XXIX,

---

12. As transcribed, translated, and glossed (in square brackets) by Andrews and Hassig in
Ruiz de Alarcón 1984:75.

13. Similarly, in prayer, the Sun is *xiuhpiltontli, in quauhtlevanjtl* 'the turquoise child, the
soaring eagle' (FC 2:202:8). In *huehuetlatolli* the Sun is *xippilli* 'turquoise childe [i.e., turquoise
prince]' (FC 6:12:35).

14. Durán 1994:127, 157, 282, 398.

and in many songs throughout the *Cantares*. For this purpose the singer may appeal to the ruler—"you, Nezahualcoyotzin" (song XVII)—or speak in the ruler's own voice—"I am Temilotzin" (song I)—at the same time recognizing that it is the supreme spirit who actually produces the needed warriors — "Life Giver creates them. He, Self Maker, brings them down" (song XVII).

4. Flowers as Weapons

4.1   As he continues reciting his *conjuro*, the traveler who is worried about bandits summons personified weapons as his further spirit helpers:

> I have brought the priest, His-*tonal* Is One Water [i.e., the staff], [or] the priest, One Death [i.e., the rocks], [or] One Flint [i.e., the knife]. *ca onichualhuicac in tlamacazqui çe atl, itonal, intlamacazqui çe miquiztli, çe tecpatl.*[15]

4.2   Likewise the *netotiliztli* singer imagines a delivery of personified weapons, representing warriors armed for battle, calling them *mitl* 'arrows' (*Romances* 10v:4), *matlatl* 'hand slings' (1v:6), *tlacochtli* 'spears' (9:7), *chimalli* 'shields' (31:10), or, more fully, *tlacochtli xochitl* 'spear flowers' (30:12), *chimalli xochitl* 'shield flowers' (18:6–7).

4.3   Weaponlike plant materials may also designate the warrior: *tzihuactli* 'spines' (10v:4), *mizquitl* 'mesquites' (13:17), *acatl* 'reeds' (*Cantares* passim),[16] or, more fully, *acaxochitl* 'reed flowers' (*Romances* 31v:10). (But *mizquitl* may also mean the warrior king specifically, as do *pochotl* 'ceiba' and *ahuehuetl* 'cypress'.)

4.4   Heaping metaphor upon metaphor, the singers may call upon *chimalmatlatl* 'shield hand-slings' (1v:6) or *tzihuacmitl* 'arrow spines' (10v:4).

4.5   Metonyms based on the warrior's weapons have their mirror image in metonyms based on the warrior's body parts: *maitl* 'hands', *yolli* 'hearts', *cuaitl* 'heads', and *nacaztli* 'ears'.[17] Such figures may be combined, as in

15. Ruiz de Alarcón 1984:75. *Tlamacazqui* 'priest', i.e., spirit power, deity (FC 6:35:12; TEZ ch. 11). The names of these "priests" are *tonalli*, or calendar signs.

16. In addition to *acatl* 'reed(s)' the Florentine Codex describes *acaçacatl* 'reed grass' with leaves that are *asperas y cortan* 'sharp and can cut' (CF lib. 11, cap. 7, para. 7, fols. 183v–84; cf. FC 11:196:3–5 and 11–13).

17. Compare the statue of Coatlicue with its belt of heads and its necklace of hands and hearts, generally interpreted as war trophies (Pasztory 1998:158–59). Less widely known are the ears: "then they went and made conquests in Xochimilco. It was to get clippings that they gave

nacazmaxochi- 'ear and hand flowers' (*Romances* 17:16). (The terms give rise to ambiguity—especially "hands" and "hearts," also used in more conventional figures of speech, comparable to the English "all hands on deck" or "from the heart.")

4.6   These are only a few of the literally hundreds of figurative names by which the warrior is known, including the names of specific flowers (e.g., *izquixochitl* 'popcorn flower', *cacahuaxochitl* 'cacao flower', *cacaloxochitl* 'raven flower', *cempohualxochitl* 'marigold', *miyahuatl* '[maize] tassel'), as well as specific birds and specific butterflies.

4.7   As in *Romances* XXVII and XXX, the rising 'smoke' (*poctli*) and descending 'dust' (*teuhtli*) of the battlefield may also designate the warrior.[18]

5. "Flower" Birds Return to Earth

5.1   In the song texts the warriors' home in the sky is frequently mentioned, called by such names as *zacuancalli* 'House of Troupials' (*Romances* iv:13) or *chimalpapalocalli* 'House of Butterfly Shields' (31v:5); and as set forth in the midwife's speech quoted above, from the Florentine Codex, the newborn male child is believed to descend directly from this celestial abode. Another passage from the Florentine Codex—the principal source for *huehuetlatolli,* here quoted in an explanatory passage—describes the warrior's home as:

> [. . .] the home of the Sun, in the sky: those who go there are the ones who die in battle [. . .] or are just captured to die later, who, perhaps, are stripers [victims of sacrifice] [. . .]; all [who die in battle or are captured and sacrificed] go to the home of the Sun. It is said that [. . .] when the Sun appears, when it dawns, then they shout and cry out to it. [. . .] And after they've spent four years, then they're changed into precious birds, hummingbirds, flower birds [. . .] chalk butterflies, feather

---

chase. When they were hunting for prisoners, it was only ears that they were stacking up in their bag so that it would be known how many they were capturing. And they were only clipping an ear from one side" (CC 17:17–20). Compare the jacket of Huitzilopochtli, painted with "severed heads, ears, hearts, entrails, livers, lungs, and prints of the hand and the foot" (FC 12:50:17–19). The ears are featured again in Codex Boturini (Pasztory 1998:201–2).

18. DICT poctli, teuhtli. For smoke and dust as techniques of warfare, see Hassig 1988:95–96 (smoke signals) and 105–7 (destructive fire); Díaz del Castillo 1956:58 ("the Indians gave great shouts and whistles and threw dust and rubbish into the air so that we should not see the damage done to them") or 1976:55 (cap. XXXIV) ("daban los indios grandes silbos y gritos y echaban pajas y tierra en alto, porque no viésemos el daño que les hacíamos").

butterflies [i.e., potential captives chalked and feathered for sacrifice], calabash-cup butterflies [i.e., sacrificial victims as drinking vessels of the gods], and they sip there where they dwell. And they come here to earth in order to sip [*or* inhale] all the different flowers: the [flowers of the] *equimitl,* or skull-rack tree; [and] the cornsilk flowers, the spear cornsilk flowers. […] *ichan tonatiuh ilhujcac, iehoantin vmpa vi, in iao-miqui […] yn anoço çan calaquilo, i çatepan miquizque. Yn aço oaoano […] muchintin vi in tonatiuh ichan, quil […] in iquac in oalmomana in oalquiçaia tonatiuh, nimâ quicaoatza, coiovia […] auh in iquac onauh-xiuhtique, njmâ ic mocuepa, tlaçototome, huitzitzilti, xochitototl […] tiçapapalotl, ivipapalotl xicalteconpapalotl, tlachichina in vmpa in mo-noian [read inonoian]. Yoan in njcan tlalticpac oalhui in quioalchichina, in jxquich nepapan xochitl in equimjtl, anoço tzonpanquavitl xilohxochitl, tlacoxilohxochitl.* (CF lib. 3, ap. cap. 3, fols. 28v–29)

5.2 If the careful listener catches an undertone in "sipping flowers," passages in the *Cantares* may suggest the deeper meaning:

Cantares song LII (34:5): Ah, these princes are scattered as eagles, painted as jaguars. Let these incense-flowers of His be sipped! *An quaauhnenelihui oceloihcuiliuhtimanique in tepilhuā ayahue maça yic-xochiuh [read yiexochiuh] onchichinalo.*

Cantares song LII (35:6–8): Let them be sipped, these plume-incense flowers. They're scattered. God sets His flowers free, [then] takes these flowers to His home. *In ma onchichinalo in quetzalyiexochitl aya moyahua quitomaya yxochiuh yehuan Dios huiya hui çan ca ye ichan y aya xochitly ca cana.*

5.3 Observe the *Cantares'* allusion to the repeating cycle of descent and as-cent ("sets His flowers free, takes these flowers to His home"). As for the dead warriors' return to earth after "four years," the songs also use the ritual number four, but with reference to space, not time. The incoming warriors arrive not "after four years," as above, but "from the four directions":

Cantares song XIV (7v:18–20): Lightning strikes from the four direc-tions. Golden flowers are sprouting. There, the Mexican princes are alive. *Çan ye nauhcampa y ontlapepetlantoc, oncan onceliztoc in coçahuiz xochitl oncā nemi in Mexica in tepilhuan.*

Cantares song XIX (15v:4–6): Come! Set them free! Do indeed stand up and noose these hearts of mine as flower garlands from the four directions. [And] O my hearts, what would befall you? *tlacuel tla xictotoma xochimecatica nauhcampa ca cenca huel xihxittomonilpitica* [read *xicxittomonilpitica*] *noyollo noyollo quen anquiChihuazque.*

5.4   In the same vein the *conjuros* ritualist calls for his warrior spirits and spirit helpers: *inic nauhcā niquintzatzilia* 'from the four directions I summon them'.[19] Subsequently, when they have done their work, 'the earth will be drunk [with the blood of their victims]' (*tlalli ihuintiz*).[20] And by the same token, 'there's earth-drunkenness' (*tlalhuintihua*) in *Cantares* song 87 (77v:3–4).

5.5   As the warriors arrive, they are "flower birds," according to the *huehuetlatolli* passage quoted above. But in the *netotiliztli* they may be various species, including *tzinitzcan* 'trogon', *zacuan* 'troupial', *toztli* 'parrot', *aztatl* 'egret', *xiuhtototl* 'cotinga', *quetzaltototl* 'quetzal', and especially *quechol* 'swan', frequently amplified as *teoquechol* 'spirit swan' or *tlauhquechol* 'roseate swan'. A roseate swan in everyday diction is indeed the roseate spoonbill (*Ajaia ajaja*), but the Linnean designation is unsuitable for translating the term as it appears in the *netotiliztli*, where we also find such forms as *ayopalquechol* 'auburn swan', *chalchiuhquechol* 'jade swan', and *cuauhquechol* 'eagle swan' among yet others, and even the verb *quecholti* 'to become a swan'. (The translational solution 'swan' is not meant to denote *Cygnus* but 'swan' in the sense of such English expressions as 'sweet swan of Avon' or 'swan knight', connoting musicianship or transport to the other world.)

5.6   The return of dead souls, it should be mentioned, was not an idea peculiar to the war cult. According to the mid-sixteenth-century Codex Telleriano-Remensis, the dead in general were summoned to earth during the annual *huei miccailhuitl* 'great feast of the dead', when people climbed up to their roof terraces and "each one made long prayers to the dead, to those who were their ancestors, crying out, 'Come quickly, for we await you.'"[21]

---

19. Transcribed and translated by Coe and Whittaker in Ruiz de Alarcón 1982:106.

20. Ruiz de Alarcón 1982:105 or 1984:77.

21. *Hazian grādes oraciones a los muertos cada vno a los que [e]rā de su linag[e] y dādo vozes dezian: Venid presto q[ue] os esperamos* (Códice Telleriano-Remensis 1964, pt. 1, plate 4; 1995:8 [folio 2v]).

6. Flowers as Fish

6.1 Metaphorically the warrior, especially a warrior en route to or from the dead land, is a *michin* 'fish':

> *Cantares* song 60 (43v:19): O hummingbird fish, O picture of gold! In the net alone are you pleasured. *Yn huitzitzili michini teocuitlaamox çan i matlatitec timahuilia.*

6.2 The usage accords with the recurring image of the other world as a watery paradise, seemingly in conflict with the idea of the sun's home. By now, however, it should be clear that there is no rule against mixed metaphors.

6.3 In the *Cantares,* the resistance hero Temilotzin appears prominently in a 'fish song', where it is made clear that the metaphor is particularly apt since Temilotzin, as the records show, jumped overboard during an enforced voyage to Spain—and disappeared in the ocean.[22]

7. "Companions" and "Pleasure"

7.1 It may be asked why a captured warrior, or "fish," would be "pleasured" in the net, as put forth in the *Cantares* passage quoted above. Here again the *conjuros* are helpful.

7.2 It will be recalled that in the traveler's incantation against bandits, the verb *ahuiltia* 'to give pleasure' is used sarcastically, meaning 'to engage in combat'. Similarly the ritualist in *Romances* song X throws out the taunt, 'So let yourselves be pleasured, you princes of Huexotzinco' (*y ma yc xonahuiyācan atepilhuān i huexotzinco*).

7.3 Compare song I: '[...] in Huexotzinco, where the dying is, there's Dancer. It's Tlacahuepan. His eagle flower princes find their pleasure in that house of green places' (*huexotzinco yn omcān i tlamihuacā yn mācêuhcātzin yni tlacâhuepan a nimān ocān on ahuiya ynxochicuapilhuā xopâcalayntec*), i.e., Tlacahuepan of Mexico is engaging the enemy Huexotzincans in combat on the battlefield in Huexotzinco, which, with its opportunity for a glorious death, is a celestial "green places" on earth.

7.4 Another of the ubiquitous terms that may be used with a double edge is *coatl* 'companion', along with its approximate synonym *icniuhtli* 'comrade

22. CMSA pp. 463–64.

[*or* friend]'. The terms often express mundane solidarity. But not always. 'Companion' *coatl* may mean 'companion [of the sun, i.e., warrior destined for death in battle]', as in the midwife's *huehuetlatolli* quoted above. In any event it must be understood that *icniuhtli* 'friend' is not used in the Western, sentimental sense of 'soul mate' or 'second self'. It means 'ally' in the military sense, as demonstrated in the Codex Chimalpopoca; for example, *yn Mexitin ca yeppa ynicnihuan catca yn chichimeca yn quauhtitlancalque* 'the Mexica had long been friends [i.e., allies] of the Cuauhtitlan Chichimecs' (CC 13:32-33); *ca monequi aocmo ynicnihuan yezque yn xaltocameca aoquic mocniuhtlazque yhuan ca monequi aoquic yntlan huallazque* 'the Xaltocameca were no longer to be their allies; they must never again be allies with them, must never again come to their side' (CC 14:20-22). Reading hastily, jumping from "flowers" to "friends," one is led to see lyricisms on the joys of friendship—imagining Catullus' *Verani ominibus e meis amicis . . .* 'Is it you, my friend of friends, who come, / Dearer to me than a million others, / Veranius . . .' when it would be better to stand a few thousand miles closer to home, keeping in mind the Lakota warriors' songs *Kolapila* (Friends): "Friends, I have said in common life the customs are many; friends, those do not interest me," "Friends, you go on; even that younger brother is coming on the warpath."[23]

8. Songs as Flowers

8.1 Of all the figurative locutions in the *netotiliztli* the one that is immediately grasped by even a casual observer is the ubiquitous *xochitl/cuicatl* 'flower/song', setting up an equivalency between the two terms. It is also readily apparent that song is a means of perpetuating a warrior's fame (*Cantares* 29:10-11: *noxochiteyo nocuicatoca nictlalitehuaz* 'I'll make my flower fame, my song renown before I go'). In a sense, therefore, the song, alternately designated *tlatolli* 'word',[24] is the warrior—all that is left of him here on earth. The various locutions alluding to this idea are double-edged, however, because in native lore the theory of sacrifice, or war death, closely parallels the theory of music. Both involve the transfer of persons from the sky world to the earth: songs (or celestial musicians who embody the songs), like war-

---

23. Davenport 1951:261; Densmore 1918:335, 338.
24. DICT tlahtolli.

riors, descend from the house of the sun, and both songs and warriors exist
in order to serve the gods. These essential points, in the case of sacrifice,
are revealed in the passages from the sixteenth-century Florentine Codex
quoted above and, in the case of songs, in the myth of the origin of music,
preserved in two sixteenth-century sources.[25] In the *netotiliztli:*

> flowers are shrilling [warbling (of birds) *or* shrieking (of warriors in
> battle)]. *ca ycahuaca xochitl. (Cantares* 69:2, DICT ihcahuaca)

> songs are shrilling. *ycahuaca cuicatl. (Romances* 38v:1)

> God has formed you, has given you birth as a flower, paints you as a
> song. *Dios mitzyocox aya xochitla ya mitztlacatili yan cuicatl mitzicuiloa.*
> *(Cantares* 27:24)

> I come created as a song, come fashioned as a song. *cuiçã [read cuicatl]*
> *nopictihuiz cuiçã noyocoxtihuiz. (Romances* 2:13–14)

> As a song you've been born, O Montezuma: as a flower you've come
> to bloom on earth. *cuicatl ye tiyol tiMoteucçomatzin xochitl ticueponico*
> *in tlp̈cqui. (Cantares* 63:7)

> As songs you've come alive, as flowers you've blossomed, O princes,
> O Zacatimaltzin, O Tochihuitzin. *Cuicatl ayolque xochitl ancueponque*
> *antepilhuāN i çacatimaltzin in tochihuitzin. (Cantares* 15:17–18)

8.2   Yet in many passages that speak of songs, or songs and flowers, there is
no immediate allusion to warfare or to warrior kings coming to life, and the
audience may imagine, at least for a moment, that only music is the topic. It
should be clear, however, that music is the subtext of war, and vice versa (see
below, sections 9.1, 9.9). The constant coupling of *xochitl* 'flower' and *cuicatl*
'song' does not indicate 'song(s)' or 'music' alone, nor simply 'warrior(s)'
or 'war'. The 'flower and song' of the *netotiliztli,* if it needs to be freely interpreted, might best be rendered 'war and music'. The fundamental notion is
a dichotomy, not an amalgam.[26]

25. For the full texts of these myths, see Appendix I. For further discussion, see CMSA
p. 21.
26. Metaphorically the two terms can be synonyms—a song can be a flower—but the two
do not blend into a third term, as in English "cloak" + "dagger" = "intrigue." Thus the well-
known formulation set forth by Garibay (1961:116), *xochitl + cuicatl = poema,* is here regarded
as incorrect. Garibay's discussion (1953–54 1:260, 383) ("[...] el poeta [...] con la imagen

8.3   Another way of looking at these "flowers" that have been brought to life is to consider that they are metaphorically, not literally, reborn on earth. The ambiguous *cuicatl ye tiyol* 'as a song you've been born' can also be translated 'in [*or* by means of] a song you've been born'.[27] Yet in either case the meaning is that you, the soul being addressed, have returned to life through the power of music. To say whether it is the mere essence or the flesh that is making an appearance would be beyond the scope of textual analysis; and the same query might be raised in connection with the *conjuros*. No one who witnesses the recitation of any of these texts will see Montezuma himself, let alone the combative spirits of the *conjuros*, suddenly materializing. At least in the song performances, Montezuma may be impersonated by a dancer.[28]

8.4   The act of "descending," expressed in the verb *temo* 'descend', or by implication in the verb *temohuia* 'bring down', characterizes the diction. Often the "flowers," or "songs," are a "mist" (*ayahuitl*), said to rain or drizzle down (*pixahui*), to pour down (as rain) (*[mo]teca*), to be shaken down (*tzetzeloa*), to be set free (*[mo]toma*), or to be scattered as they come (*moyahuatihuitz*).[29] Occasionally it is said that they are brought down in a 'pack basket' (*matlahuacalli*). Observe that songs are 'lifted' or 'raised' (*[m]ehua*) by the earthly singer but 'brought down' by supernatural power. Arriving on earth, they are *nepapan* 'divers [*or* various, many, a multitude]'.[30] It may be said that they 'are (out)spread' (*mani*), meaning that they stand as a group over a sizable area (not that they are recumbent). They are active: they 'stir' (*[hui]molihui*).

8.5   As noted above (section 2), the dead warriors are *yolque* 'live ones [*or*

---

trivial en la poesía náhuatl, metafóricamente llama 'flor' al canto"; "flores = cantos"), by contrast, may be judged correct.

27. The Florentine Codex, quoting a brief passage from a song of the *netotiliztli*, interprets the phrase *cuicatl ye tiyol* [...] *in tl p̄cqui* in this very way (*toconiamaceoa, cujcatl tiioliz tlalticpac, aaiave: vevetitlan tinemiz* 'bien mereces ser loado, con cātares, y bien mereces que tu fama, viua en el mundo, y que los que baylan en los areytos, de [*read* te] traygan en la boca enrededor de los atabales' [you deserve to be praised with songs and you deserve that your fame will live in the world and that those who dance in the dances will bring you forth in their mouths beside the drums]) (CF lib. 6, cap. 21, fol. 95).

28. As in fact he was, in a *mitote* witnessed in 1645 by the Jesuit historian Andrés Pérez de Ribas ("[...] at the head of [the dais] [was] placed the seat of the emperor Motezuma. [...] There were [...] fourteen in the dance, or *sarao*, not including the emperor, who came in at the end"). Translated from the Spanish in Pérez de Ribas 1944, 3:325–27 (bk. 12, ch. 11). See also CMSA pp. 88–91.

29. For synonymy see DICT temo 1, moyahua 1.

30. DICT nepapan 2; CMSA p. 26 ("The legion of the dead").

revived ones]', and they are fittingly said to be *huetzcani* 'laughing ones'. As the text has it, 'I come shaking down these laughing ones' (*nictzetzelotihuitzy o huetzcani*).[31]

9. Vocables as War Cries

9.1 Even outside the *netotiliztli*, music and warfare are in some sense inter-changeable. As set forth by the *huehuetlatolli* orator in his lengthy admoni-tion to the newly installed king:

> Agitate and bring to life the pleasure things [i.e., the musical instru-ments], the drum and the rattle. That's how flood and blaze [i.e., war] is brought to life, brought to mind, forged and drilled [i.e., crafted]. *xicolinj xiciocoia in avillotl in vevetl, in aiacachtli: in vncan moiocoia, in vncan molnamjquj, in vncan mopitza, momamali in teuatl in tlachinolli.* (CF lib. 6, cap. 10, fol. 45)

9.2 In the words of the mysterious Conquistador Anónimo (1971:374):

> It is one of the world's most beautiful sights to see their squadrons in battle, because they proceed with marvelous order and with great style [...]. While they fight, they sing and dance, giving out with the world's most ferocious cries and whistling sounds [...]. [...] *è una delle belle cose del mundo vederli à la guerra in compagnia, per che vanno maraviglio-samente in ordine & galanti [...]. Nel tempo che combattono cantano & ballano & tal volta danno i piu fieri gridi & fischi del mundo [...].*

9.3 Similarly, the conquistador Bernal Díaz del Castillo (1956:58 and 1976:55) writes:

> I remember that when we fired shots the Indians [...] sounded their trumpets and drums and shouted and whistled and cried "Alala! Alala!" *Acuérdome, que cuando soltábamos los tiros [...] los indios [...] tañían atambores y trompetillas y silbos, y voces, y decían: Alala, Alala.*

9.4 Compare the untranslatable vocables in the *netotiliztli*:

ala (*Cantares* 19:16)
chitalalala (*Cantares* 67v:8 and 10)

---

31. CM 27v:14–15. Cf. 11:20, 61:24; RSNE 11:19.

papa (*Cantares* 12:14, 63v:18, 66v:13)
yapapa (*Cantares* 19:11)
yapa-yatañ-tilililin (*Cantares* 17v:24)
ylilili (*Romances* 34:13)

9.5   The whistling (Nahuatl *mapipitzoa*) mentioned by Bernal Díaz is heard on the dance floor as well as the battlefield.[32] Likewise, verbs based on the cry "papa" refer to sounds heard in either locale:

> *papauia:nitla* 'dar alaridos cõ boces los que baylan en el mitote [for dancers to give noisy cries when they do the mitote]' (MOL), lit., to use "papa" on people or things.
> *teñpapauia:nino* 'alaridos dar en la guerra [to give out war whoops]' (MOLS), lit., to apply "papa" to oneself at the lips.[33]

9.6   Note that the Spanish (and American English) term 'mitote', designating certain Aztec and modern Mexican dances, derives from the same Nahuatl verb, *itotia:nin* 'bailar o dançar [to dance]', as the noun *netotiliztli* (MOL).

9.7   In the *netotiliztli*, accoutrements of the dance (*ecacehuaztli* 'fans', *pantli* 'banners', *xochicuahuitl* 'flower trees'), as well as musical instruments (*hue-huetl* 'drums', *teponaztli* 'log drums', *ayacachtli* 'rattles', *tetzilacatl* 'gongs', *qui-quiztli* 'conch horns', *oyohualli* '[leg] bells [worn by warriors]', *coyolli* '[war-riors' jingle] bells'), are regularly mentioned. These items, metonymically, may signify the dancer or warrior.[34]

9.8   By the same token the dance floor, *petlatl* 'mat', or its location, *tecpan* 'palace', or *ithualli* 'court [*or* patio]', may be thought of as a field of combat. The characteristic yelling of the warrior, *icahuaca* 'to shrill [*or* scream]', is interchangeable with the musical shrilling *icahuaca* 'to shrill [*or* sing (of birds)]'.[35]

9.9   As previously suggested (section 8.2), it follows that war itself, or action on the battlefield, is in some sense the same as *cuica* 'to sing', *tlatoa* 'to speak',[36] or *notza* 'to pray', which "entertains," or "serves," the supreme spirit.

---

32. DICT mapipichtli, mapipitzoa.
33. DICT papahhuia:tla. On the literal meaning of verbs ending in *-huia*, see Andrews 1975:358–59 or 2003:586–90. For the general object *tla-* 'things *or* people', see GN 4.1.
34. *Romances* 1v:7 (*yecaçēhuaz*), 1v:8 (*ãçālipāticā*), 1:6–7 (*huehuetitla*), 1v:11 (*chalchiuhtetzil-acatli*), 1:16–17 (*ôcēloyohualichā*). DICT ehcacehuaztli, pantli, huehuetl, tetzilacatl, oyohualli.
35. DICT ihcahuaca.
36. DICT tlahtoa.

For warriors the reward is a life of bliss in the celestial paradise, as shown above; and, on earth, *tleyotl mahuizzotl* 'fame' and glory'. As the text states, "Prayers and services to him are everywhere. His fame and glory are sought on earth" (*Romances* song IV).

10. Vocables as Weeping

10.1 Although some of the many vocables in the *netotiliztli* may be interpreted as war cries, by far the majority are related to interjections that express anguish. Compare, for example, the ubiquitous vocables *aya, hue, hui, huiya, iyo, o, ohuaya, ohuaye, ohuiya, yahue* with the interjections *ay, hue, hui, iyo, iyoyahue, o, oh, yahue, yoyahue,* any of which may be translated 'ah!' or 'woe!' or 'alas!' Most frequent of all is the characteristic *ohuaya,* evidently related to the interjections.

10.2   The expressions of lament reflect a widespread technique for coercing pity from the gods, strongly recommended in the *huehuetlatolli* and carried out in both the *conjuros* and the *netotiliztli.* As advised by the *huehuetlatolli* orator:

> Call out, cry out to the master, our lord [. . .] and then he will take pity on you, he will give you what you deserve, what you ought to have. *xicnotza, xictzatzili in tlacatl, in totecujo [. . .] auh vncan mjtzicnoittaz, vncan mjtzmacaz, in tlein molhvil momaceoal.* (CF lib. 6, cap. 18, fols. 76v-77)

10.3   As if heeding this advice, the *conjuro* ritualist repeatedly speaks with the voice of *icnopiltzintli, centeotl* 'Pitiable Little Child, Corn Spirit' (i.e., the child of the gods who was buried alive so that crops could grow from the earth). The myth of this corn spirit is recorded in a sixteenth-century Aztec version and is still current in Mesoamerica. In a modern Nahuatl variant from northern Veracruz State the child corn-god continues to be called *pilsintsij,* and in one version it is said that the little boy "began to weep at being so badly treated." Among Huichol and other native groups of the Western Sierra Madre, where the analogous Corn Woman myth is preserved, it is reported that the story is told with much weeping.[37]

37. The Aztec version is in Jonghe 1905:31–32; the Veracruz variant, in Sandstrom 1991:187, 245–46. For other Mesoamerican variants, see Bierhorst 2002:68–74, 90–98, 220–21, 222–23. An

10.4   Accordingly, in one of the Aztec *conjuros* the ritualist breaks into actual lamentation, using the vocables of *netotiliztli*:

> Aya ohuiya oh ayaye ohua aye ohua! I am poor! I am Pitiable Little Child, I am Corn Spirit! *ayauhuia oh, ayaye, oa, aye oa. Ninotolinia, niycnopiltzintli, niceteotl.*[38]

10.5   Similar strings of vocables may be seen throughout the *Romances*, for example:

> *ô aye ohuâya ohuaya* (1v:10)
> *oayye yyayye ayya yyohuia* (4:1–2)
> *ôhuayyayye / ohuayyayye yye ahuayya ahuaya ohuaya ohuaya ayee*
>   *huaya* (4v:4–5)
> *aye oaye ô aya* (4v:9–10)
> *haya o ooo yayye a ooo aya o aya o ay* (11:1)
> *huiya yyayya* (25:12)

10.6   The expression *ninotolinia* 'I am poor', moreover, is one of the staples of *netotiliztli* phraseology. The idea, evidently, is that the pitiableness of the singer will bring forth the "remembered" warriors:

> I remember them all, I who am not pleasured, not happy on earth. I am poor. *çâ moch niquilnamiqui ŷn anahuiya hanihuelamati tlalticpâ oo çâ ninotoliniya oyahue ya yliya yye ohuaya ohuaya* (leaving untranslated the mournful *oo* that precedes 'I am poor' and the final *oyahue*, etc.). (*Romances* 38:6–10)

10.7   Or, more explicitly (and note the vocables):

> *Romances* song XXIX-A (36:3–4): Let's have weeping for eagles, for jaguars. *ma nechoquililo ŷ cuauhtla oçêlotl · ohuaya* (leaving untranslated the final *ohuaya*).

---

alternate corn myth, in which the food originates within a mountain, is in Taggart 1983:87–97; Bierhorst 2002:86–90.

38. Ruiz de Alarcón 1953:92 (trat. 2, cap. 14). Apparently unaware of the corn myth and misreading the name *ce[n]teotl*, Ruiz de Alarcón mistakenly explains the vocables as an outburst of joy (*algazara de alegría*) over the prospect of a successful outcome. Cf. Ruiz de Alarcón 1982:158 and 1984:113. On the name Centeotl, see Ruiz de Alarcón 1984:322.

Romances song V (6v:6–12): This I say, I Cacamatl: I recall the kings
Nezahualpilli and Nezahualcoyotl, are they summoned? Are they
seen? Here beside the drum I recall them (*more literally,* I just say
it, yehuaya! I am Cacamatzi' i! huiya! I recall the kings. Nezahualpil'
ah! Are they seen, are they summoned? Nezahualcoyotl huiya! Beside
the drum I recall them, ohuaya ohuaya). *çā niquitohuā yeehuaya çā
nicacamatzi i huiya çā niquimilnamiqui yn tlatohuanime netzāhualpila
ayyahue cuix ōmotā cuix omnoçā* [read *cuix ommotta cuix ommonotza*]
yn netzahualcoyootl huiya huehuetitla niquimilnaqui [read *niquimilnamiqui*] *ohuaya ohuaya.*

10.8   As the *huehuetlatolli* orator recommends:

Attend to the drum and the rattle, which are a means of awakening
the city [to war] and, so, of giving pleasure to the Ever Present, the
Ever Near [i.e., the supreme power], beseeching him, seeking his aid,
calling out to him in sadness. *xicmocujtlavi in vevetl, in aiacachtli yn
ijxitiloca in atl, in tepetl: auh in javiltiloca in tloque, naoaque, in jtlai-
tlanjliloca, in jtlatoltemoloca injc tlaoculnonotzalo.* (CF lib. 6, cap. 14,
fols. 60v–61)

10.9   So the singer, grieving, in obvious sadness, cries:

Romances song XXXI (37v:12–13): "Let me weep, let me sing." *ma ya
nixoca y ma ya nicuica y* (leaving the vocables *ya* and *i* untranslated).

10.10   And in the singers' words the incoming warriors and warrior kings themselves, ritually brought to earth, are *ixayotl* 'tears', *ixayauhtli* 'eye mist', *choquiztli* 'sobs', *choquizxochitl* 'sob flowers'—and *cococ* 'miseries', *tlaocolli* 'sorrows', *ellelli* 'agonies':[39]

Romances song XIV (15:13–15): May your agonies be off to war. *tlaoc a
melel i çô yazqui yaoyotl a ohuaya ohuaya* (leaving the vocables *a, i,* and
ohuaya untranslated).

10.11   Since the vocables occur not only as free-standing interjections but as
prefixes, suffixes, and infixes, all translations of Aztec songs have omitted
these persistent intrusions, or most of them, for the sake of clarity. This prac-

39. DICT ixayotl, ixayauhtli, choquiztli, cococ, ellelli.

tice, for better or for worse, has helped to strengthen the impression that Aztec songs are "poetry" rather than ritual.

11. Concrete and Abstract Nouns

11.1 As the basic elements of the *netotiliztli* idiom emerge, it becomes apparent that the singer is making a distinction, though not always clear-cut, between the incoming warriors and his fellow ritualists on the dance floor (who are also regarded as warriors) — that is, between the imagined and the real, the ghosts (so to speak) and the mortals.

11.2 The concrete nouns *icniuhtli* 'comrade [or friend]' and *icuitl* 'brother' can designate a member of either group. Thus the term of address *antocnihuan* 'you who are our friends [concrete form]' may refer to either the singer's fellow ritualists or the imagined warriors arriving from the sky world, while the abstract *icniuhyotl* 'comradeship(s)' and *coayotl* 'companionship(s)' always mean ghost warriors.[40]

11.3 The awkward '-ship(s)', of very limited use in English — compare the obsolescent "your lordship(s)" — is better omitted in translation.[41] Hence 'comrades', 'companions', rather than 'comradeships', 'companionships', as in *icniuhyotl aya tocōcenquixtia tlalticpac ye nican ohuaya ohuaya* 'you assemble comrades [abstract form] here on earth' (leaving the vocables untranslated) (*Cantares* 69:29).

11.4 The abstract forms *cuicayotl* 'songs', *xochiyotl* 'flowers', *hueyotl* 'braves [i.e., outstanding warriors]', *cuauhyotl* 'eagles', *oceloyotl* 'jaguars', and others as well, may be included in this category.[42] Possessive forms often occur, but the standard distinction between "alien" and "organic" possession does not seem to apply. In other words, the rule that abstract *xochiyotl* 'flower', for example, can only be possessed by a plant, while the flower that a person holds or owns must be designated by concrete *xochitl*, is disregarded in the

---

40. On the translation of abstract nouns see GRAM 8.9. Garibay's definition (1964:105) *icniuhyotl* = "brotherhood or guild (of poets)" is not preferred here. As applied to the *netotiliztli*, Molina's definition *compañia* = *icniuhyotl* (MOLS folio 28) may be better understood as "company" in the military sense.

41. As noted in Karttunen and Lockhart 1987:101, 111 (*totecuiyo* 'our lordship' to be understood as 'our lord', i.e., God).

42. For *Cantares* occurrences, see DICT.

idiom here under consideration, as shown by the forms *noxochio* 'my flowers [abstract form]', *moxochiotzin* 'your precious flowers [abstract form]'.[43]

12. The War Ethic

12.1   The ambiguous expression *ninotolinia* 'I am poor', alternately translated 'I am suffering', may simply be used by the singer to elicit divine pity,[44] as indicated above. But in certain contexts it means 'poor [in deeds]' (i.e., cowardly, not warlike); and in still other contexts, 'suffering [in this life]' (i.e., miserable on earth and eager for blissful reunion with the supreme power). By contrast the accomplished warrior is "rich," especially the captured warrior who wins the "riches" of "knife death," or sacrifice.

12.2   The midwife, it is reported, advises a newborn boy 'of all the suffering and torment that will befall him on earth' (*in ca muchi tetolinj, tecoco, in jpan muchioaz tlalticpac*), promising him that 'he will die on the battlefield, or be sacrificed [as a captive]' (*iaoc momjqujliz, anoçe teomjqujz*) (CF lib. 6, cap. 31, fol. 146).

12.3   In one of the lengthier, more elaborate *huehuetlatolli* texts, addressed to the god Tezcatlipoca in time of war, the orator pays tribute to:

> [...] our bereaved eagles, our bereaved jaguars, who have no pleasure, who are discontent, who live in torment, who live in pain on this earth. [...] *in tocnoquauh, in tocnocelouh, in aiavia, in avellamati, in toneoatinemj, in chichinacatinemj in tlalticpac.* (CF lib. 6, cap. 3, fol. 11v; cf. FC 6:14:30–32)

12.4   And offers the prediction:

> [...] may they in peace, in repose attain the sun, which endures, shines. [...] *manoço ivian, iocuxca itech onaciz in tonatiuh in manjc in tlanexti.* (FC 6:12:32–33)

12.5   These unmistakable postulates, instilling the worthlessness of life and the value of death, find repeated echoes in the *netotiliztli* in *Cantares*:

---

43. CM 68v:2, 43:4. The rule is in Andrews 1975:243, CARO 83.

44. Similarly, in the *conjuros*, Andrews and Hassig find "admissions of poverty as a ploy for compassion" (Ruiz de Alarcón 1984:259).

I'm suffering bereavement [...] on earth. *ninotolinia icnopilotl [...] in tlp̈c.* (69:11–12)

We're to leave the enduring earth. *ticyaoncahuazque in tlalli manic.* (35v:19)

Let bereavement be destroyed! *maoc ompolihui ycnopillotl.* (13v: 21–22)

No one's home is earth. *ayac huel ichan in tlp̈c.* (69v:2–3)

Not forever on earth! *annochipa tlp̈c.* (17:17)

We only come to dream; it is not true, not true that we come to live on earth. *ça tontemiquico ahnelli ahnelli tinemico in tlp̈c.* (14v:3–4)

Nothing we say here is real [...] it is a dream [...]. *ye antle nel o tic ytohua nican [...] temictli [...].* (13:4)

12.6   Evidently the Aztec theory reflects a general Native American war ethic, emphasizing the impermanence of earthly life, as revealed in warriors' songs from the North American plains and upper midwest:

Is this real, this life I am living? (Pawnee)[45]

I cast it away, my body. (Ojibwe)[46]

the earth only endures. *maka' kiŋ leće'la tehaŋ' yuŋke'lo.* (Lakota)[47]

I live but I cannot live forever, only the great Earth lives forever, the great sun is the only living thing. *háw 'ahgáw 'al 'ah 'óhboy góongtdaw, 'oy dóhm deyl kgée 'óhboy k'aw, 'oy pbáhee deyl kgée 'óhboy daw.* (Kiowa)[48]

And in warriors' prayers, for example:

I do not want to live long. Were I to live long, my sorrows would be overabundant, I do not want it! *bi·wirəxba·'k`e ci·'ərək` bari'atsisək`.*

---

45. Brinton 1890:292. The song belongs to one of the Pawnee war societies, or "lance" societies, whose members, according to native testimony, "held their lives in such light esteem as to be called unreal" (Densmore 1929:53). In the words of another song, "You see them but they are not real, / They are the Lance dancers" (ibid.: 54).

46. Schoolcraft 1845:347.

47. Densmore 1918:357.

48. Rhodes n.d.:18.

bi·wirəxba·'k̓e ci·'ərək̓ ba·m barasarakawi'ə a`ka·'ci bari'atsisək̓.
(Crow)[49]

12.7   But voices like the following, which are not rare in either the *Cantares* or the *Romances,* carry an undercurrent of reluctance even if they basically accept the doctrine:

> *Romances* song XVIII (20v:13–21:7): Alas, I have no pleasure here, no happiness on earth. Is this my lot? Is this my fate? Ah, bereavement is all I've come to know in this company here. Let there be borrowing [of incoming warriors], O friends. And only here. On earth! What will Life Giver's heart be requiring one of these days? We must travel to his home, O friends. Then let us be pleasured! *yyoya·huee - / oyahui xahue / anahuiya o / - anihuelamatin / tlalticpac o ye nicâ - / ohuaya ohuaya aca yuhcâ ye niyol / yuhcan nitlacat / a ycnopilotli · / çã nicmatico ye nican y tenahuâc â - ohuaya ohuaya maoc netlatlaneo* [read *maoc netlatlanehuilo] nicâ - / y yatocnihuân i · / çâniyo nican · / ay tlalticpac a ohuaya ohuaya ya moztla huiptla / que conequiz yyolo / ypalnemohuâ / toyazq̃ ye yncha·/n atocnihuâ maoc tonahaahuiyacan / ohuaya ohuaya.*

12.8   Note the term "borrowing," indicating that the warrior's life on earth is intended to be "brief," lasting no more than a "moment," soon to "wither" (like a flower), as the texts often say. Other passages are more plainspoken:

> No one can be Life Giver's friend. *ayac huel icniuh [i]n ipalnemohuâ.*
> (*Romances* 5:3–4)

> "Let's have no more lordly marching. Let's forget war and conflict."
> *macaçō ayac yn teconenemi* [read *teucnehnemi] cualayotl cocolotl maçô ylcahui.* (5v:11-13)

12.9   The weight of the *netotiliztli,* nevertheless, falls squarely on the side of sacrifice, with occasional reminders aimed at cowards, doubters, and dissenters, as in *Romances* song I: '[...] who will seek them, who will meet them here beside the drum? [...] Who among us will fail to entertain, to gladden God Self Maker?' Or, more pointedly, as in *Cantares* song XII:

---

49. Lowie 1933:441–42 and 1956:334. Lowie (1956:334) comments: "[...] he asks only for release from his torture. Why linger? Earth and sky are everlasting, but men must die: old age is a scourge and death in battle a blessing."

Clever with a song, I beat my drum to wake our comrades, rousing them to arrow deeds, whose never dawning hearts know nothing, whose hearts lie dead asleep in war, who praise themselves in shadows, in darkness. Not in vain do I say, "They are poor." *Nictzotzonan nohuehueuh nicuicatlamatquetl ic niquimonixitia ic niquimitlehua in tocnihuan yn ahtle ynyollo quimati yn aic tlathui, ypan in inyollo yaocochmictoque in inpan motimaloa in mixtecomatlayohualli ahnen niquitohuay motoliniay.*

12.10   The "human," the "sane" attitude is to embrace the "flood and blaze" that represents war (see especially *Romances* song V). And if shame fails, there's praise. As stated in *Romances* 36v:10, "Only for fame and renown does one die in war." And the dying is squarely faced: warriors are 'forsaken' (*cahua*); they 'splinter' (*poztequi*), 'shatter' (*teini*), 'ruin' (*po[h]polihui*), 'wither' (*cuetlahui*), and are 'gathered up' (*pe[h]pena*).

12.11   Ultimately the authority for military action comes from the supreme spirit. As the songs repeatedly ask, "What does God say?" (i.e., "What does God decree?" or "What does God want [or require]?"), demanding the answer, "War."[50] The right pursuit is *cualanyotl cocollotl* 'war and conflict' (*Romances* 5v:12); the warrior should 'foam [i.e., seethe with anger]' *pozoni* (*Romances* 7:11, *Cantares* passim). The warrior's mandate is clear; and yet, doubts must be resolved, calling for argument.

12.12   The argumentative strain that runs through the repertory has an apparently pre-Cortésian component in the old native attitude toward a faithless and untrustworthy supreme spirit. As the saying went, *aiac vel icnjuh, aiac nellin qujlhuja Tezcatlipuca* 'no one can be Tezcatlipoca's friend, to no one does he tell the truth' (FC 4:35:23). The adage crops up in *Romances* song IV (as noted above): *ayac huel icniuh [i]n ipalnemohuā* 'no one can be Life Giver's friend'. And again in song XVIII: *q̄xquich i ye neli quilhuiya · / yn · amo nello* 'to how many does he tell the truth, does he not tell the truth! [*freely,* how many does he "yes" and "no"!]'. But in *Cantares* song VII the querulous tone takes on an unmistakable Christian coloration, as noted in "Dating the Songs" in the Introduction. Establishing the precise boundary between an older native attitude and the newer nativistic way of thinking, which incorporates Christianity, is by no means a simple task.

---

50. See the final stanza of *Romances* song IX and CM 4:18 *teoatl tlachinolli quitoa* 'he decrees war' (cf. 17v:1, 17v:28, 32v:1, etc., and DICT ihtoa:tla 1).

12.13   It should be remembered when confronting a song that appears to be entirely negative, such as *Romances* song XIX, that the text may not mean what it seems to mean. A warrior's song of the Pawnee Lance Society may be compared in this connection:

> It has been said, / a woman did say it: / "The dance [of the Lance Society], no! / It is not the true thing for you, [my newborn son,] / the lance [of the dancers] that is walking around [in their ceremony]." *nari-ru-rit riwaka / tzapat tiwaku / Taku kaki / nariksha / Kitzichta ra huriwi.*[51]

This is apparently an admonition against war, exactly the opposite of the midwife's word of encouragement quoted above in section 2.1. But the collector of the text writes that "the inner meaning of the song is the reply" — that the newborn boy, when grown, should in fact join the war party, because (according to native exegesis), "Where will the woman send her son that he will not meet death?"[52] An essential point is that the Pawnee dances, like the earlier Aztec dances, were public performances sponsored by an established native order (warily permitted in later times, in New Spain, by a colonial authority ill equipped to analyze content). To suppose that negativity under such circumstances could be given a hearing for any purpose other than to receive scorn would be unrealistic. Similarly, to fantasize, as some have done, that Aztec songs represent private musings would be to ignore ethnography and historical evidence.

13. Drunkenness

13.1   Intoxication is mentioned or implied throughout the *netotiliztli*, often in connection with *octli* 'wine [i.e., pulque]'; the unidentified hallucinogen *poyomatli*, or *poyon*, variously given in English as 'poyon' or 'narcotic'; and the milder stimulants *iyetl* 'incense [refers to tobacco]' and *cacahuatl* 'cacao'.[53] The warriors are said to *i* 'drink', *cua* 'eat', or *chichina* 'inhale' these substances.

13.2   With reference to ritualists playing the part of warriors in a calendrical ceremony, the Florentine Codex describes those 'who had become drunk,

---

51. Curtis 1968:113–14, 136–38, 543.
52. Ibid.
53. DICT octli, poyomahtli, iyetl, cacahuatl.

unruly [like] warriors, daring, foolhardy, full of spirit, lively, proud of their valor, playing the part of men' (*yn aqujque, mihivintia iautlaueliloque, mixtlapaloanj, acan ixmauhque, iollotlapaltique, iollochicaoaque, quipopoanj yn jntiiacauhio moqujchnenequj).*[54]

13.3   Drunkenness may also describe the joyful condition of deceased warriors in the sky world, where they 'sip the various flowers' (*qujchichina in nepapan xuchitl*) 'in such a way that they seem intoxicated' (*injc iuhqujma ivintitinemj).*[55]

13.4   Or, it may describe the hoped-for predicament of one's enemies on the battlefield, allowing them to be more easily captured—allowing them to "lie in our hands," as the songs frequently say. In time of war the *huehuetlatolli* orator prays to Tezcatlipoca:

> Intoxicate our foes; inebriate them, make them drunk. May they cast themselves into the hands of, may they deliver themselves to, may they come unaware upon our pitiable eagle warriors, our pitiable jaguar warriors, who rejoice not, who are discontent, who live in torment, who live in pain on earth. *ma xicmotlaoantili, ma xicmjvintili, ma xicmoxocomjctili yn toiaouh, ma imac oalmotlaça, ma qujoalmomaca, ma ica oalmomotla in tocnoquauh, in tocnocelouh, in aiavia, in avellamati, in toneoatinemj, in chichinacatinemj in tlalticpac.* (FC 6:14:27–31)

13.5   Or, finally, captives taken in battle may be given *octli* 'wine', or *teooctli* 'sacred wine', immediately before being sacrificed. The practice is repeatedly mentioned by Durán, whose modern translators Fernando Horcasitas and Doris Heyden find that the "sacred" version of the beverage "gave valor to those who were about to die" and may have contained narcotic additives.[56]

14. Acts of Creation

14.1   To bring forth the agents of supernatural power, the *conjuros* ritualist—rather than merely summoning the spirits—may claim to have "made" them, as in the medical incantation addressed to the personified powers of tobacco and water that will be needed in the cure:

---

54. As transcribed and translated by Anderson and Dibble in FC 2:49:3–6.
55. FC 6:13:8–11.
56. Durán 1971:178n. Cf. Durán 1994:157, 172, 186n.

Indeed, right here, I've come to set up the Yellow Priest [i.e., the to-bacco], the White Priest [i.e., the water]! The one who comes is I, the Priest, Sorcerer Lord! I've made you, I've given birth to you! *Ca ye nican oniquizaco* [read *onicquetzcaco*] *coçauhqui tlamacazqui, iztac tla-macazqui; nehuatl onihualla nitlamacazqui, ninahualtecutli: ye onimitz-chichiuh, onimitzyolliti.*[57]

14.2   In the same vein the *netotiliztli* singer announces:

As a flower you've been created, you've been brought to life, O prince. You've been summoned from the Place of Duality [i.e., the other world where human life is created]. *xochitla yyhuiya / y toyoooloc* [read *toyo-coloc*] *haya toniyatlacati titepilçin yn i tinahuatiloc yn omeyocana.* (*Romances* 10v:12–14)

14.3   The same idea, with variations, is stated and restated throughout the *neto-tiliztli*, as the incoming "princes," or warriors, are said to be made, given birth, created, or brought to life.[58] Occasionally, as in *Romances* song II, they are said to be the *nacayotl* 'flesh' of the creative power or its agent; and in general they are *ilhuizolli* 'marvels' (as in song XIV).

15. Acts of Craftsmanship

15.1   Although the incoming warriors—as "songs" or "flowers"—may be simply "created," they are often crafted, so to speak, after the manner of the jeweler, the featherworker, the painter, or the florist.

15.2   Just as the jeweler creates by *pitza* 'smelting' and *mamali* 'drilling', then *zo* or *zozo* 'stringing', his *acatic* 'tubiform beads' and *ololihuic* 'round beads',[59] using gold, jade, and turquoise, so the ritualist can claim:

I drill my songs as though they were jades, I smelt them as gold. *Nic-chalchiuhmamali teocuitlatl nicpitza ye nocuic.* (*Cantares* 23:26)

In beauty I compose these songs of mine, I, a Cempohualtec, and these are my braves [*lit.*, great ones],[60] round beads, tubiform beads.

57. Ruiz de Alarcón 1953:139 (trat. 6, cap. 3). Cf. Ruiz de Alarcón 1982:225 and 1984:164. Comparable passages are in ibid., trat. 2, caps. 4, 5, 8; trat. 4, cap. 3; trat. 6, caps. 1, 3.

58. DICT chihua, tlacati, yocoya, yoli. See also section 8, above ("Songs as Flowers").

59. The jeweler's craft is described in FC 9:75:16 (*pitza*), 9:80:19 (*mamali*), 11:223:8 (*ololtic, acatic*). Cf. DICT.

60. Over a dozen attestations are found in the *Cantares* (see DICT hueyotl 1).

nocoyectlalia nocuic niccempohualtecametla [read *nicempohualtecame-tla*][61] *nohueyohua ololihuic acatic.* (*Cantares* 38v:10–11)

15.3 The featherworker, crafting a mosaic, *zaloa* 'mounts' the *ihuitl* 'feathers [or plumes]',[62] and, thus inspired, the ritualist can say:

As trogon feathers I mount, I recall, the root songs. *nictzinitzcanihui-caloaya* [read *nictzinitzcanihuiçaloaya*] *niquilnamiquia nelhuayocuica-tla.* (*Cantares* 3:5–6)

15.4 The painter of pictographic screenfolds or *amoxtli* 'books' — freely, 'pictures' — gives his images *tlilli tlapalli* 'outline and color',[63] prompting the ritualist to say:

And so you're giving outline to these comrades, these companions, these nobles. In colors you recite the ones who'll live on earth, and so you're hatching eagles, jaguars, in your painting place. *yc tictlilania cohuayotl / a yn icniuhyotl a y tecpilotl huiya tocotlapalpuhua y nemitzi* [read *nemiz i*] *y tlalticpaco yc tictlatlapana cuayotl · oçeloyotl · y motla-cuilolpani.* (*Romances* 35:9–13)

15.5 The craft of the florist supplies the *icpacxochitl* 'crown of flowers', the *xochicozcatl* 'flower necklace' — and, more elaborate still, the *xochimecatl* 'flower rope [or garland]', requiring a close look at the various verbs that express twisting or turning. These, the verbs that activate the *xochimecatl*, are one of the distinguishing features of the *netotiliztli*.

16. Verbs of Rotation (and "Garlands")

16.1 The Nahuatl verbs *cueyahua, huicoma, ihcuiya, ilacatzoa, malacachoa, ma-lina,* and *tzahua* (including the reduplicatives *cuecueyahua, huihuicoma,* and *mamalina*), which as a group may be translated by the English verb 'twist', broadly defined, appear throughout the *Romances* and the *Cantares,* often in context with "flowers." Of such verbs the two most commonly found in the songs are *ilacatzoa* and *malina.* These may be either transitive or intransitive; and *ilacatzoa,* in addition, has the special intransitive form *ilacatzihui.* Used in tandem, as attested in the Florentine Codex, they describe the crafting of

---

61. Imitating a Gulf Coast dialect (see DICT cempohualtecatl).
62. FC 10:166:20–35.
63. The painter of screenfolds is described in FC 10:28:17–29 (cf. FC 10:29:19).

a decorative floral item called *mecatl* 'garland', or *xochimecatl* 'flower garland' (more precisely 'rope of flowers').[64] In the *netotiliztli*, as would be expected, the *mecatl* are warriors, especially incoming warriors and warrior kings produced by the ritualist or the ritualist's imagined agents:

> *Romances* song XIII (13v:14–16): Flower garlands have been twirled [*or* twisted, i.e., created], and these are your flowers, your good words [i.e., songs], O princes. *xochimecatl oo / yhuã momamali / yn amo-xochihui / y yectlin âmotlatol antepilhuãno* (leaving untranslated the vocables *oo yhuã*).

> *Cantares* song XXIX (20v:7–11): Eagles are spun [*or* twisted], jaguars are recognized. / With eagle flower garlands the city goes hunting [i.e., for captives]: what's spun [*or* twisted] are jaguar flowers, the princes Montezuma and Cahualtzin. *onmomamalina in quauhyotl ye ōmiximati oceloyotl a ohuaya etc / Quauhuixochimeatica oye a'antoc y in atlon yan tepetl oceloxochitla in onmomalintoque in tépilhuan y Moteucço-matzin oa in cahualtzin.*

> *Romances* song XXXIII (40:9–11): He starts to sing: flower garlands are whirled [*or* twisted, i.e., created], these hearts of yours [i.e., your warriors], O singer! *pehua cuica xochinmecatlã momamalinã · moyoliyo · ticuicanitli.*

> *Cantares* song LXVIII (58v:30): These garlands roar, these fish are flying. *ȳ mecatl yhcoyocaya cã michin patlania.*

> *Cantares* song LXX (63:1–2): O Holy Spirit, you arrive! You come bringing your swans, these angels, these flower garlands. *spilito xanto çan tihualacico can tiquîhuicatihuitz in Moquecholhuan a yn ageloti xochimecatlo.*

16.2   In the last example the incoming warriors are called *angelotin* 'angels', a usage that also has — in the *Cantares* at least — the synonyms *centzonxi-*

---

64. *Auh yn omoçoçoc, suchitl, mec momamalina, mjlacatzoa, vel viujac viujtlatztic, totomaoac, vel tomactic* 'and when the flowers had been threaded, then [*mec*, a variant of *nec*] they were twisted, turned [to make garlands] — long, very long, thick, very thick'. Or, as freely translated by Sahagún: *flores [...] las ensartauan, en sus hilos, o mecatejos: tenjendolas ensartadas, hazian sogas torcidas dellas gruesas, y largas* 'flowers [...] they threaded them [to make] their strings, or strange *mecates*; after having threaded them, they twisted [these strings of flowers] into [heavier strings, or] ropes that were thick and long'. CF lib. 2, cap. 28, fol. 59; cf. FC 2:101:17–18.

quipilli 'innumerable ones' and *ilhuicac chane* 'heaven dwellers'.[65] In other songs, emphasizing their status as progenitors, they may be called *nonan nota* 'my mother, my father', *teci tecol* 'grandmother, grandfather', or simply *nelhuatl* 'root' or *nelhuayotl* 'rootstock'.[66]

17. Verbs of Rotation (and Pastoral)

17.1   Since the Nahuatl verbs of rotation, or some of them, can mean 'to twist around something in a helical fashion', it is tempting to search the syntax to see if such a meaning can be accommodated in translations of the *neto-tiliztli*. The lure is especially strong in passages that have hunting or fishing imagery, as in *Romances* song I, where we find the hero Temilotzin using a snare (*ilpia* 'to tie, snare, *or* capture'). One asks whether the accompanying rotational verbs, *icuiya* and *ilacatzoa*, could mean 'twist up', or 'ensnare', in this case.

17.2   The possibility is even more compelling in the various passages that mention "flowers"—or "songs" as though they were flowers. Couldn't the syntax be read in such a way that the principals are 'enlaced', 'wreathed', or 'entwined' with flowers, or the song itself is a kind of flowery wreath wrapped around one's waist or shoulders, especially in passages where the warrior is said to be "arrayed" or "adorned"?[67]

17.3   The image of untrammeled nature conjured up by "twining" or "wreathing" plant materials, with its tacit suggestion of rural innocence, is one of the staples of European pastoral tradition—by the late 1500s already absorbed, creatively, into the intellectual life of New Spain. Developed by Latin poets of the Augustan age, drawing on Greek models, pastoral diction and pastoral attitudes were revived by the Italian Renaissance and promptly disseminated in Europe—with a vigorous branch in sixteenth- and seventeenth-

65. Comparing a text from the *Psalmodia christiana* (Sahagún 1583:171v) with a passage from the Florentine Codex (FC 3:47:1–19), Burkhart (1989:85) writes, "The angels are implicitly identified with dead Aztec heroes, who in the sun's heaven took the form of birds." For angels as *centzonxiquipilli* 'lit., 400 × 8000', see MS 1628-bis, new folio 273, line 12. For angels as *ilhuicac chane*, see *Doctrina cristiana* 1944:74v. For *Cantares* occurrences, see DICT.

66. DICT tahtli/nantli, cihtli/colli, nelhuatl, nelhuayotl 2.

67. The "adornment" is figurative, as can be seen in passages where the adorning "flowers" are "sighing" (CM 5:19), are "swans" (CM 46v:29–30), are "war flowers" (CM 72:8–10), etc., suggesting that the warrior as captor is "dressed," "arrayed," or "adorned" with captives, or wears them as a "flower crown," or holds them as a bouquet (*macxochitl* 'hand flowers [*lit.*, flowers in or at the hand]').

century Mexico, where the countryside took on a New World flavor and the innocent shepherds became Indians.

17.4   Inasmuch as pastoral, or its special phraseology, survived in English poetry well into the nineteenth century, writers of English have ready-made "clasping ivy twined" (Alexander Pope) and "twined flowers" (John Keats) at their disposal, without harking back to the Augustan "let the garlands wave and blow" (Catullus), "vagrant stems of ivy, foxglove, and gay briar" (Virgil), or "would you with ivy wreathe your flowing hair" (Ovid).[68] It is not without interest, moreover, that the works of Virgil, Catullus, Ovid, and other Latin poets were well known in New Spain during the sixteenth and early seventeenth centuries—imported in editions published in Spain, anthologized in local publications, translated into Spanish, and intensively studied in institutions of learning.[69] Turning to the homegrown product, in lyrics variously known as *romances* 'ballads' or *italianillas* 'little Italian ones',[70] we find among the—astonishingly numerous[71]—poets of New Spain:

> [a native chieftainess] encircled with flowers and foliage. *rodeada de flores y arboleda.* (don Antonio de Saavedra Guzmán, 1599)[72]

> [And] here [beside the *laguna de México* 'Lake of Mexico'] the shepherds play their games, / Here the shepherdesses dance their dances. *Aquí sus juegos juegan los pastores, / aquí sus bailes bailan las pastoras.* (Doctor Eugenio de Salazar, 1530?–1605?)[73]

> O shepherd [...] happy flowers [...] wreathed in flowers. *Pastor [...] alegres flores [...] envuelto en flores.* (Bernardo de Balbuena, 1561?-1627)[74]

---

68. Pope 1956:24; Keats 1951:383; Davenport 1951:272 (Catullus), 292 (Virgil), 470 (Ovid).

69. Osorio Romero 1980:58–59 and passim.

70. Méndez Plancarte 1964:88–172 passim (*romances*); 95n (*italianillas*).

71. The historian of Mexican literature Carlos González Peña (1968:56) writes, "The super-abundant production of poetry—which has always been characteristic of Mexico—began to show itself even in the sixteenth century. [...] In the literary contest held in 1585 during the third provincial Mexican Council, three hundred poets took part." In a quotable line of the day it was said that at the court of the viceroy "there are more poets than dung" (Dowling 1994:43).

72. Méndez Plancarte 1964:98.

73. Ibid.:72.

74. Ibid.:116, 122.

[A shepherd who imagines his deceased friend] wreathed in as-
sorted flowers. *enbuelto en uarias flores.* (Francisco de Figueroa, before 1577)[75]

[A heartsick shepherd addressing his cruel love as] the vine I adore,
entwined in the embrace of another elm. *entretexida mi amada vid, y
en otro olmo abraçada.* (Damasio Frías, before 1677)[76]

[And:] Dance, ye [native] Mexicans [...] for Mary is triumphant
[...] make garlands for her. *Bailad, Mexicanos [...] pues triunfa María
[...] hacedle guirnaldas.* (Francisco Bramón, 1620)[77]

17.5 By the time the *romances* 'ballads', or *cantares* 'songs', of the native *mexicanos* became a subject of study, the phraseology of pastoral, along with the
attitudes that informed it, came readily to mind as a key to interpretation.[78]
As an exercise, one might take the following passage:

Here come the Colhuan nobles, spinning [*lit.,* here the Colhuan
nobles become spun *or* twisted]. Here the Colhuan Chichimecs, our
lords, are whirling [*or* turning]. *Nican momalinaco in colcahuahcatec-
pillotl huiya nican milacatzoa in colhuahcachichimecayotl in toteuchua.*
(*Cantares* song XV 7v:24–25)

—and ask: What precisely does this mean? It may be granted that the verbs
can be read differently (or at least an alternate reading is remotely feasible
even if unsupported by sixteenth-century textual attestations):

Here the Colhuan nobles become entwined [with flowers?], here the
Colhuan Chichimecs, our lords, are wreathed [with flowers?].

17.6 The problem with the "entwined" or "wreathed" translation is that these
verbs are being used without the near proximity of flowers or any other bo-
tanical materials to serve an adverbial function—as also in this stanza:

75. Peña 2004:226. Although the poets Figueroa and Frías (see the following quotations)
did not reside in Mexico, the verses in question were compiled in Mexico as part of the anthology *Flores de baria poesía* (1577).

76. Peña 2004:456.

77. Méndez Plancarte 1964:164.

78. Thus Carochi in his *Arte* of 1645 gives *ilacatzihui* 'to be twisted' and in the same breath,
translating a phrase from "the songs of the Indians," has *ilacatzihui* 'to be entwined' (CARO
76–76v, Carochi 2001:284–85).

It's the Commander [i.e., Temilotzin]! O Temilotzin, you summon
your comrades! You recall them, and in this way they're whirled [*or
twisted*] by dint of misery, these, your tears. *Çan tlacateccatl titemi-
lotzini tiquiyanotza mochihua tiquelnamiqui yeic malintoc cococ ycaya
mochoquiz aya.* (*Cantares* 43v:27–28)

17.7   Far removed from pastoral, the historical Temilotzin (*tlacateccatl* 'commander' of Mexican troops during the Conquest) now serves as the agent
of supreme power (as in section 3), bringing forth warrior comrades, using
several of the ritual techniques that have been mentioned above: summoning (section 1), recalling (sections 10 and 14), creating by twisting (section
15), and eliciting pity (section 10).

17.8   It is true that the verbs of rotation are used in sixteenth-century Nahuatl
writings on plant morphology to describe the helical form of certain roots
and tendrils. But the helical or tapestry-like figures in which nature imitates
art, or art imitates nature (as in the pastoral diction of European poetry),
do not seem to be part of the semantic baggage of these Nahuatl verbs until
the 1640s.[79]

18. Verbs of Rotation (and the Creation Myth)

18.1 Just as the *conjuros* ritualist invokes the myth of human creation in the hope
of making an injured patient whole again,[80] the *netotiliztli* singer alludes to
the same myth (the myth of human creation) as a means of bringing sky
warriors to life—incorporating the term *ilacatzoa*, semantically the most
flexible of the several verbs of rotation:

The flower tree stands in Tamoanchan, God's home. There! You're created! "We've been summoned. Our Spirit, Life Giver, whirls us as lord
songs." What I'm smelting is as gold: I'm carving our good songs as
jades. "Four times and as turquoise! Tamo, God, Life Giver whirls us

79. See note 78. Another example: Bartolomé de Alva's Nahuatl adaptation of Calderón's
comedia *El gran teatro del mundo,* about the same date as Carochi's *Arte* or a little earlier, has
momamalin yn huitzitzilxochitl. Though untranslated, this can plausibly be understood, in context, as 'hummingbird flowers have been intertwined' (Alva ca. 1640:2v). For sixteenth-century
usages applied to roots and tendrils, see FC 11:206:13, 206:29, 207:17, 209:12, 210:21.

80. To mend a broken bone, the ritualist identifies with the god Quetzalcoatl, who created a
new race of humans in the paradisal Tamoanchan, using bones retrieved from the underworld
(Ruiz de Alarcón 1984:190–92, 295–96, 371 [trat. 6, cap. 22]).

four times in Tamoanchan!" *Xochinquahuitl onicac in tamoan ychan dios yecha* [read *ye ichan*], *oncan tiyocoloc tinahuatiloque teuctlatoltica techylacatzoa in çā yehuan toteouh yn ipaltinemi. Yhui yn teocuitlatl in nicpitza nicchalchiuhtequi yectli tocuic yhuin teoxihuitl icni* [read *inic*] *nappa, techilacatzohua nappa tamo, tamoa ychan yehuā Dios ypalnemo-huani.* (*Cantares* 15:1–6)

18.2   The myth varies considerably over its range (which seems to be confined to the southwest quarter of the North American continent). But a look at some of the variants should show that the verb *ilacatzoa* has been plausibly translated in the passage quoted above.[81] The essential idea is that a circular motion, repeated four times, duplicates the twisting of winds, thereby im-parting the breath of life in a process of imitative magic. For convenience, references to the circular motion, the wind, and the number four are here italicized:

> One day Coyote wanted to make people. [...] Coyote said to his wife, "Make a big *round* basketry water bottle." She made it. Coyote [...] took the basket and filled it half full of seeds. Then he stopped up the opening. He took a pipe, filled it with Indian tobacco, took one whiff of smoke, and *blew it into the basket.* [...] The basket was full of something. Coyote picked it up and *four times danced round in a circle with it.* [...] He put the basket down. Already there were plenty of people inside [...]. He poured the people out, saying, "[...] Well, I have made plenty [...]." (Washo)[82]

> [...] we must see what can be done to make human beings [...]. [...] They went to the good land of day. In *four revolutions or gyrations of the upper worlds,* we became human beings. (Osage)[83]

---

81. The translation follows Garibay 1965:139 (*techilatzoa nappa* 'nos hace girar cuatro veces [i.e., spins us four times]'), disagrees with Schultze-Jena 1957:72–73 *techilacatzohua nappa* 'wickelt uns [...] viermal [i.e., wraps us four times]'. However, a Zuni prayer describing the procedure that ritualists have followed in making prayersticks, or "plume wands," representing human beings to be sacrificed to the gods, states, "[...] four times clothing their plume wands / They made the plume wands into living beings" (Bunzel 1932:710)—suggesting that Schultze Jena's idea of "wrapping" or "swaddling" (see SIM 164 and Olmos 1972:226, MOLS emboluer niño = niquilacatzoa) should not be dismissed out of hand.

82. Lowie 1939:333.

83. Dorsey 1888:394–95.

[...] after the fourth call, the gods appeared ... [carrying] two ears of corn [...]. The gods laid one buckskin on the ground [...]; on this they placed the two ears of corn [...]. Then they told the [spirit] people to stand at a distance and allow the wind to enter. [...] While the *wind was blowing,* eight of the Mirage People came and *walked around the objects on the ground four times* [...]. When the Mirage people had finished their walk [...] the ears of corn had disappeared; a man and a woman lay there in their stead. [...] It was the wind that gave them life. *It is the wind that comes out of our mouths now that gives us life.* When this ceases to blow we die. In the skin at the tips of our fingers we see the trail of the wind; it shows us where the wind blew when our ancestors were created. (Navajo)[84]

The gods said, "Who will there be?" [...] Then Quetzalcoatl went to the dead land, to the dead land lord [...]. He said to him, "I've come for the precious bones that you are keeping." [...] The dead land lord replied, "Very well. *Blow my conch horn* and *circle four times round my precious realm.*" [...] Then he *blew on it,* and the dead land lord heard him, and again the dead land lord spoke to him: "Very well, take them!" [...] Then [Quetzalcoatl] carried them to Tamoanchan. And when he had brought them, the one named Quilaztli, Cihuacoatl, ground them up. Then she put them into a jade bowl, and Quetzalcoatl bled his penis on them. Then all the gods did penance [...] then they said, "Holy ones, humans, have been born." *in teteo quitoque aqui in onoz* [...] *auh niman ye yauh in quetzalcohuatl in mictlan itech açito in mictlanteuctli* [...] *quilhui ca yehuatl ic nihualla in chalchiuhomitl in ticmopiellia* [...] *quito in mictlanteuctli ca ye qualli tla xoconpitza in notecçiz, auh nauhpa xictlayahualochti in nochalchiuhteyahualco* [...] *nima ye quipitza quihualcac in mictlanteuctli · = auh ye no çepa quilhuia in mictlanteuctli ca ye qualli xoconcui* [...] *niman ic quitquic in tamoanchan · auh in oconaxiti niman ye quiteci itoca quilachtli yehuatl iz çihuacohuatl nima ye ic quitema in chalchiuhapazco · auh niman ye ipan motepoliço in quetzalcoatl niman mochintin tlamaçehua in teteo* [...] *auh niman quitoque otlacatque in teteo in maçehualtin.* (CC 76:18–77:2)

84. Matthews 1969:69.

18.3   As the site or proximate site of human creation, the otherworldly Tamoanchan lends added meaning to such passages from the *netotiliztli* as:

> *Romances* song XI (11:18–11v:7): "I come as a flower tree from Tamoan-
> chan, the flower seat, come whirling these, these laughing ones, these
> flowers, burgeoned flowers, [song-]root flowers." [...] "I am cre-
> ated in Tamoanchan." *nicmalitihuiz xochicuahuitlo huehuezcani xo-
> chitl a y tamohuâchā / xochipetlapana ayyahue / mimilihuic xochitla
> yeehuaya a nelhuayoxochitli [...] nin■yecoya [read ninoyocoya] a /
> tamohuānichani.*

> *Cantares* song XXII (17v:22–23): From Tamoanchan, where flowers
> stand, from there beyond, you come, O lords, O Montezuma, O Toto-
> quihuaztli. You've arrived [...]. *Yn tamoan icha xochitl ye icaca ompa
> ye yahuitze yantoteuchua huiya timoteucçoçomatzin, in totoquihuatzin yn
> āme'coque.*

18.4   In the second of these two passages there is no verb of rotation, but if
there were it might be *ilacatzoa, malina*[85] — or any one of the others, since
they appear to be interchangeable, at least in the *netotiliztli,* as indicated in
the following section.

19. Verbs of Rotation (and "Whirling")

19.1   The interchangeability of *malina* and *ilacatzoa,* and of *ilacatzoa* and *icuiya,*
can be seen in passages quoted above (17.5, 17.1), where the paired verbs are
treated as approximate synonyms. The first of these two pairs may even be
used imperatively in a single command:

> *Romances* song X (11:5–8): Spin! Whirl [*lit.,* be twisted!], you princes
> of Huexotzinco, Xayacamach and Temayahuitzin! *ximilacaçoca ximo-
> malinacān ātepilhuan i huexotzinco y xayacamachan i temayahuitzin.*

19.2   In the indicative mode, though no less coercively, *malina* and *huicoma* are
coupled:

---

85. Even in prosaic contexts Molina allows these verbs to take human subjects. See MOL
malintiuetzi.ti 'caer dos enel suelo asidos'; MOLS embouer niño 'niquilacatzoa'.

Cantares song LXXX (67v:16–17): The flower tree is whirling, twisting, drizzling down in this rainy house of yours. *xochinquahuitl malinticac huiconticac ya pixahuiinticcaco ye moquiapan.*

19.3   *Malacachoa* and *malina*, also, may replace one another, as can be seen by comparing formulaic phrases in which 'flowers' (potential captives that the warrior imagines as already lying in his hand) are produced, i.e., 'blossom' or 'come forth', as though a flower garland were being crafted, or twisted, into existence:

Romances song VII (8v:14–16): Shield flowers are spinning [*or* twisting (*malacachoa*)]. Plume popcorn flowers lie in our hands. *çâ momalacachohuaya / chimali ya xochitl - yn quetzalyzquixochitli - tomac onmania.*

Cantares song XXX (21:15): War flowers are blossoming. Shield popcorn flowers lie in my hand. *Ȳ yaoxochitl oncuepontimani chimalizquixochitl aya nomac in mania.*

Romances song XII (12v:2–3): Whirling [*or* twisting (*malina*)], blossoming. *naliticac oo - vaye omcueputicaqui* [read *malinticac oo huaye oncueponticac i*].

Cantares song LXIV (53:13–15): Let these holy flowers come forth. Let them lie in your hand. These songs, these words of yours, are whirled [*malina*] as flowers [*lit.*, twisted flowerwise]. *ma quiça om a yectli xochitl ma momac onmania onxochimalintoc amocuic amotlatol.*

19.4   And note that *ilacatzoa* can replace *cuecueyahua*:

Cantares song XXXVI (23v:1–6): As though they were plumes he twists them, he, Totoquihuaztli. Let the singer come. Let the singer come. / Life Giver! As a trogon, as a swan, a cotinga, you seem. Your heart is pleasured, it imbibes the painted flowers. Songs are painted! / You've opened out your plumelike wings. You're whirled as trogon feathers, O Auburn Swan. *quetzalte huehuelin quicuecueyahua in totoquihuatzi ma cuȋca huitz ma cuȋca huitz etc / Tzinitzcan quechol xiuhtotötl ypan timomatia ypalnemoa moyol ahuia i yeehuaya coyachichinaya tlacuilolxochil ihcuiilhuin cuicatl a etᵃ / Çan moquetzalahtlapal o çan timoçoçoa tzinitzcanyhuitica timilacatzoa in tayopalquechol.*

19.5   Any of the several verbs under consideration may be correctly given in English as 'twist' (Spanish 'torcer'), with the understanding that the meaning ranges through various kinds and degrees of torsion with or without rearrangement of the entity being revolved or rotated. Because the English 'twist' carries a heavier connotation of rearrangement, or distortion, than the corresponding Nahuatl verbs, and is therefore potentially misleading, English 'twirl', 'turn', 'spin', or 'whirl' has been given preference in these translations.

20. The Payment

20.1   Whether by cajoling, insisting, dancing, singing, metaphorical "twisting," or other ritualistic means, the summoning of dead warriors, or "lords," from the house of the sun does not come without cost. There must be a process of *ixtlahua* 'to pay' or *patiuhtli* 'payment'. In other words, lives must be given in exchange. Here, then, is the philosophical basis for the practice known in Nahuatl as *tlacatica moxtlahua* 'to make the human payment'.[86] As expressed in the *Cantares* (23v:16–18):

> You are feathered; as chalk you're thrashed, O Tlacahuepan, you that will have thus departed for the Place Unknown. It seems that you're a payment for the lords, O Tlacahuepan. *timopotonia tiçatica in ye timox-conoa ha in tlacahuepa huiya yca toyao quenonamica huiya ahua yhua ya ohuaya aye ahua yio yahui / O anca ye tinpatiuh in teteuctin a in tlaca-huepa huiya.*

20.2   Although the term *patiuhtli* appears in the *Romances* only in song VI, the concept is helpful to an understanding of the manuscript as a whole. In number V, for example, the resistance hero Cacamatl, murdered by Spaniards in 1520, is impersonated by the latter-day ritualist, who has him summoning deceased lords from the more distant past, at the same time asking whose deaths, perhaps including his own, will serve as payment:

> This I say, I Cacamatl: I recall the kings Nezahualpilli and Nezahual-coyotl, are they summoned? Are they seen? Here beside the drum I re-

---

86. The vocabulary is attested in CC 5:11, 5:24, 9:8, 20:26, 22:37, 22:38; and in CM (DICT patiuhtli, patiyohua, patla:tla). See the discussion with regard to Aztec songs in CMSA pp. 30–31; in relation to American lore generally, in Bierhorst 1994:211–27.

call them. / And who will pass away? Jades? Gold? Will someone pass away? Am I a turquoise shield? Never again will I be put together? I am arrayed in plumes here on earth. Here beside the drum I recall them.

20.3   Throughout the *netotiliztli* the exchange, or payment, may be signaled by a perturbation of the universe:

this earth is shaking. *tlalli olini.* (*Cantares* 31:2)

the earth is rolling over. *tlalli mocuepa.* (*Cantares* 9:5–6)

the earth rolls over, the sky shakes. *tlalli mocuepaya ilhuicatl olinia.* (*Cantares* 33:23–24)

this jaguar earth is shaking and the screaming skies begin to rip. *Ocelotlp̈c olini yehuaya oyohualli ylhuicatlin nanatzcatimomana.* (*Cantares* 63:19)

the skies are roaring. *tetecuica yn ilhuicatl.* (*Romances* 6v:2–3)

20.4   In a broader context the matter is discussed by the anthropologist Bruce Trigger in terms of an exchange, or flow, of energy between sky and earth:

While it is important to understand Aztec prisoner sacrifice in ecological and functional terms, it is no less important to recognize it as being one specific elaboration of a set of beliefs that extended from the Tupinamba of the Amazonian forests as far north as the Iroquoians of the northeastern woodlands of North America. This cult, or network of cults, involved sacrificing prisoners to the sun in the belief that this was necessary to maintain the cosmic energy flows upon which all life on earth depends.[87]

20.5   Those who have believed that the *Cantares* and the *Romances* contain metaphysics may turn out to be right after all.

21. "Not Twice"

21.1   At various points in the repertory the ritualist finds it necessary to deal with the harsh reality that death may be permanent. If it is, this contradicts the doctrine of return and exchange. As the texts have it, "we die forever" (song

87. Trigger 1991:559.

XIX), or, in a phrase characteristic of the *netotiliztli,* "not twice does one live" (song XVI).

21.2 The singer confronts the "not twice" objection in a variety of ways. He may simply state it, then drown it out in a virtuosic display of "crafting," "creating," or "bringing down" the required ghost warriors. The fullest example is the 55-stanza *Cantares* song XVIII, which rehearses all aspects of the "die forever" argument, then swamps it in a triumphant coda ending with "everyone alive," "flower garlands coming from beyond," in a glorious "war of flowers."

21.3 Or he may turn the objection to advantage, illogically it would seem, suggesting that permanent death is the just desert of enemy warriors or, alternately, that since the warrior does not live "twice," he may as well enjoy the "flowers" of combat while he can.

21.4 Or the singer may wallow in the objection, becoming morose. In this way he inspires the divine pity that releases warriors from the sky world, allowing them to return to earth.

21.5 More decisively and in true ritualistic fashion, the singer may simply decree that the objection be removed, using the phrase *tlaca ayoppatihua* or its variant *tlaca hayopâ* 'Let there be no "never twice"!' (*Cantares* 71v:3, *Romances* 34:1).

22. Mexico

22.1 Unlike the *conjuros,* which are based on religion exclusively, the *netotiliztli* draw upon history and politics; and evidently for this reason they were called "profane" by nonnative observers, who distinguished them from another native song-genre, the *macehualiztli,* recognized as "sacred."[88]

22.2 While the battles waged in the *conjuros* are between the agents of personal harm and the spirits of succor, the warfare imagined in the *netotiliztli* favors Mexico against its mundane enemies. With Mexico (that is, the twin boroughs of Tenochtitlan and Tlatelolco) stand its partners in the so-called Triple Alliance: Acolhuacan (with the city of Texcoco as its seat) and Tepanecapan (seated at Azcapotzalco until the Tepanec War ca. 1430, thereafter at Tlacopan). Mexico's traditional antagonists are Chalco, a confederation to the south, and, especially, Huexotzinco and Tlaxcala, a pair of

---

88. The distinction is made in Motolinía 1971b:386–87 (parte 2, cap. [27]) and in Cervantes de Salazar 1985:463 (lib. 4, cap. 102); see also CMSA p. 92 and the Introduction, above.

confederacies on the other side of the mountains some distance to the east. These longtime enemies of the imperial power at Tenochtitlan, not incidentally, became the allies of Cortés in the siege of Mexico, 1521.[89] In the songs, blame for the Conquest is shifted from the *conquistadores* to the native enemies, notably Huexotzinco-Tlaxcala, while the city of Mexico, tragically destroyed, fondly remembered, becomes an object of cult.

22.3   The entire situation is easier to grasp in the *Cantares,* with its many songs commemorating actual battles,[90] than in the more generalized songs of the *Romances.*

22.4   In the *Cantares,* Mexico is named sixty times, Tenochtitlan twenty times, Tlatelolco six (here omitting various figurative names for Mexico that would add another twenty).[91] The Eagle Gate at the south side of the main square in Tenochtitlan is named three times; Coyonacazco 'coyote's nose', the neighborhood at the northern tip of Tlatelolco, where Mexicans made their last stand against Cortés, appears four times; and Chapolco (or Chapoltepec or Chapoltepetitlan), the location of Mexico's water supply, weighs in with no less than seven mentions (as it reminds the singers that Mexico, in defeat, has been elevated to the paradisal waters of the sky world). Several songs openly treat the Conquest; and Mexico itself, not merely its warriors, is portrayed in otherworldly terms, suggesting an apotheosis:

> Brilliant flowers stand blooming [as a group]. [And] where these pictures stand, this Mexico lies shining. / Indeed [O God] within your pictures, these paintings, lies the city Tenochtitlan. *Tlahuilli xochitl oncuepontimani amoxtli manca Mexicon ia ohuaya tonatimania ahuaya & / Cenca ye mamox hi cenca y tlacuilolitic onmania in atlo yan tepetl in tenochtitlan.* (*Cantares* 53:18–21)

> Montezuma, you creature of heaven, you sing in Mexico, in Tenochtitlan. / Here where eagle multitudes were ruined, your bracelet house stands shining. *Ylh.ᵗˡytiqui tiyocolloc timoteucçomatzin Mexico tontlato-*

---

89. The events of 1521 are synopsized, with references, in Brundage 1972:282–90, 331–32. Ultimately even Mexico's Triple Alliance partners, Acolhuacan and Tepanecapan, came to the aid of Cortés.

90. The Conquest of Mexico is rehearsed or lamented especially in CM songs 13, 60, 66, 68, and 91 and in what Gordon Brotherston (1997:15) has called the "invasion" sequence, CM songs 69–72.

91. DICT acapechohcan, amochco, atlan 3, atlihtic 3, atlixco 2, atl/tzacualli, chalchiuhatl 1, chalchiuhtepetl, huexotzinco 2, tlilapan 2, matlalcueyeh, xictli 3.

huay in tenochtitlani ahuaya ahuaya ohuaya. / Nican in nepapan quauh-
tli ypolihuiyan momaquizcal i tonaticac. (65:2–4)

These uttered words [*or* songs] of theirs, it seems, are stirring as a
blaze and from the four directions, giving Tenochtitlan City its place
within the dawn. They are Montezuma and Acolhuacan's Nezahualpilli. *O anca tlachinolmilini intlatol ye coyaihtoa y nauhcampa yyaoo qui-*
tlahuizcallotia in atlo yan tepetl ȳ tenochtitlan y Moteucçomatzin Neca-
hualpillin acolihuacā. (23:9–11)

Ah, this Mexico arrives in that Chapolco yonder, aya! *ahanahaya nican*
in Mexico oncā chapolco yeco ayan. (56v:2)

22.5   In the *Romances,* Mexico or Tenochtitlan is mentioned only eight times,
with the Eagle Gate appearing just once (at 10:19). But note veiled allusions
to the siege of Mexico throughout the *Romances* (e.g., in songs I, V, VII, X,
XII, XIV, XVIII; see the Commentary).

22.6   The question arises whether any of the songs in the *Romances* could be
non-Mexica, particularly Texcocan, since the manuscript has been preserved with a Texcocan document and the *Romances* glossator has an apparent interest in Texcoco. Arguably song XXXIII, which speaks of the Acolhuans (i.e., Texcocans), could be singled out. But the fact remains that the
Cantares and *Romances* texts as a whole overwhelmingly brand the surviving
netotiliztli as a Mexica phenomenon.

23. Montezuma and Nezahualcoyotl

23.1   For reasons that are not fully clear,[92] Montezuma and Nezahualcoyotl receive more space in the old native and early colonial literature than any of
the other Aztec kings. In his compendious *Diccionario biográfico de historia*
antigua de Méjico, incorporating all the significant references throughout the
chronicles, Rafael García Granados needed 126 pages for Montezuma (23
for Montezuma I, 103 for Montezuma II) and 34 for Nezahualcoyotl. The
nearest competitors are Nezahualpilli with 13 and Axayacatl and Tezozomoc
with 11 each.

23.2   Since most of this sixteenth- and seventeenth-century literature is

---

92. But see "The Future of Nezahualcoyotl" in the Introduction.

Mexica-oriented, why so much attention to Nezahualcoyotl, ruler of Texcoco (1431–72)?

23.3   A partial answer is that Nezahualcoyotl, though a Texcocan, was related
to the royal house of Tenochtitlan and, as troop commander and strategist,
served as the architect of Mexico's victory in the Tepanec War, ca. 1430.[93]
Without this turn of events, the great age of imperial Mexico would not have
been possible. Durán embroiders on the theme:

> [Nezahualcoyotl, by throwing in his lot with the Mexica,] simply
> shows the love he had for the [Mexica] Aztecs, who were his kinsmen.
> In all the histories, in all that can be read about him, he is shown to be
> a valorous and spirited man. He performed great feats in wars, which
> he often attended in person. He was especially brave in the long wars
> waged against the Tepanecs [...] [and he even pretended that the
> Mexica had waged war against Texcoco and that he had surrendered
> to them] in order to live in peace with the [Mexica] Aztecs, to respect
> their authority, to honor them and extol their name. In this way the
> entire country would fear them and be subject to them because of
> their fame as conquerors of such a great kingdom.[94]

23.4   The *netotiliztli*, likewise, give more space to Montezuma and Nezahualcoyotl than to any of the other kings. In the *Cantares* and *Romances* combined, Montezuma (I and II) and Nezahualcoyotl (often called Yoyontzin)
receive about 60 mentions apiece. The *Romances* mentions Montezuma
6 times and Nezahualcoyotl/Yoyontzin 23 times. That the *Romances* tilts so
heavily toward Nezahualcoyotl probably indicates conscious selection on
the part of the pro-Texcoco compiler—or the pro-Texcoco singer(s) who
served as the source.

23.5   The various references to Nezahualcoyotl, as suggested above, do not
necessarily mean that the songs in the *Romances* are non-Mexica, even if
the manuscript is a Texcocan compilation. Further, it should be noted that
"Texcoco" never appears in any of the songs in either the *Romances* or the
Cantares and the name "Acolhuacan" only rarely (and never in the transfig-
uring phraseology reserved for Mexico/Tenochtitlan).

---

93. On the Tepanec War, CC 30:31–48:45. On the role of Nezahualcoyotl, CC 34:33–40:1,
44:29–38, 45:28–47:40, 48:31.
94. Durán 1994:128–29 (ch. 15).

23.6   As a postscript it may be pointed out that Nezahualcoyotl, though be-
loved of modern, nonnative historians and even biographers, dropped out
of oral tradition after about 1600. Montezuma, however, remained alive (or,
better, returned to life), joining the ranks of perennial Indian kings and mes-
sianic figures.[95] Of these the most recent, apparently, is the Quiché Maya
hero Tecun Uman, who had met the Spanish conquerors of Guatemala in
1523—and, it was said, returned during the Guatemalan civil war of the
1980s, bringing with him an army of 2 million warriors for the Indian cause.[96]
(Most recent, that is, if the return of the Tzeltalan hero Votan in the State of
Chiapas in the 1990s can be discounted as a non-Indian blandishment.)[97]
The most powerful, perhaps, was the Montezuma whose cult flourished in
the pueblos of New Mexico from the 1600s to the early twentieth century,
for whom sacred fires were kept burning against the day when he would
return as the native people's deliverer from Spanish oppression.[98] Among
the most poignant is the Moctezuma of the twentieth-century Popoluca of
Oaxaca State, where the Aztec king who had greeted Cortés had come to
be regarded as a culture hero—still being kept prisoner in Mexico City.[99]
Finally, as a linguistic note, it may be added that by the twentieth century
the term *montezuma* had become integrated into the Guaymí language of
western Panama as the word for 'king' or 'tribal leader'.[100]

24. Ritual as Poetry

24.1   When all is said and done there will still be the reader who approaches Aztec
songs as poetry, who hopes and believes that they are precolumbian, and
who is willing to see them as "universal statements about an unchanging and
essential human nature."[101] Can these expectations be met?

24.2   The answer perhaps is yes. First, because the songs in performance, with

95. Bierhorst 2002:200–206.

96. For Tecun Uman in history, see Carmack 1973:301–3; in legend, Shaw 1971:223–24; in the 1980s, Carmack 1988:69.

97. On Votan, see Bierhorst 2002:162. On the return of Votan, see Ross and Bardacke 1995:195–98.

98. Parmentier 1979:617–20. The "Montezuma" of the New Mexico pueblos has been compared to the "Montezuma" who led the Yucatec Maya uprising of 1761 (Patch 1998:73–74, 76, 81–82).

99. Foster 1945:215.

100. Alphonse 1956:44; Verrill 1929:205, 213–14.

101. Kernan 1990:2.

their abundant entertainment aspects, were obviously intended to refresh the spirit, as poetry must, even to the point of satirizing the underlying ritual (as several of the irreverent, even ribald, texts in the *Cantares* manuscript can demonstrate). Second, because there is every reason to believe that the rhetorical apparatus, even whole stanzas, and probably whole songs in some cases, was imported into the mid-sixteenth century from a pre-Cortésian past. And third, because the idiom is rich in the metaphorical content that makes universal truths—better to say realities—if not acceptable, at least easier to endure.

24.3　　Basically the *netotiliztli* functions as a single guiding metaphor connecting two articles of belief, each independently attested: (1) the dogma that slain warriors, residing in the sky world, are returned to earth; and (2) the idea that song, originating in the sky world, is brought to earth by the singer (see secs. 5 and 8.1, above). Playing on the similarity between the two ideas, the metaphor calls for the warrior to be regarded as a song—the warrior *is* the song—and it is this equation, counterintuitive for the unattuned listener, that provides the central mystery of the *netotiliztli*. To grasp it is to grasp the "poetry" of the entire genre.

24.4　　Yet comparisons with the poetry of far-removed traditions need not be ruled out, even if songs in the European pastoral mode (discussed above) offer only a false echo. The singer's subservience to an agent, or muse, suggests a parallel with the Homeric epics; the pro- and anti-war voices recall the dialogue between the god Krishna and the reluctant war chief Arjuna in the Vedantic poem *Bhagavad Gita*; and, in form, the brief stanzas bear a resemblance to the "links" of Japanese *renga*, or linked verse, in that the sequencing from one link to the next may thoroughly, perhaps intentionally, baffle the uninitiated. Thus the *netotiliztli*, however ritualistic, culture-specific, even obscurantist, can be said to operate in the company of world literature.

Guide to the Vocabulary

Except for proper nouns, which may be located in the Concordance to Proper Nouns, the main vocabulary items used in the English translation of the *Romances* will be found here, together with the number of the paragraph in which each item is discussed or mentioned in the preceding essay, On the Translation of Aztec Poetry.

adorn 17.2
agonies 10.10
appear 1.7
array 17.2, 20.2
arrive 1.7, 2.1, 2.2, 16.1, 18.3, 22.4
arrow 4.2–4, 12.9
await 5.6
banner 9.7
begin, *see* Appendix I
bell 9.7
bereavement 12.5–7
blaze 2.1, 2.4, 9.1, 12.10
blossom 2.1–2, 8.1, 19.3
born 8.1–3
borrow 12.7–8
break open, *see* hatch
brief 12.8
bring down 1.7, 1.12, 3.5, 8.4, 21.2
brother 11.2
bud 2.2
burst open, *see* hatch

cacao 13.1
cacao flower 2.2, 4.6, 13.1
ceiba 4.3
chalk 5.1, 20.1
color 15.4
come 1.7, 3.1, 5.1, 8.1, 8.4–5, 16.1, 18.3
companion 2.1, 2.3, 7.4, 11.2–3, 15.4
comrade 2.2–3, 7.4, 11.2–3, 12.9, 15.4
conch 9.7
conflict 12.11
cotinga 5.5
court 9.8
crave 2.2, 2.4
create 3.5, 8.1, 14.2–3, 15.1, 18.3
crown of flowers 15.5
cypress 4.3
dance 9.7
dance cry 9.5
descend 1.12, 8.4
drill 9.1, 15.2
drink 13.1

patio 9.8
payment 20.1–3
picture 15.4
pleasure 2.3, 3.1, 7.1–3, 9.1, 10.8, 12.7
plume 15.3
poor 10.4, 10.6, 12.1, 12.9
popcorn flower 4.6
pour down 8.4
pray 9.9
prince 14.2–3, 16.1, 19.1
quetzal 5.5
rain 8.4, 19.2
raise (a song) 8.4
rattle 9.1, 9.7, 10.8
raven flower 4.6
recall 17.7
reed 4.3
renown 12.10
require 12.11
rich 12.1
roar 16.1, 20.3
root 16.2
roseate swan 5.5
ruin 12.10
sadness 10.8–9
sane 12.10
scatter 8.4
seek 12.9
seethe 12.11
services 9.9
set free 8.4
shake down 8.4
shatter 12.10
shear, *see* shorn
shield 4.2
shorn 2.5
shrill 8.1, 9.8

sing 9.9
sling 4.2
smelt 15.2
smoke 4.7
snare 17.1
song 8.1–3
sorrows 10.10
speak 9.9
spin 17.7, 19.1, 19.3–5
spine 4.3
splinter 12.10
spread 8.4
sprout 2.1–2, 5.3
stir 8.4, 22.4
strew, *see* scatter
strike up, *see* Appendix I
string 15.2
suffer 12.1
summon 1.7, 3.1, 3.5, 5.4, 14.2, 17.6
sun 2.1, 3.2, 5.1, 12.4
sun flowers 2.5
swan 5.5
tassel 4.6
trogon 5.5
troupial 5.5
turn 15.5, 17.5, 19.4
turquoise 15.1–2, 18.1
twice 21.1–3
twirl 16.1, 19.5
want 12.11
weep 10.3, 10.7, 10.9
whirl 17.5–6, 18.1, 19.1–5
whistling 9.3, 9.5
wine 13.1, 13.5
wither 2.2, 12.8, 12.10
word 8.1, 16.1, 19.3, 22.4

Romances de los Señores de la Nueva España

Ballads of the Lords of New Spain

Guide to the Transcription

The reader of the *Romances* manuscript soon discovers that the scribe omits or inserts *n*'s and *m*'s—or exchanges one for the other or doubles them—without an apparent system. Another peculiarity is that the sounds /s/ and /ts/, often written ç and *tz*, are interchanged indiscriminately. Further, untranslatable song syllables, or vocables, appear in most passages, sometimes as *i, ya,* or *iya* within a word, often as *i, ya,* or some other meaningless syllable at the end of a word, producing distortion. A great many other vocables, such as *yehua, cahui,* and the ubiquitous *ohuaya,* are free-standing. All have been reproduced in the transcription without any signal to distinguish them from lexical material, just as in the manuscript, and with no assurance that they have been segmented in a way that accurately reflects oral delivery. (For a concordance to vocables, see DICT pp. 729–36.) The following additional points may be noted:

Copyist's errors. Obvious mistakes are abundant, characters misread, whole syllables dropped. Corrective footnotes, where needed, are supplied with the translation.

Roman and italic. The transcription uses two fonts: roman for the heavily penned main text, *italic* for the more lightly penned jottings of the glossator.

Slash, dash, and bullet. A forward slash, /, found in some passages, evidently marks the boundary between words. A short dash, given in the transcription as a hyphen, -, has the same function, as does the bullet. No doubt it is the copyist responsible for the main text who uses the short dash. The slash, where short and heavily penned, must also belong to the main text, while a thinner, longer slash, often squeezed in as an afterthought, presumably comes from the glossator. The transcription does not distinguish between the two kinds of slash; and wherever the boundary marker is taken to be incorrect, the character string has been closed up, nevertheless preserving the slash, dash, or bullet.

Brackets. Occasional directions to the reader, as well as manuscript line numbers at the beginning of each line, are enclosed in square brackets, [ ], following the usual method of indicating editorial additions.

Paragraph mark. The pilcrow, or paragraph mark, ¶, has been kept throughout, just as it appears in the manuscript (at the beginning of each stanza). It is not an editorial addition.

Stricken and illegible characters. A line through a character, as in ~~a~~, means that the copyist has stricken it, yet it is still legible. If a character is blotted or otherwise unreadable it appears as the symbol ■.

Abbreviation marks: arc and tilde. The superscript tilde, ˜, and the superscript arc, ⌒, occur throughout the manuscript, indicating that one or two unwritten characters follow the marked character, viz., *n* or *m* if the marked character is a vowel; *ue* or, rarely, *ui* if it is a *q; a* if it is the *p* in the combination *tlpc* (for *tlalticpac* 'earth', or, as it would seem, the mark converts the entire combination *tlpc* into the full word *tlalticpac*). Either symbol written over an *n,* however, simply converts the *n* to the familiar Spanish *ñ*. (Because the arc and the tilde are variously slanted, flattened, or curled in the untidy *Romances* manuscript, they are often indistinguishable, and the printed transcription, forced to make choices, is therefore provisional in this regard. For more information on the arc and the tilde, see GRAM sec. 4. A third typographic symbol, the overbar, ¯, might have been introduced in cases where the arc or the tilde has been flattened nearly perfectly, but because of the many gradations it is not clear that the copyist intends this. Rarely the arc, where slightly pointed, might be interpreted as a circumflex, ^, instead of an arc, ⌒; but again, the scribe fails to make this plain, and the circumflex has not been used in the transcription.)

Abbreviation mark: the vertical stroke. Rarely (at 14:14, 23v:16, 24:16, 27v:19, 40v:16) a vertical stroke, ', appears over a *q,* converting it to *qui* (as discussed in Anderson et al. 1976:34).

Diacritics. The arc and the tilde (see above) may be considered diacritics rather than abbreviation marks when appearing over vowels, indicating nasalization, which, as already implied, is anything but consistent in the *Romances* manuscript.

Calligraphic flourishes. As in other, contemporaneous manuscripts the *i* is sometimes written with an apostrophe in place of the usual dot. This flourish, even where ill formed and therefore susceptible to being taken as a diacritical mark, has not been carried into the transcription. A more difficult case is the nasalization of the vowel immediately following the ç. The copyist almost always marks such a vowel, using a slanted tilde or an arc, though often the mark strikes the eye as a flourish perhaps inspired by the cedilla under the preceding *c* (as noted in Karttunen and Lockhart 1980:36). Because nasalization is usually a possibility in such a position, the troublesome strokes have been resolved as either arcs or tildes (both of which are customary for this purpose). Thus the transcription, where it errs, errs on the side of overinclusion, indicating nasalization where a mere flourish might have been all that the scribe intended.

Glossator's numbering. The glossator, or presumably the glossator, has numbered the folios and the stanzas, using arabic, or occasionally roman, numerals (and an odd number 12 appears on the first folio to the right of the title). These have been reproduced, in italic, in the positions where they occur in the manuscript.

In sum, a most vexing paleograph, especially in view of the "diacritics." As reproduced in the transcription, the marked characters are:

$$\hat{q} = \text{que } or \text{ qui}$$
$$\dot{q} = \text{qui}$$
$$\bar{p} \; or \; \hat{p} = \text{pa (appears only in } \textit{tlalticpac)}$$
$$ñ \; or \; \hat{n} = ñ$$
$$\text{and}$$
$$â, ê, ŷ, ô, û \; or \; ã, ẽ, ỹ, õ$$
$$= \text{an } (or \text{ am}), \text{ en } (or \text{ em}), \text{ in } (or \text{ im}), \text{ on } (or \text{ om}), \text{ on } (or \text{ om})$$
$$or \text{ an } (or \text{ am}), \text{ en } (or \text{ em}), \text{ in } (or \text{ em}), \text{ on } (or \text{ om})$$

The possibility that some of the marks, or their variations, could indicate vowel length or the glottal stop (as in â, á, à, a', etc.) has been ruled out. The main caution is that in some cases, always with vowels, an ornamental flourish might have been the original significance, as noted above. Yet even in those instances, barring an occasional careless slip, nasalization is conceivable. The manuscript does frequently indicate a long vowel by doubling, as in *xoochitl* 'flower', but seemingly never, or almost never, includes a glottal stop. A rare exception occurs at 21:6–7: *tonahaahuiyacan* 'let us be pleasured', where the first *h* represents the stop. The strange-looking *mâcêuhcātzin* 'Dancer' at 1:18—where the actual phonology calls for *mah-ceeuhcatzin,* or *mahceeuhcantzin,* allowing for a nonsignificant nasal before the *tz* (and with an *h* to indicate the glottal stop after the first *a*)—is here regarded as an anomaly.

[folio 1]

1

+

❡ romanses de los señores de la	*12*
nueba españa—

3	❡ *1* tlaoc tocuicaca tlaoc tocuicatacan [4] yn xochitonalocalitec âya
atocni[5]huani câtliq̃ yni quinamiqui can[6]ni quitemohuã yayo ca q̃on
huehue[7]titla ye nicân an ohuaya ôhuaya
8	❡ *2* çã nixochitlatlaôcoya namocniuh[9]tzin y çã chichimecatetecuitli
tecâye[10]huâtzin aquin aoc timochin tica[11]huiltizq̃ tichuelamachtizq̃
moyoco[12]tzin yehuâya Dios y tla câ nipâ ye câ ten [13] tlaxcalan o
xoxochipoyocuicâ tla puyo[14]cuicã yn xicotecatli yn temilotzin [15]
çan cuitlitzcaltecuitli tlã ohuaya ohuaya
16	❡ *3* cuauhtamiyohuâchânoo ôcêloyohua[17]lichâ huexotzinco yn omcãn i
tlami[18]huacã yn mâcêuhcãtzin yni tlacâhue[19]pan a nimãn ocãn on
ahuiya yn[1]

[folio 1v]

1

1	[1]xochicuapilhuã xopâcalayntec o o[2]huâye hahuâyya onye ohuaya
ohuaya

[I]

3 Friends, let us sing, let us go sing in the house of sun flowers.[1] And who
will seek them, who will meet them here beside the drum?[2]

8 "I grieve in sadness for these flowers,[3] I, your poor friend,[4] Chichimec
Lord Tecayehuatzin. Who among us will fail to entertain,[5] to gladden
God Self Maker?" At flood's edge yonder in Tlaxcala let him sing
narcotic flower songs.[6] Let Xicotencatl, Temilotzin, and Lord
Cuitlizcatl sing narcotic songs. Let us hear "ohuaya ohuaya."[7]

16 In Eagle Tamoanchan, the home of jaguar bells,[8] in Huexotzinco, where

the dying is,[9] there's Dancer. It's Tlacahuepan. His eagle flower
princes find their pleasure in that house of green places.

1. Literally, 'flower heat-of-the-sun house', taking the third *o* as a vocable. However, the translation offered here treats *xochitonal[li]* as a variant of *tonalxochitl* (freely, 'sun flower'), meaning
any kind of flower associated with the sky world (the term *tonalxochitl*, assigned by sixteenth-
century authors to various species, cannot be given a Linnean translation). Probably *xochitonal-o-
calli* (or *xochitonal[l]ocalli*) is a nonce term inspired by such similar locutions as *xochipapalocalli*
'house of flower butterflies' (CM 52v:19, 52v:21, 63:6), referring to the warriors' paradise (or the
battlefield or the dance floor as it represents paradise). For synonyms, see DICT calli.

2. Literally, 'which are these [*câtliq yni*, cf. FC 2:88:23 *iehoan y* 'they are these'] who meet
them, where are they who seek them right [*ca quen*, see DICT quen 5] beside the drum here'.

3. Literally, 'flower-wise I grieve intensely'.

4. The suffix -*tzin* connotes pitiableness when used with the first person. DICT -tzin 9.

5. Literally, 'who not at all [of] we all will entertain [...]'. DICT *ayoc* or *aoc* 'not at all'.

6. Read *can nipa ye can [a]ten[pan]* 'at flood's edge yonder' (for other examples of dropped syllables in this manuscript, see 6:17, 6v:11, 9:7, 10:1, 21:1, etc.). Note the double locative *can [...] can*
(DICT can 2), and cf. CM 55v:13 *oncan [...] atempan* 'there [...] at flood's edge' (i.e., in battle),
and below, 1v:4–5 *omcâ [...] aytec* 'yonder [...] in the middle of the flood'.

7. *Tla ohuaya ohuaya*, literally, 'let there be ohuaya ohuaya [the untranslatable sounds of vocal
music]'.

8. *Oyohualli* 'bell(s)'. Alternately *yohualli* 'darkness'.

9. *Tlamihuacan* 'place where one dies', from *tlami* 'to die' (CARO 114)—a construction disallowed by Andrews (2003:498), who would prescribe *tlamihuayan* (but see also *ximohuacan*,
24v:12, below). Cf. DICT tlami 4, tlamiyan.

3   4 ¶ çâ cacahuaxochiticâ tlapâpahuiti[4]huiçê ye omcâ yn xochiahahuiya
     [5] aytec ã yehuantzin conitquitihui[6]tze ynteomcuitlachimalmãtla
     [7] yecaçêhuaz teônaxochincuauh[8]cocolticâ q̂çâlipâticâ
     toteahuil[9]ticô xopâcacalaytic oo hahuãyya [10] ô aye ohuâya ohuaya
11   5 ¶ chalchiuhtetzilacatli / ycahuaca oo[12]huaye xochiyahuachquiyahuitl
     [13] omquiztoc yn tlaticpac çâcua[14]cala ymacann ixtilavaquitequi [15]
     ye temoya y espiritu santo y dios a[16]ye o ayya ohuaya
17   6 ¶ xoxopã y opã temoyan ipalnemo[18]huan çâ mocuicayzhuayotia
     mo[19]xochiapana huehuetitlan moma[1]

[folio 2]

2

+

[1]linã ye motech onquiçã an yhui[2]ti xochitli ye o ayya yye mã
xonahui[3]yacan ã ohuaya ohuaya
4   7 ¶ [superscript:] *ye onihualla* [line script:] antocnihuãn i
     no[superscript:]*cô*[line script:]q̶u̶i̶cozcaçoya, nic[5]tzinitzcamanaya, ni
     c̶t̶l̶a̶u̶h̶[superscript:]*teoo*[line script:]quecholhui[6]molohuã,
     nicteomcuitlaycuiya, [7] nicquetzalhuixtoylpiz, yn icniuhyotli, [8]
     niccuicaylacãtzoz cohuâyotli yn tec[9]pa■ nicquixtiz, an ya tomizin,
     quini[10]cuac tomitzin,n otiyaq̂, [superscript:] *ye mictlan* [line script:]
     y yuhcã tzan [11] tictlanehuico yn ohuaya ohuaya
12   8 ¶ ye omyanihuala ye omninoqueça [13] ã cuiçã nopictihuiz cuiçã
     noyocoxti[14]huiz antocnihuã nechhualihua [15] dios [superscript:]
     teotl [line script:] nehua nixochhuãtzin nehua [16] nitemilotzin noohuâ
     ye noteycni[17]uhtlaco nican an ohuaya ohuaya

3 As cacao flowers they come sounding the dance cry,[10] finding flower
    pleasure yonder in the middle of the flood, come carrying their gold
    shield hand-slings, their fans.[11] "With flood-flower eagle sadness, with
    plume banners we come entertaining in this house of green places."

11 Jade gongs shrill. A drizzling rain of flowers falls to earth. From the
    House of Troupials, from the bosom of the fields the Holy Spirit,
    God, descends.[12]

17 From Green Places he descends. It's Life Giver. He provides himself
F2 with song petals, he adorns himself with flowers here beside the
    drum. They're whirled, they come from you, these drunken flowers.
    Be entertained!

4 "Friends, I've come to string them as jewels,[13] spread them out as
    trogons, make them stir as spirit swans, twirl them as gold, these
    comrades. As plume-captives I'll snare them.[14] I'll song-whirl these
    companions, in this palace I'll bring them forth. Ah, all of us, then in
    a moment all of us will have departed for the dead land.[15] For we only
    come to borrow them.

12 "I come, I appear! Friends, I come created as a song, come fashioned as
    a song.[16] God sends me here. I have flowers, I am Temilotzin. I've
    come to assemble a company of friends."[17]

---

10. *Cacahuaxochitica* 'as cacao flowers'. For -*ca* 'as', see DICT 1. -ca 2; cf. 2. ic 4.

11. For *yehuantzin* read *yehuantin*.

12. Read *ixtlahuaquitec i* 'in the midst of the [Elysian] fields'. Cf. CM 9:21 *ixtlahuac itec* and DICT ixtlahuatl.

13. DICT zo:tla 'to perforate or string something [as a gem, to make a necklace]'.

14. Alternate reading: *nicquetzalxi[t]to[mon]ilpiz* 'as plumes I'll snare them'. See the Remarks in the Commentary for song I.

15. The text has *y yuhcā* for *yn yuhcan* or *ye yuhcan*, 'that place [beyond]'. The glossator writes directly above it: *ye mictlan* 'the dead land'. The seemingly metathetic *tomizin* or *tomitzin* 'all of us', normally *timochin*, is reflected in CM 48:10, where *michi* replaces *mochi* 'all'. Cf. CM 3v:11 *çan cuel achic nican timochi tonyazque o ye ichano* 'only for a moment here, and all of us will be departing for His home' (recurs at CM 25:20).

16. For *cuiçā* read *cuicatl* 'song' (the error *ç* for *c* occurs more obviously at 9v:2; and the error, or apocopation, *cuicā for cuicatl* occurs also at 14v:7). Cf. CM 27:24 *Dios mitzyocox aya xochitla ya mitztlacatiliyan cuicatl mitzicuiloa* 'God has formed you, has given you birth as a flower, paints you as a song', CM 63:7 *cuicatl ye tiyol tiMoteucçomatzin xochitl ticueponico in tlp̄cqui* 'as a song you're born, O Montezuma: as a flower you come to bloom on earth'. On the omission of the first-person subject prefix in reflexive verb forms, see CARO 126 or GRAM 3.4.

17. *Nonteicniuhtlaco*. Molina gives the core meaning of the verb *icniuhtla:nite* as *amigos hazer a algunos* 'to cause people to be friends' or, more fully, *dar a conocer a otros paraque se amen* 'to cause others to become acquainted so they will love one another' (MOLS 9v, MOL 33, cf. Andrews

ya esta trasuntado

tamôhua
ni a ca te   4 titloq̃ tinahua ay dios
huatl   [superscript:] *totecoyo*
2 y ma o■■■■   [line script:] ayac ypalne
â quimati

3 ahuilotl i machtic mati
yca çā totlaocol yye■

[folio 2v]

2

1   9 2   **·ℭ·** nihualaciz ye nicâ ye niyoyotzin [2] yhuiya çā nixochiyeelehuiya
ehua[3]ya nixochitlatlapanaco tlalticq̃ noco[4]yatlapana yn
cacahuaxochitli nocô[5]yatlapana ycniuhxochitli ye tehuā [6]
monacāyo titecpiltzinn i necāhual[7]coyotl tecuitli yoyotzin i yyahu
ohui [8] y yya hayyo ya oha ha ay yohuiya
9   10 ℭ tzan nicyatemohuitihuiz nocuiqu i [10] yectli yhuā nicyatemohuiya,
[11] titocnihuan anaya cohuatihua [12] yehuan ycniuhtlamachoya y [13]
yahua hui y yya hayyo ya oha [14] y yuayyo ohuiya
15   11 ℭ Achin ic nonahuiya oo achin ic opā[16]pactinemi noyolo yn
tlalticpac[17]quin ye niyoyotzinn i■ nixochiyee[18]lehuiya oo nixochicu
icuiycātine[19]miya ohuaya ohuaya [1]

[folio 3]

3

+

1   12 ℭ [1] nicnenequi niq̃elehuiya yn icni[2]uhyootl yn tecpilotli yn
cohuāyo[3]tlin nixochiyeelehuiya oo nixochi[4]cuicuicâtinemiya
ohuâya ohuaya

[II][18]

1 "I'm coming,[19] I, Yoyontzin, craving flowers, hatching flowers here on earth, hatching cacao flowers, hatching comrade flowers."[20] And they're your flesh, O prince, O Lord Nezahualcoyotl, O Yoyontzin.

9 "I come bringing my good songs, bringing them down. We're friends. May all be comrades, may all know friends.[21]

15 "On earth I'm briefly pleasured. These hearts of mine — they briefly live in happiness,[22] and I'm Yoyontzin, craving flowers, flower-chirping.

F3 1 "I'm desiring, craving friends, princes, comrades. I'm craving flowers, flower-chirping.

1975:357 or 2003:585–86). Molina's *icniuhtla:nite* = *hazer amigos a los enemistados* 'to make friends out of enemies' (MOL 33, also CARO 81) is an applied meaning, not relevant here. In the present case, as in the *netotiliztli* generally, the singer means "friends," or "allies," in the sense of battlefield comradeship, much desired by spirit warriors coming into contact with their earthly counterparts (see CMSA p. 26 section entitled "Sodality and Reunion"). Thus the singer's statement is personal, though not without a political overtone. On the military, or political, use of *icniuhtli* 'ally', see TRAN 7.4. We may then interpret the passage at hand to mean that a warrior-singer out of the Mexica past appears on an imagined battlefield to make common cause with earthly Mexica, thus fulfilling the promise announced in the opening stanza by the verbs 'seek' and 'meet', spelled out more clearly in the second stanza of song II: "We're friends. May all be comrades, may all know friends" — restating *Cantares* 64:28, *yn icniuhyoticanya titoyximati huehuetitlana* 'we, in comradeship, become acquainted beside the drum' (CMSA pp. 356–57).

Here (in the manuscript) follow four fragments of indeterminate affiliation, with the heading *ya está trasuntado*, 'already transcribed'. Several of the terms may be analyzed: [1] *tamohuan[chan] [. . .] ca tehuatl* 'Tamoanchan' [. . .] indeed it is you'; 2 [. . .] *quimati* 'he knows it'; 3 *ahuillotl [. . .] mach ticmati / ica za totlaocol [. . .]* 'pleasure [. . .] do you know it? / thus there's just our sorrow [*or* our created one]'; 4 *titloque tinahua[que] ay dios / ayac ipalne[mohuani . . .]* 'O Ever Present, O Ever Near, oh God! / no one [is the friend of] Life Giver', to which the glossator adds *toteucyo* 'Our Lord' (cf. 5:3–4 *ayac huel oo / ayac huel icniuh [i]n ipalnemohuā* 'no one, no one can be the friend of Life Giver'; CM 24:30–24v:2 *Titloque tinahuaque Diose tonicniuhtlatzihuiz [. . .] ypalnemoani ticiehuiz tontlatzihuiz titechonmotlatiliz* 'O Ever Present, O Ever Near, O God, you will weary of friends [. . .] O Life Giver, you will tire, you will weary, you will "hide" [i.e., kill] us').

18. The song also appears as CM song 25 (18v:16–19:10); and stanzas 3–4 appear yet again at CM 68:28–32.

19. *Nihualaciz* 'I am to arrive here'.

20. This may mean 'breaking open', as an egg hatches or a flower bursts into bloom, thus 'giving birth (to)'. Or it may mean that the comrades, or 'flowers', are destined to be broken in battle. DICT tlahtlapana:tla, tlapana:tla, tlapani.

21. Literally, 'all have comrades, all have knowledge [*or* acquaintance] with regard to friends'.

22. Alternate translation: 'This heart of mine, it briefly lives in happiness'.

5   *13*   ohu aca yuhqui teocuitlatl o ohuaye [6] acā yuhqui cozcātli · ŷ q̂çāli
           pâtlahuac [7] q̂n ipâ ye nicmatia yectli ya mocui[8]yc aya tontatzinni o
           yehuâ dios i [superscript:] *totecoyo* [line script:] ycan [9] nonahuiya a■
           ynca nonitotia hue[10]huetitlan oo xopâcalayntequi ye niyō[11]yôtzin
           haya ha noyol quimatin ohuā[12]ya ohuaya

13   *14* ¶ ma xiquihueliçôçônan moxochihue[14]hue ticuicânitli yeehuâya
           moxochiaya[15]câch in ma yzquixochitl ihuā cacahua[16]xochitli ma
           humoyahuâya ma ô[17]çêçêlihui ye nican a huehuetitla[18]n oo ma
           tahuiyacani ohuaya ohuaya

19   *15* ¶ ha ca xiuhq̂chool tzinnizcâ tlauhq̂[20]chol ōcann ocuicâ tlatohuaya y [1]

[folio 3v]

3

[1] xochitl a yc pâqui oo ha ylili o ha y[2]lililili ohuiya oo hayya ohuaya
[3] ohuaya

4   *16* ¶ ah uca ya yncâqui yn xochihuauh[5]tli yn huehuetitlan ah ayyahue [6]
           y ye yntech onemi nemiya y ye q̂[7]çâliquechol i tototli ynpâ
           mo[8]chuhtinnemin oo y neçahualcoyo[9]tzin ô
           xochicuicuiŷcantinemi [10] oo yn xochitla yc pāqui oo ha ylili oo [11] a
           ylililili ohuiya oo haya ohuaya [12] ohuaya

3

14   *17* ¶ ye no cēpā ya cuica no ya hualāciz ha [15] o ya mōyecoya toxochi oo
           aya tocuiqui ■ [16] yya oayye yya yye ayya yyohuia

17   *18* ¶ ma ça moq̂çâ a ōhua ni■cuihuan i [18] onoq̂ omcate yn tepilhuan oo
           [19] netzahualcoyotzinn i cuicanitl huia [1]

[folio 4]

4

+

[1] çontecochchatzin · liya oayye yyayye [2] ayya yyohuia
3   *19* ¶ xococui moxochihua yhuān i meca[4]çehuaz ma yca ximototin çâ
           tehua [5] nopiltzin çâ ye tiyoyotzinn ayyohui[6]ya

7   *20* ¶ ma xococua yn cacahuatl yn caca[8]huaxochitl ma ya omnihuā ŷ ma
           [9] ya netôtilo ma necuicatilo ani[10]ca tocha anica tinemizq̂ toyaz ô
           ye [11] yuhcan i yaô ahuayya oo huiya huia

5 "I value these good songs of yours as gold, as jewels, as broad plumes, O father, O God.²³ With these I'm pleasured. With these I dance beside the drum in this house of green places, I, Yoyontzin. My heart enjoys them."

13 Play your flower drum skillfully, singer. And your flower rattle. Let there be popcorn flowers, cacao flowers. Let them scatter, let them sprinkle down beside the drum. Let's be pleasured.

19 There! The turquoise swan, the trogon, the roseate swan is singing,
F3V   warbling, happy with these flowers.

4 There! A flower tree stands beside the drum. The plume swan is in it. It's Nezahualcoyotzin. He's like a bird, flower-chirping, happy with these flowers.²⁴

III

14 Again they make music, and they will arrive. Our flowers, our songs are created.²⁵

17 Brothers, let them appear. And here they are, the princes!²⁶
F4   O Nezahualcoyotzin! O singer! O Tzontecochatzin!

3 Pick up your flowers, your fans, and dance with these, my prince Yoyontzin.

7 Pick up this cacao, these cacao flowers, and let them be sent away.²⁷ Let there be dancing and music. Our home is not here. We're not to live here. You are off to that place.

---

23. Superscript *totecoyo* 'Our Lord'.

24. Read *ah oncan ya ihcac yn xochicuauhtli* 'Ah! There stands a flower tree'. For *onemi nemiya* read *onnemiya*; for *ynpâ mochuhtinnemin* read *ypan mochiuhtinemi*. Cf. CM 19:7–8. The textual *xochihuauhtli* 'flower amaranth', where CM has *xochicuahuitl,* would seem to be an error. Unless here, *huauhtli* 'amaranth' does not occur in either the *Romances* or the *Cantares*. Note that *cuauhtli* is a variant of *cuahuitl* (see DICT).

25. Read *moyocoya* 'they are created'. Or read *moyeco ya* 'they have been created' (cf. DICT *yecoa:tla* 2). Cf. 11v:6, below.

26. Literally, they're there (*onoque*); there are princes (*oncate in tepilhuan*).

27. Read *ma xococui* 'pick [them] up', as in the preceding stanza; and *ma ya ommihua* 'let them be sent away', to accord with the text that follows. But if the reading is *ma xococua yn cacahuatl yn cacahuaxochitl ma ya omihua* 'eat cacao, cacao flowers, let them be imbibed', it would accord with 9:21 'let's drink — let us eat — cacao flowers'.

12   21 ⸿ maçâ tlatoliya maçân itoloni cui[13]catl yn ma no nehuatl y
          niquino[14]notzā yn tepilhuan i çintlalcohuâ[15]tzinn i cahualtzin
          motecuiçôma[16]tzin netzahualcotla ohuaya ohuāya
17   22 ⸿ y huelamāti ye noyol paqui noyool on[18]nococaco y ycuic ma
          onnetotilo [19] mach och çâ no yhui omca nixpan [1]

                    [folio 4v]

     4

     [1] nima niquihuica yn tepilhuân oo [2] oo ynn opa ximohua / ohuayo
     ohua[3]ya q̂nonamicana [4] ôhuayyayye / ohuayyayye yye ahuayya [5]
     ahuaya ohuaya ohuaya ayee huaya
6   23 ⸿ Ya nnihualatzic euia nicuicanitli [7] mochi noxochihui nicmamali[8]nā
          niq̂çālicuilohuā yn anye ô a[9]ya yhuā cânan tocohuini aye oaye ô
          a[10]ya yhuā cana ohuāya ohuāy

                    el poder grande del criador
                         4   *ya esta tra*
                                                    suntado

12   24 ⸿ aca huel icha moyocoyatzin yehuaya [13] Dios [superscript:] *totecoyo*
          [line script:] yn nohuiya noçâlo / nohuiya [14] no chiyalo / yehua
          temolon itleyotzi [15] mahuizyo / tlalticpac ohuaya ohuaya
16   25 ⸿ ohuaya - quiyocoya / yeehuaya mo[17]yocoyatzin / yehuaya dios
          [superscript:] *totecoyo* [line script:] yn nohuiya [18] notzâlo / nohuiya
          no chialo / yehua [1]

                    [folio 5]

                                                         5

                         +

     [1] temolo·n itleyon imahuizyo / tlal[2]ticpac ohuaya ohuaya
3   26 ⸿ ayac huel oo / ayac huel icniuh [4] n ipalnemohuā / cani noçâlo /
          hue[5]l itlocqu inahuac oo nemohuā / [6] ye nicann i tlalticpac / yyao
          ohui[7]ya
8   27 ⸿ q̂nami y quihuelmati / cani noçâlo [9] huel itlocqu inahuac oo /
          nemo[10]huā / ye nicân i tlalticpac / yyao [11] ohuiya
12   28 ⸿ ayac neli ye mocniuh / ypalne[13]mohuā çân ihui xochitla ynpā [14]
          totemati tlalticpac monahuac an [15] ohuaya ohuaya

12 Let there be words, let songs be spoken. I, too, want to speak with the princes, Citlalcoatzin, Cahualtzin, Montezuma, and Nezahualcoyotl.

17 My heart is happy, my heart is glad. I have heard their music. Let there be dancing. Just so. For now.[28] Before my eyes. And then I will take

F4v   away these princes to the place where all are shorn, the place unknown.

6 I have come, I the singer. I whirl them all, all my flowers. I paint them as plumes.[29]

IV[30]

12 God Self Maker's home is nowhere.[31] Prayers and services to him are everywhere. His fame and glory are sought on earth.[32]

16 God Self Maker makes ohuaya.[33] Prayers and services to him are

F5   everywhere. His fame and glory are sought on earth.

3 "No one, no one can be Life Giver's friend. Where there are prayers to him, near him and in his presence, can there be life here on earth?"

8 What does he enjoy? Where there are prayers to him, near him and in his presence, there can be life here on earth.

12 "O Life Giver, really no one is your friend. You merely treat people as flowers on earth and in your presence.

---

28. Read *mach oc zan no yhui oncan* 'Indeed just now, absolutely thus at this time'. DICT mach 2, oc 4, no iuh, oncan 2. The oddly formed *h* in *och* (read *oc*), evidently a copyist's careless duplication of the preceding *h* in *mach,* is similarly formed at 6:16 (fifth character from the end of the line).

29. The translatable text is followed by a string of vocables, including some unusual ones. Cf. the similar *cani, toco, ton-cohuili,* etc., in the Concordance to Vocables in DICT pp. 729–36.

30. Gloss: 'the great power of the Creator'. And to the right: 'already transcribed'.

31. Superscript *totecoyo* 'Our Lord'. His home is "nowhere" because he seizes authority everywhere, as explained in FC 4:33:34–37.

32. Literally, 'he is called to' (*notzalo*); 'he is waited upon, i.e., venerated' (*chiyalo*). For *itleyotzi mahuizyo* read *itleyotzin imahuizyo* 'his fame, his glory'.

33. Superscript *totecoyo* 'Our Lord'. Cf. CM 13v:3–4 *Çan ca ilhuicatlytec oncan ticyocoya motlatol can yehuā Dios* 'Oh, God! You're making those songs of yours in heaven'.

16 29 ⸿ omtlatzihuiz y moyollo / yeehuaya [17] çã cuel achic yn motloc
monahuac [18] an / ohuaya ohuaya

19 30 ⸿ Techyolopolohua/n ipalnemohua[20]ni / techihuitiya o nicaan a/ya
oo[1]

[folio 5v]

5

[1]huaye / ayac huel i çõ tlan oquiçã [2] omtlatohua tlalticpac / ohuaya
[3] ohuaya

4 31 ⸿ yn çãn ic ticamana ▪ / yn quenin [5] conitohuã toyollo / yeehuaya
oo[6]huaye / anyac huel i çõ tlan oquiçã [7] omtlatohua tlalticpac /
ohuaya [8] ohuaya -

5

de cacamatzin ultimo rey de tezcuco
quando se bido en grãdes trabajos acor
dãdose del p▪▪[▪▪?] y maj[ta▪] *grande de su pa*[e] *y aguelo*

10 32 ⸿ yn atocnihuane tlaoc xococaqui[11]cã macaçõ ayac yn teconene[12]mi
cualayotl cocolotl maçõ yl[13]cahui maçõ pupuliuhui yecã
tlal[14]ticpac ohuayo ohuaya.

15 33 ⸿ noçã nomã ye nehuatl nechonito[16]-a y / yalhuã tlachcon catcã
con[17]nitohua comolhuiya ach q̃ tlatla[18]cã / ach q̃ tlatlamati / ac çãn
i mo[19]mãtin mochi conitohua am yn a[20]nel nitlatohua tlalticpac
ohuaya [21] ohuaya

16 "Your heart will grow tired. Briefly near you and in your presence!
19 "Life Giver maddens us, makes us drunk on earth. No one can escape
F5v   from Him who rules on earth."[34]
4 Just so. We annoy him.[35] What is this our hearts are saying? No one can
escape from Him who rules on earth.

V[36]

10 Friends, listen to this: "Let's have no more lordly marching.[37] Let's
forget war and conflict.[38] Let those things be done with here in this
good world."
15 Even me. They talk about me, too.[39] Yesterday there was the ball court.[40]
This is what they were saying, what they were telling each other:
"How can he be human? How can he be sane?"[41] Who knows all that
they say? But is it not true that I speak on earth?

---

34. Read *ayac huel in zo itlan onquiza* 'no one can indeed from Him escape'. Cf. MOL *tematitlampa niquiça* 'descabullirse, o escaparse de entre las manos de algunos'; *tetlan niquiztiquiça* 'descabullirse de ĕtre otros'.

35. *Ticamana* 'we annoy him' echoes *omtlatzihuiz y moyollo* 'your heart will grow tired' (5:16). Cf. CM 30:3–4 *mahmana tlatzihui* [...] *ipalnemoa* 'he becomes annoyed, grows weary [...] he, Life Giver'.

36. Spanish gloss reads: *de Cacamatzin ultimo rey de Te[t]zcoco quando se vido en grandes trabajos acordandose del p[oder] y maj[es]ta[d] grande de su pa[dr]e y abuelo* 'of Cacamatzin, last king of Texcoco, when he found himself in great difficulties, recalling the power and great majesty of his father and grandfather'.

37. Literally, 'Let there be no one who marches as a lord' (*teucnehnemi*). *Nehnemi* 'to move or march [in battle]' (FC 4:70:11, 12:97:5, 12:104:22). On *nehnemi* 'march' see note to 40v:3.

38. Literally, 'bellicosity [and] fights'. DICT cualani, MOL *cocollotl* 'riña [fight]'.

39. *Noza nohmah ye nehhuatl nechonihtoah* 'just even already me they speak (ill) of me'. For *no* and *za* as intensifiers see DICT. For *nohmah* 'even' see FC 10:183:31 *oc noma no mopotonja in jnmac* 'they even paste feathers on their arms'. For 'speak (ill)' see DICT ihtoa:te 2.

40. Captives were sacrificed at the *tlachco* 'ball court' in the main square of Tenochtitlan (FC 2:134:2–4).

41. *Ach quen tlatlaca* [apocopated *tlatlacatl*] *ach quen tlatlamati* 'How is he human? How does he have understanding [*freely,* sanity]?' Compare the description of the incompetent ruler, as translated by Anderson and Dibble: [...] *aiocmo teixco, teicpac tlachia: auh in aiocmo can icnoio in jiollo* [...] *injc aoc tlatlamati, injc aoc teixco tlachia* [...] *ca ovellapolo, ca aocmo ça njman qujmati* '[...] no more hath he regard for others, and no more is he anywhere compassionate [...] so he is evermore presumptuous, evermore impudent [...] is completely crazed; he no longer understandeth at all' (FC 6:25:17–6:26:8).

[folio 6]

6

+

1　34 ⁋ ayahuiztli moteca ōhuaye ma [2] quiquiztlā yncahuācan nopan [3] pani
tlalticpac huiya çeçelihui [4] mimilihui yahualihui xochitli [5]
ahuiyaztihuiz yn tlalticpac â o[6]huaya ohuaya

7　35 ⁋ o ach iuhqui nel ye ychan totatzin oo [8] a yn Dios a a/yyahue ach in
iuhqui [9] xoxopâni q̂çāliyaxochiticâ [10] om tlalicuilohua tlalticpac
[11] ye niconn ipalnemohuani ohua[12]ya ohuaya

13　 ⁋ chalchiuhteponaztli / mimilito[14]c an ayyahue

36 omchalchihuilaca[15]piçôhuāya yn itlaçô dioss aya a [16] yn ilhuicac a
ayyahue yhuh q̂cho[17]lle cocozcatl huihuilotihuiz yn [18] tlalticpac /
a ahuaya ohuaya

19　 ⁋ cuicāchimalayahuitlacochqui[1]

37

[folio 6v]

6

[1]ya/hui ya tlalticpa/a/qui nepa[2]pa xochitli / omyohuala ycâ ya
te[3]tecuica yn ilhuicatl aya teomcui[4]tlachimalticâ ye omnetotilo
ohua[5]ya ohuaya

6　 ⁋ çā niquitohuā yeehuaya çā nicaca[7]matzi i huiya çā

38 niquimilnami[8]qui yn tlatohuanime netzāhualpi[9]la ayyahue cuix
ômotā cuix om[10]noçâ yn netzahualcoyootl huiya [11] huehuetitla
niquimilnaqui ohua[12]ya ohuaya

13　 ⁋ ac nel a yaz · yn chalchihuitl teocui[14]tlatl mach acâ omyaz huiya

39 cuix ni[15]xiuhchimali ayoc çepā noçâlo[16]loz iin y q̂çâlayatica
niquimilolo ya [17] tlalticpāc aya huehuetitla niquimi[18]ylnamiqui
ohuaya ohuaya

———　　———

19　　　　　　　　titoco · titoco · titoco · titoco - titoco · ti

20　　　　　　　　tocoti

F6 1 The smoke rolls.[42] Ohuaye. Let the conch horns scream with me here
on this earth. The budding swelling flowers are scattering down.
They come with pleasure here on earth.[43]

7 This is how it would be in the home of our father God, how it would be
in green places: Life Giver painting the earth with plume-incense
flowers.[44]

13 Jade log drums are sounding; God's loved ones, jade-fluting in the skies;
swan feathers heavy with jewels, bending on earth.[45]

19 A song shield spear mist, raining on earth. And with this multitude of
F6v flower bells the skies are roaring. There's gold shield dancing.[46]

6 This I say, I, Cacamatl: I recall the kings Nezahualpilli and
Nezahualcoyotl, are they summoned? Are they seen?[47] Here beside
the drum I recall them.[48]

13 And who will pass away? Jades? Gold? Will someone pass away? Am I
a turquoise shield? Never again will I be put together?[49] I am arrayed
in plumes here on earth.[50] Here beside the drum I recall them.

[two-tone drum cadence:] titoco titoco titoco titoco titoco titoco ti

---

42. Cf. CM 84v:12 *ayahuitl moteca* 'the smoke rolls [from a harquebus]'. *Ayahuihtli* would be
a possible variant of *ayahuitl*, easily misunderstood as *ayahuiztli* if the scribe were reading from a
copy that had the descending *h*. (The *ayahuitl* at CM 84v:12 does have the descending *h*.)

43. Read *ahuiyahtihuitz* 'they come being pleasured' (treating the verb *ahuiya* as though it had
the preterite form *ahuiyah*). The scribe seems to have copied a descending *h* as though it were a
z (see GRAM 4.2). See also 10v:20 and 38v:8.

44. Read *quetzaliyexochitica*. Cf. 18:1, 37:10. See also TRAN secs. 5.2, 13.1.

45. Read *yhuiuh quecholli cocozcatl huihuitolotihuitz yn tlalticpac* 'feather(s) of swan (in relation
to) jewels come severally bending on earth' — said of flowers laden with dew in CM (1:8). *Huito-
loa* 'to bend' is here used intransitively. On dropped syllables see the note to 1:12.

46. Literally, 'divers [*or* many] flowers, bells, by means of them it is roaring, the sky, by means
of [*or* with] gold shields there's dancing'. DICT *nepapan* 'many'.

47. Read *cuix ommotta cuix ommonotza* 'are they seen, are they summoned?' Alternate translation: 'Do they find one another, converse with one another?'

48. Read *niquimilnamiqui*.

49. Pieced together (as a work of craftsmanship), or: composed (as a song). FC 10:167:19,
FC 10:166:11–12, FC 10:169:24.

50. *Quetzaltica* 'by means of plumes'. The *aya* is most likely a vocable but could be read as
aya(tl) 'cloak'; thus *quetzalayatica* 'by means of a plume cloak'.

[folio 7]

7

+   *de tlaltecatzin*

6

2 ⸿ aya nicpiaco tepetl cana ytoloya [3] xochitlacuilohuāya · yehuaya
40 [4] dios i coohuayotl · ni tocahuililoc [5] ye mocha a titlaltecatzi
tonel[6]tzitzihui ya tonayatlatohua ya cayyo [7] o ohuiyya
8 ⸿ yye yhua tocuica yehua noteoohui [9] yehua diiyosa ya
41 toneltziçihui ya tona[10]yatlatohua ya cayyo ohuiya
11 ⸿ tlauhquechol çeliya puçõ/tima/ni [12] ya / moquipâcoxochiuh
42 / tinoon oo / hue[13]lica tzihuatl / cacahuayzquixochitl / [14] çâ
tinetlanehuilo ticahualoz / [15] tiyaaço ximohuaz yuhcãn ay[16]yoo /
ohui·ya
17 ⸿ yn tiyecoc ye nica/n imixpano / tete[18]cuiti·n aya timahuiztlachihuala
43 mo[19]nequezca naasiuhtoz q̂zalpetlapa [20] tonicac aya
cacahuayzquixochitl [21] çâ tinetlanehuilo ticahualoz tiya [1]

[folio 7v]

7

[1] atz∎ çô / ximohuaz yuhcan ayoo / o[2]huiyya
3 ⸿ a can - xochicacahuatl yn putzontima[4]niya xoo/chitl ectla nocoyayn
44 [5] taa / an noyol quimati quihuiti ye [6] noyoliya yyo ohuiya
7 ⸿ ayaa / yeeçe ye nicaa tlaa/la ycpac [8] âtetecuita nopilohuan
45 aa / a noyol [9] quimati quihuiti ye noyoliya
10 ⸿ a ca ninetlamata niquitohua y [11] aa/naya maca niyahuiya ompa [12]
46 ximohuaya tlaçôtli noyol yn ne∎[13]hua nehua çâ nicuicanitl / [14]
teocuitlayo ha noxochihu acay[15]yo

2 "I come to guard the city, [in that] somewhere I am uttered."[52] With
   flowers God is making paintings: they're companions! You've been
   left in your haven, O Tlaltecatzin, and you're sighing, you're warbling.

8 Together with him you sing—he is my spirit, he is God. You're sighing,
   you're warbling.

11 The roseate swan is reviving. Flowers of your crown, O mother,[53]
   O fragrant woman, are foaming abroad. O narcotic popcorn flowers!
   You are merely borrowed. You will be forsaken, you will pass away,
   [for] all that are here will be shorn.[54]

17 You've arrived among the princes, O honored creation. You've made your
   appearance, O turquoise parrot.[55] You're standing on this plume mat.
   O narcotic popcorn flowers! You are merely borrowed. You will be
F7V   forsaken, you will pass away. Yes, all will be shorn in that place
   [beyond].[56]

3 Ah, this flower wine I've drunk is a flower cacao foaming abroad.[57] My
   heart is savoring it. It has made my heart drunk.

7 Here on earth no more, you princes, you nobles![58] My heart is savoring
   it. It has made my heart drunk.

10 Ah, for I grieve, saying: Don't let me pass to the place beyond, where all
   are shorn. My singer's hearts are precious. My flowers are gold.[59]

---

51. Gloss: 'of Tlaltecatzin'. The ten stanzas of song 6 recur as CM song 48, with the title 'Song
of Tlaltecatzin of Cuauhchinanco', but with stanzas 7 and 8 combined into a single stanza (CM
stanza 6) and RSNE stanza 6 omitted, so that CM song 48 has only eight stanzas (1, 2, 4, 5, 3, 6,
9, 10, with reference to RSNE).
   Presumably the cadence belongs with song 6; in CM, cadence notation always precedes the
text.

52. CM 30:23 has *nitoloyan* 'I am uttered [*or* I am spoken of]'. The RSNE text, if allowed to
stand, would read: '"I come to guard the city." Somewhere this is uttered'.

53. For *tinoon* read *tinaan* [for *tenan*], as in CM 30:29.

54. *Yuhcan* 'here'. DICT iuhcan 2. CM 30:31 has *nican* 'here'.

55. Literally, 'This is your appearance, O my turquoise parrot'. CM 30v:2 has *noxiuhtoz* 'my
turquoise parrot'. DICT -*nequetzca* 'action of appearing'.

56. Alternate reading: *azo ximohuaz* 'won't all be shorn?'

57. CM 30:27 nocoyayc, meaning *noconic* 'I have drunk it'. The *ya* is an intrusive vocable. CM
30:27 *octli* 'wine' in place of *ectla*. And for the meaningless *taa an* CM has merely the free-standing
vocable *oo*.

58. Read *Aya yez ye nican tlalticpac antetecuitin nopilhuan* 'No longer will it be here on earth,
O you lords, my princes'.

59. The singer seems to be treating the terminal *acayyo* as a vocable. But CM runs this together
with the next stanza and has *anca yc*, meaning *anca ye* 'it seems that . . .', instead of *acayyo*.

16   ⸿ y niquiyacahua çâ / niquita nochan [17] / xochimamani / mach hueey
47   chal[18]chihuitl oo/huaye / ậçâli patla[19]huac mach nopatihu âo /
      ynca [20] ninoquixtiz ꝗmaniya / acan [1]

[folio 8]

                                                                    8

                              +

[1] çan niyaaz / nipolihuitiuh / huayy[2]oo / ohuiyya
3   ⸿ ha omya tinocaya / a noteeco yehua[4]ya diyosa · / niquitohua
48   ma ni[5]yauh ma ya ninoquimilo / nicui[6]canitli / ma ya yhui ma ya /
      acâ [7] tel-tel mach acaa / açiqui noyol [8] ayyo
9   ⸿ a can yuh niyaz / xochihuicotica / ye [10] noyoliyo / huaya / ye
49   quetzalneneli[11]hui chalchiuhtli ya / tlaçôtli yectla [12] mochiuhtoc
      âya / acan machiyo[13]ticac tlalticpaccâ · yhuiyaa / om[14]hua
      ynhuiyanayyo

15   *de atlyxco*   7

16   ⸿ xochiteuhtl imanicâ / cuicaoyo[17]hual imãcan/n in atlyxco
50   yn / ya [18] om xochicanlitec an / omhuaya ohua[19]ya
20   ⸿ çâ ye omnahuiltiloya / yn ipalnemo[1]
51

[folio 8v]

8

[1]huā / yn atepilhuan i · xoochitica y / [2] ma onnetotilo / ya om
      xochican[3]litec an / omhuaya ohuaya
4   ⸿ omn itzmolitimani oohuaye / yn ca[5]cahuaxochitla / yn
52   izquixochitla / [6] y meesico y / mimilihui oo / cueputi[7]mania /
      omvaya ohuaya
8   ⸿ çâno y maniya yn tecpilotl / yn cuauh[9]tin oçelo / mimilihui
53   oo / cueputima[10]niya / omhuaya ohuaya
11   ⸿ a ynca yycc ocuetlahuiçôo - çâ chimali[12]xochitli / ya omnahuac
54   a yxtlahua[13]quitecâ / omhuaya ohuaya
14   ⸿ çâ momalacachohuaya / chimali ya [15] xochitl - yn
55   quetzalyzquixochitli - to[16]mac onmania / ya omnahuac a
      yx[17]tlahuaquitecâ / omhuaya ohuaya

16 I leave this home of mine I see, that lies in flowers. Are they great, these
jades, these broad plumes? Could they be my payment? It is thus that
F8   I'd be born in future time!⁶⁰ It seems I go to my destruction.⁶¹

3 Ah! I am forsaken,⁶² O Lord, O God. And I say: Let me pass away and
be arrayed, singer that I am. Let it be this way: let someone be the
gems.⁶³ And one of my hearts has arrived!⁶⁴

9 Only thus would I pass away, my hearts as flowers twirling,⁶⁵ scattered
as plumes, becoming jades, precious and good, beyond compare on
earth.

VII⁶⁶

16 The flower lords,⁶⁷ the song bells, are in Water Face,⁶⁸ this house of
flowers!

20 Life Giver is entertained with flowers, O princes. Let there be dancing
F8v   in this house of flowers.

4 Cacao flowers, popcorn flowers are sprouting in Mexico. They're
budding, they're blossoming.

8 Lords, eagles, jaguars are standing as a multitude.⁶⁹ They're forming
buds, they blossom.

11 And so these shield flowers are to wither in Anahuac, in the fields.⁷⁰

14 Shield flowers are spinning. Plume popcorn flowers lie in our hands. In
Anahuac, in the fields.

60. In place of *ynca*, CM has *ica* 'thus'.
61. For acan read *anca* 'it seems', as in CM 30v:8.
62. CM has *A oya ninocahuaya* 'Ah! oya [vocable] I am forsaken ya [vocable]'.
63. CM has *tete'l* for *tetetl* 'gems'.
64. Read *mach acah acic in noyol* 'indeed some one of my hearts has arrived'. But CM has *mach aca[h] caciz ye noyol* 'won't someone capture my hearts?'
65. CM: *çan ca iuh noyaz xochihuiconticac ye noyoliol*.
66. Gloss: 'of Atlixco'.
67. Strictly, 'flower dust, its place of being located' (*xochiteuhtli imancan*). But *teuhtli* 'dust' and *teuctli* 'lord' give rise to a pun (DICT teuhtli). If 'dust' is the intended meaning, it could refer to the method of obscuring combat maneuvers (TRAN 4.7n).
68. Figurative name for Mexico. DICT atlixco. The glossator sees a reference to the geographical Atlixco. But cf. stanza 3: Mexico.
69. DICT mani 3.
70. For the presumed vocable *yycc* read *yyoo*.

18   ꞇ q̃tza/çālaxochitl oo / tlachinolxochi[19]tli / canyyo y
56   tonequimilol - yaom[1]

[folio 9]

+

9

[1]xochitla omhuaya ohuaya
2   ꞇ ohu atepilhuaa / acuauht amoçelo [3] ximoquimilocân
57   ixtlahuaqui[4]tequi yaomxochitla omhuaya ohuaya

5   8

6   chalcayotl i tlatocacuicatl

7   ꞇ y chalco ycalicoya - tlacochtli nepani [8] tiçâtl a y▪huitl i amos·cala
58   yn ima[9]cân achitzila Dios e ychana ovaya ohua[10]ya
11   ꞇ ye temoya xochitli ye temoya yaye [12] ycuic yehuaya Dios aya
59   oohuaye ay [13] noca tlatohuā mochan i q̃çaltotootli [14] y teohua
      tecuitli oya cuepuqui mo[15]xocha ohuâya ohuaya
16   ꞇ xochithualco pehuā hayauhthuâ[17]li macâ mapipichohua
60   yyehuaya [18] Dios / ocan iye metlacahuani ye [19] momcuic huhuaya
      ohuaya

20   9

21   ꞇ yy ma ye toconica ma ye tococuacā [1]
61

[folio 9v]

9

[1] cacahuaxochitli ye yc tonahui[2]yaca oya çuepuqui moxocha
ahua[3]ya ohuaya
4   ꞇ cacahuaxochitla quihuitiaya [5] noyolo / yeehuaya / quihuiya
      noyo[6]lo / yeehuaya / ma yc ninapâtiuh [7] cano ye yuhcan i ma ynca
      huel o[8]yatiuh noyolo ye maca y cuetlahui[9]ya xochitla ohuaya
      ohuaya

18 These plume flood flowers, these blaze flowers are our only adornment.[71]

F9   These are war flowers.

2 Princes, eagles, jaguars, adorn yourselves in the fields. These are war flowers.

VIII

A Chalcan piece, a lord song

7 Chalco's come to fight. The spears have been scattered,[72] the chalk and the plumes, where this house of pictures lies. But briefly in God's home.[73]

11 Flowers descend, his songs descend: O God, he speaks in your home, here![74] and he's a quetzal, a spirit-owner lord.[75] Your flowers have opened.

16 In the flower court he strikes it up, in the mist court he sounds the whistle cry.[76] God is cheered by your songs.[77]

IX

21 Let's drink—let's eat—cacao flowers. Let's entertain ourselves with

F9v   these. Your flowers are opening.

4 Cacao flowers make my heart drunk, ah, my heart drunk. Adorned with these, let me pass away to that place [beyond]. Let my heart go with them. May these flowers not wither.[78]

71. Read *çanyyo* 'only'.

72. Or strewn. DICT nepanihui. On dropped syllables see the note to 1:12.

73. For *achitzila Dios e ychana* read *achitzi[n]ca Dios ichan,* assuming the copyist has read *c* as a curled *l*.

74. Read *nocan tlatohua mochan* 'here he speaks in your home'. For *nocan* as a variant of *nican* 'here' see DICT nican.

75. *Teohua tecuitli,* better *teohuah teuctli* 'spirit-owner lord', a title held by various Chalcan leaders (DICT teohuah 3). Note that in the first stanza the place name "Chalco" may mean the king, or leader, of Chalco (GN 3:1).

76. For *hayauhthuâli macâ* read *ayahuithualli imancan* 'where the mist court is'.

77. Read *mellacuahua-ni yc* (with *ni* as a vocable). DICT ellacuahua:mo.

78. Literally, 'Let it be that with them I am adorned; to where indeed is that place, let it be with them truly that my heart goes along, indeed let it not be that the flowers wither'. DICT canon, iuhcan, yahtiuh.

10   ¶ ma yuh niyahuin iuhcâ ma nocpac[11]xochihui mâ yuh niyahuin iuhca
      ma [12] nocpacxochihui ma noxochicozq̂ ma [13] yca malintiuh ye
      omco xochitli [14] ma y cuetlahuiya xochitla ohua[15]ya ohuaya
16   ¶ ytech onenemiya oohuaye - yn itla[17]tol - yehua yn dios çā
      cohuatecatli [18] ya oohuaye yzta coyotla ohuaya o[19]huaya
20   ¶ quihualtemohuiya - ynhuiti xo[1]

[folio 10]

10

+

[1]chitla ytech onaçia tocuiyc tonatihu aa[2]yyave ytech onaçia S maria
q̂nona [3] ehua yyahue q̂noni quitohuâ ya ye[4]huaya Dios yya
oohuiya

10 *huexutzinco tlatocacuicatl*

6   ¶ on oqui q̂çâcoya yhuehueuh y yehua [7] ya Dios xicyahueliçoçona / yn
      [8] tepiltzinn i yehua yoyotzinn i / oc [9] xonahuiyacan atepilhuan a
      [10] ohuaya ohuaya
11   ¶ y ma yc xonahuiyācan atepilhuā[12]n i huexotzinco yn
      xayacama[13]chan i / calmecahua o / matsan y [14] huitzinn i /
      temayahuitzin/n iz cā ha [15] moxochiuh / a yz ca yn tocuic ma
      ti[16]quehuaca / ma tonahuiyacana / [17] ohuaya ohuaya

10 Let me pass away. Let me have my flower crown.[79] Let me have my
      flower necklace. May these flowers, then, go twirling as they pass
      beyond.[80] May these flowers not wither.[81]

16 They're marching at God's command.[82] They're simply Coatecatl—and
      Iztac Coyotl!

20 He brings them down, these drunken flowers.[83] These songs of ours
F10   reach Our Lord the Sun.[84] They reach Santa María. What? What does
      God say?[85]

                                X[86]

6 For a moment God's drums come forth.[87] Play them beautifully, Prince
      Yoyontzin. For a moment take pleasure, you princes.

11 So let yourselves be pleasured, you princes of Huexotzinco:
      Xayacamach, Calmecahua, Matzin,[88] and Temaxahuitzin.[89] Here are
      your flowers, our songs. Let us sing them, let us take pleasure.

---

79. Literally, 'Let it be thus that I pass away to that place; let there be my flower crown'. The
copyist then rewrites these two phrases, no doubt a slip of the pen.

80. Literally, 'let it be that in this way they go twisting already to there [i.e., the battlefield],
the flowers'. DICT oncan 1.

81. Read *maca y*, as in the preceding stanza.

82. On *nehnemi* 'march' see the note to 40v:3.

83. *Ihuinti xochitl* 'these that are drunken, these flowers'. Alternately *ihuintixochitl* 'these intoxicating flowers' (DICT ihuintitl, xochitl).

84. Read *to[te]cuiyo tonatiuh* 'Our Lord the Sun [i.e., Jesus]'. Cf. SPC 233v *Iniquac oualmomā
tonatiuh in Iesus, etetl tonatiuh in momanaco: iece ca tlamauiçoloc, auh onoceppa cecentet* 'when arose
the sun which is Jesus, three suns appeared: definitely indeed people marveled, and again they
became one'. See also CM 42:9 *huel nelli tonatiuh o y Jesu* 'the true sun, Jesus'.

85. DICT quenon, quen 6.

86. Nahuatl gloss: 'a lord song of Huexotzinco'.

87. Read *In oc i quizaco ya ihuehueuh i yehhua ya Dios* 'for a moment it issues forth [or they
issue forth], the drum(s) of him, him that is God'. Alternate translation: 'for a moment they are
brought to life [or born], the drums [...]'. DICT quiza 7, quiza 8. Cf. CM 13v:24 *canin tlacati
tohuehueuh* 'where are our drums born?'

88. The character string *huitzinn i* has been (carelessly?) written twice, here and again in the
following phrase. Thus for *matsan y huitzinn i / temayahuitzin/n iz cā [...]* read *matsan y tema-
yahuitzin/n iz cā [...]*. And for the nonsensical *matsan* read *matzin*, as in IXT 2:215. (The odd *ts*
written for *tz* appears also at 12:16.)

89. For *temayahuitzin* read *temaxahuitzin*, as in Muñoz Camargo 1892:102 (lib. 1, cap. 12).

18 ⸿ oçelocal imacã tzihuacpetlatli [19] yonoca ayyahue
cuauhquiya[20]hua[1]

[folio 10v]

10

[1]qui toniyaycaq̃ chichimecaltecuitli [2] y huexotzinco
teomxiuh·tiçãyo [3] y monesconol tocoyeyecohuã y
mo[4]tzihuãquimiuh yca titemoc y hue[5]xotzinco ya ohuaya ohuaya

6   ⸿ matlahuâcaltica nemamana[7]lotoc yyeehuâya yn iyahuia ye[8]huân i
diosa yn tenmayahuitzin [9] viya xayacamachaam oya mizqui[10]octica
onequimiloloya ohuaya ohua[11]ya

12 ⸿ xochitla yyhuiya / y toyoooloc haya [13] toniyatlacati titepilçin yn i
tina[14]huatiloc yn omeyocana ohuaya o[15]huaya

16 ⸿ ma chalchihuitl oo / ma teocuitlatl o [17] yn quetzali patlahuac yye
nequimi[18]lolo yxtlahuacan i yaonahuac a [19] ohuayo ohuaya

20 ⸿ tamocohuacale tamocxaquina[1]

[folio 11]

11

+

[1]le haya o ooo yayye a ooo aya o aya o ay

2   ⸿ yzcohuatzin i tenoxtitlani ahuayya [3] yyamo aye neçahualcoyoltli
hui[4]ya ma yzquixochitli ma cacahua[5]xochitli ximilacaçoca
ximomali[6]nacãn ãtepilhuan i huexotzinco [7] y xayacamachan i
temayahui[8]tzin yn ohaya oaya o ay

18 At the house of jaguars,[90] at the spine mat, at Eagle Gate you stand,[91]

F10V　　O Chichimec Lord of Huexotzinco! You create them chalked as turquoise, these, your thrashed ones.[92] And with these arrow spines of yours you've descended. In Huexotzinco.

6 They're all being offered in a pack basket.[93] O God! O Temaxahuitzin, O Xayacamach! And all are adorned with mesquite wine.

12 As a flower you've been created,[94] you've been brought to life, O prince. You've been summoned from the Place of Duality.[95]

16 Let there be jades, let there be gold, broad plumes. All are adorned on the field of war.

F11　20 Tamo-cohua-cale tamoc-xahui-nale haya oooyayye a oooaya oaya oay.[96]

2 O Itzcoatzin of Tenochtitlan, O Nezahualcoyotl. Let there be popcorn flowers, cacao flowers. Spin! Whirl,[97] you princes of Huexotzinco, Xayacamach and Temaxahuitzin.

90. *Ocelocalli imancan.*

91. Read *toniyaycaqui,* to be understood as *tonihcac i* (with terminal vocable *i* and omitting the intrusive vocable *iya*) 'you stand'.

92. Read *monexconol,* possessive form of the noun *nexconolli,* perhaps better *nixconolli (ne-, ixconolli)* 'thrashed one', from the verb *ixconoa:mo.* See DICT ixconoa:mo, cf. MOL *ixconoa:nitla* 'desgranar mostazos, o otras cosas semejantes'. This and other verbs with similar meaning ('thresh', 'thrash', 'tread upon', 'beat') occur in CM. For comparable usages, see DICT ixconoa: tla, huitequi:te, huitequi:tla.

93. Offered for sacrifice. DICT mahmana:mo.

94. Read *toyocoloc.*

95. CONC omeyocan.

96. The entire stanza is composed of vocables, although the element *tamo* may be related to Tamoanchan, the mythical place where humans are created. DICT tamoanchan. DICT pp. 729–39 (Concordance to Vocables) -cal-, xahue, xahuiya, etc. The *q* is probably a misreading of the descending *h,* as at 6:5 and 38v:8. The textual *tamocxaquinale* is a presumed copyist's error for *tamoxahuinale;* cf. 34v:10–12.

97. Literally, 'be spun [*or* turned], be twisted!'

11

tototi tototi

11   ⸗ teoxihuizhuayo y monacayo mo[12]yolo yehuā / chichimecatlo viy[13]a
      yehua teni · chalchihuitl y / mo[14]yolo yehua ye yzquixochitli
      ca[15]cahuaxochitli - ahua y yao ayya [16] yye ma tahuiyacana ohuaya
      o[17]huaya ·

18   ⸗ nicmalitihuiz xochicuahuitlo [19] huehuezcani xochitl a y
      tamo[20]huâchā / xochipetlapana ayya[1]

[folio 11v]

11

[1]hue / mimilihuic xochitla yeehua[2]ya a nelhuayoxochitli
q̂tzalytec[3]pa tocuica titlaylotlaqui tomalin[4]tica y ahua yya oh ayya
yye ma ta[5]huiyacana ahuayo ohuaya

6   ⸗ nin■yecoya a / tamohuānicha[7]ni · nepapā xochitli / coçâhuic [8]
      xochitli - timaliticac yn tohuehue[9]uh · yn tayacach aya - çāniyo
      ni[10]caa-n aya titocnihuan i ovaya [11] obaya

XI[98]

[two-tone drum cadence:] tototi tototi

11 May your flesh, your hearts be leafy green,[99] O Chichimec,[100]
O Tenitl![101] These are jades, these are popcorn flowers, cacao flowers,
your hearts. And let's be pleasured.

18 "I come as a flower tree from Tamoanchan, the flower seat, come
whirling these, these laughing ones, these flowers, burgeoned flowers,
F11V   song-root flowers."[102] From within these plumes you sing,
O Arbiter.[103] You're whirled! And let's be pleasured.

6 "I am created in Tamoanchan."[104] As a multitude of flowers, golden
flowers, you're whirled. Our drums, our rattles! Here [on earth and
here] alone! O friends!

98. Song 11 stanzas 1–2 and 5–6 also appear as stanzas 3–4 and 1–2, respectively, in CM song 69, canto C. In addition stanzas 7–8 of song 11 incorporate some of the material in CM song 69, canto C, stanzas 7–8, so that canto C of CM song 69 offers a nearly complete variant of song 11, failing only to match its stanzas 3–4.

99. Read *tla xihuizhuayo*. CM 61:21 *Çan ca xihuizhuayo*.

100. Title assumed by kings. The variant text, CM 61:21, has *chichimecatlon teuctlo* 'Chichimec Lord', applicable to earthly kings or to the supreme spirit (DICT chichimecatl teuctli). CM 31v:17–18 *Pixahuin tzetzelihui ye itzmolinia yn ixochiuh y in icelteotl çan chichimecatl teuctla ohuaya* 'They fall in a raining mist, they sprinkle down, they freshen: they're flowers of the Only Spirit, Chichimec Lord'.

101. For the textual (apocopated?) *teni* read *tenitl*, name given to any of various non-Aztec peoples regarded as fierce and barbarous (FC 8:77:12 *tenitl*, FC 10:187:15–24 *tenjme*, cf. FC 4:25:37 *tenjcaiotl*). Hence a nonce name for any warrior? Applied also to the supreme spirit? In context, CM 61v:11–13 *[. . .] moxochiuh yaotzin [. . .] teicnomati [. . .] '[. . .]* your flowers, Yaotl [i.e., Enemy, Warrior] [. . .] He shows mercy [. . .]' may refer to God. See the numerous epithets of the supreme spirit listed in CMSA pp. 38–39. If *teni* were allowed to stand, it might still refer to the supreme spirit, taken as a variant or corruption of *tene* 'word owner [i.e., speaker]'; Tezcatlipoca is called *necoc tene* 'speaker on both sides' in FC 6:14:21. However, if the CM 61:22 variant, *Telitl*, were taken as correct, the reference would be to Telitl, king of Tenayocan in the Tepanec region, ca. 1430 (CC 40:10, 46:20).

102. Literally, 'root flowers'. But see DICT *nelhuayotl* 'root', *cuicanelhuayotl* 'song root'.

103. Tlailotlac, a title held by various kings and officials, including judges, hence the free translation 'Arbiter'. Repeatedly applied to God in CM. DICT tlailotlac.

104. Read *ninoyocoya* 'I am created' (DICT yocoya:mo). Or read *ninoyeco ya* 'I have been created' (see DICT yecoa:tla 2). Cf. 3v:14, above; also 2:13–14, 10v:3, 10v:12. (The illegible character in *nin■yecoya* might be an *a*. Note that *a* is mistakenly written for *o* at 16v:4 and elsewhere.)

12   ҫ y ҫâ tictlanehuico - y tlalticpacqui [13] ҫee / tiyahui / cano ximohua
yehuā - [14] ma nonocuiltono ma yc ninapâ[15]naya o xochitli ҫâniyo
nicaa[16]n aya titochihuani ohuaya ohua[17]ya

18   ҫ xochitl ycpac ye nicā xochique[19]ҫâli q̂chol maahuiliya mahui[1]

[folio 12]

12

+

[1]huiliaa xochitla ycaca ohuaya ohua[2]ya

3   ҫ ma coyachichina y nepâpa xochitlo [4] maahuilia mahuiliaa xochitla
[5] ycaca ohuaya ohuaya

6   ҫ cano tihui hue cano tihui om timi[7]qui oc nelo yn tinemi oc
ahuiya[8]loya oc ahuiltilano yehuaya [superscript:] *totecoyo* i [line
script:] Dios i [9] acā ҫâniyo nicann i tlalticpac[10]qui huelic xochitli
yhuān i cui[11]catl yhuān i tlalticpac ye neli ye [12] nel tihui ohuaya
ohuaya

13   ҫ xonaahuiyaca·n atepilhuâ/n a[14]chichimeca y / ҫā tiyazque ye
yuh[15]ca pupucatzi i oviyan i tlaylotlaqui-[16]n i tacolihuatsin / ayac
tepetiz a[17]yac mocahuaz - yn tlalticpâc a [18] ohuaya ohuaya

[folio 12v]

12

12

Canto en alabança de
Axayacatzin Rey de Mex^{co} y de Neçahualpiltzintli de tezcuco
y chimalpopoca de tlacopā

2   ҫ xochicuahuitl naliticac oo - vaye [3] omcueputicaqui a omca ye
mo[4]chā - yehuâya dios a [superscript:] *totecoyo* [line script:] -
ohuaya ohua-[5]ya

6   ҫ y nepâpa tototl hualquicâ a om[7]tlachichina ya omtlatohuā ye [8]
mocha - yehuaya Dios a [superscript:] *totecoyo* [line script:] · ohuaya
[9] ohuaya

12 We merely come to borrow them on earth, we merely go away where all
    are shorn.[105] Let me be rich, let me dress myself in these. These
    flowers![106] Here [on earth and here] alone! O friends!

18 Upon these flowers here a flower plume, a swan, is pleasuring, is
    pleasuring where flowers stand.

3   Let him go inhale this multitude of flowers, pleasuring: he's pleasuring
    where flowers stand.

6   Where we go, where we go to die, do we yet have life?[107] Is there yet a
    place of pleasure, yet a pleasure land, O God?[108] Delicious flowers,
    perhaps, are only here on earth. And songs.[109] On earth. It's true, yes,
    true: we pass away.

13 Be pleasured, princes, Chichimecs! To such a place as Smoker
    [Mountain] must we go.[110] O Arbiter! You! Father-keeper at the
    Waters![111] None shall have a city. No one shall be left on earth.

F12V

XII[112]

2 The flower trees are whirling, blossoming in your home, O God.[113]

6 All the birds are coming out, inhaling, singing in your home, O God.[114]

---

105. For *çâ* [...] *çee* read *za* [...] *za* 'merely [...] merely'.

106. But if *xochitl* is joined with the preceding vocables *ya o*, the reading is *yaoxochitl* 'war flowers', as in song 7, stanzas 7 and 8.

107. Literally, 'still is it true that we live?'

108. Superscript *totecoyo* 'Our Lord'.

109. The repeated *yhuān* 'and' is here treated as a copyist's slip.

110. For *yuhca[n] pupucatzi[n]* 'such a place, [of] Smoker', the better text at CM 61v:5–6 has *ichan Popocatzin* 'Smoker's home' and a marginal gloss *mictlan* (i.e., the Dead Land), presumably with reference to the volcano Popocatepetl (see Durán 1971 ch. 18, DICT popocatzin).

111. *Acolihuatzin*, literally 'water(s)-forefather-owner', i.e., the supreme spirit as custodian of the afterworld? See DICT acolhuacan, atl, colhuacan 2, colitl, colli 2. But if Acolihuatzin is taken as a variant of Acolhua(tzin), or Aculhua, the reference could be to the founding "prince" of Acolhuacan (CONC Acolhuatzin). The glossator, seeing "Acolhuatzin" at 39v:14, evidently regards this as a name for Nezahualcoyotl (who was an Acolhuan; that is, a native of Acolhuacan). Cf. 40:1–3, below, and see the Remarks in the Commentary for song XXXIII.

112. Gloss: 'song in praise of Axayacatzin, king of Mexico, and of Nezahualpiltzintli of Texcoco, and Chimalpopoca of Tlacopan'.

113. Superscript *totecoyo* 'Our Lord'.

114. Superscript *totecoyo* 'Our Lord'.

10 ℭ chalchiuhcoyoli câcahuâcatima[11]mi mahui y motepeuh / y
yehuâ[12]ya dios e [superscript:] *totecoyo* [line script:] -
ypalnemohuani - ŷpâ [13] chachalacatoc / çâcuatototla - zi[14]nizcā
tlauhĝchol ompāpatla[15]tinemi yn tepilhuāni / oo / aya[16]hui / ya
oaya a / ohuaya ohuaya

17 ℭ at oc achitzincā nicâ / at otlahuelma[18]tia / acā quiyocoya / yehuaya
diosi [superscript:] *totecoyo* [line script:] / [19] oo / ayahuiya ōayaa /
ovaya ohua[20]ya

[folio 13]

13

+

1 ℭ nicçâcuamoyahuaya omo huaye [2] chalchihuixelihui tomāc
omani[3]ya - moxopanixochiuh teyn ti[4]nopiltzin y-n ay
taxayacâtzin/n o[5]huāya ohuaya

6 ℭ yz cā hamoxochiuh / ximoquimilo[7]cā antepilhuā - haya
chimalpopo[8]cazin - - neçâhualpilo / ohuâye han[9]mochipâ
tlalticpacâ / ohuaya a[10]huaya

11 ℭ ma totlaocox ii / ŷ tinopiltzi/n aŷ te[12]cuitzintli ya / ay taxayacâtzin
ye [13] chalchimalacayotimâni mahu i[14]n motepeuh / ay mexico y -
om ĝ[15]tzalmiyahuâyoticac â / ohuaya ohua[16]ya

17 ℭ omiyamomali/ni mizĝtl yn pu[18]chotl - ahuehuetl - ye chalchimala
[19]cayotimani mahu / in / motepeuh [1]

[folio 13v]

13

[1] ay mexico y - omĝçalmiyahua[2]yoticac a / ohuaya ohuaya

13

3 ℭ xochicalitequi / xochimamani - [4] o cānin o çeçequiztoqui - yn
icni[5]uhyotli - yn cohuāyotli yn tecpi[6]llotli / via / yn a teyolquima
yec[7]tli yntlatol / moçeçemeltia yn [8] tepilhuan a / ohua ohuaya

9 ℭ ye xochitica y / ye onnequechna[10]hualo cuicatica oom /
momama[11]litoqui yn a teolquima / yectli [12] yntlatol moçeçemeltiya
- [13] yn tepilhuan a / ohuaya ohuaya

10 God Life Giver,[115] these jade bells are shrilling in your city.[116] Troupials are chattering. Trogons, roseate swans are flying. And these are princes.

17 For but a moment is he here? Is he content? Does God create
F13   someone?[117]

1 I scatter them as troupials, they're strewn as jades, they lie in our hands, your Green Place flowers, shattered, O Prince Axayacatl.

6 And here they are, your flowers: adorn yourselves, you princes Chimalpopoca and Nezahualpilli. Not forever on earth!

11 Don't grieve, my prince, Lord Axayacatl. Your city, Mexico, spreads a crown of jade, covered in plume tassels.

17 The mesquites, the ceibas, the cypresses are whirling. Your city, Mexico,
F13V   spreads a crown of jade, covered in plume tassels.

XIII

3 In this flower house they stand as flowers. It's where they're all assembled, and they're comrades, they're companions, they're noble ones. And ah, their words are good heart pleasers. The princes are entertained.

9 There's mutual embracing among these flowers. As songs they've been twirled.[118] And ah, their words are good heart pleasers. The princes are entertained.

115. Superscript *totecoyo* 'Our Lord'.
116. Read *chalchiuhcoyolli ihcacahuacatimani in mauh in motepeuh.*
117. Superscript *totecoyo* 'Our Lord'.
118. For *-ca* 'as' see DICT 1. *-ca* 2.

14 ⊙ xochimecatl oo / yhuā momamali / [15] yn amoxochihui / y yectlin
âmo[16]tlatol antepilhuāno / yn anconito[17]huā om / antepilhuan ā
ohuaya [18] ohuaya

[folio 14]

14

+

1 ⊙ nihualchoca y / nihualycnootla[2]mati çā nicuicânitl hvia y / a [3] ca
anichuicaz i toxochi om oo[4]huaye / ma yc ninapantiaz - ca[5]no
ximohuâya oohuaya / nihual[6]laocoya ohuaya ohuaya

7 ⊙ a ca çān iuhqui xoochitl aya / y ypâ [8] momâti / yn tlalticpacqui - çā
quel [9] achic tocontotlaneehuico ahuili [10] xochitli xonaahuiyacâ
oohua[11]ye nihuallaomcoya ohuaya [12] ohuaya

13 ⊙ antochan oo / yn tinemi ye nicâ [14] yn tlaticq̄ / çân ihui çân achic / çâ
[15] tictotlanehuiya / oohuaye / ximo[16]quimilocann âtepilhuan a -
o[17]huaya ohuaya -

18 ⊙ yn çāniyo o ye nicā paqui toyollo - [1]

[folio 14v]

14

[1] achi titocnihuā tototlanehuicō - an[2]çē tochan i tlalticpac ô o / yn
cāni xo[3]ca y / oohuaye ximoquimilocan[4]n antepilhuān ā / ohuaya
ohuaya

14   *de chalco tlacamaçatl*

6 ⊙ ô / ayyacohui / yaom ayahui / nococa[7]co yectiuâya / cuicâ y ye
ychan i [8] tepilhua y cohuacuechtliya o[9]vaye tzinizcân amoxochitica
yn [10] teocuitlanepapaniuhtoc / yn[11]câ ximapanâ tlalticpac ahuâyya
[12] o / ahuaya o ayye ohuaya ohua[13]ya

14 ⊙ çâ ye ôcan oo maniya xochitli ya [15] cuitli / ychan i yehua - tecuitli
[16] ya tlatq̄qui chalchiuhtlatona[17]q̄ / çâ tzinizcān amaxochiticâ teo
[18]cuitlanepapanniuhtoc ŷca xima[1]

[folio 15]

15

[1]panâ tlalticpac ahuayya ôniha-hua[2]ya oya ohuaya ohuaya

14 Flower garlands have been twirled, and these are your flowers, your
good words, O princes, these that you utter, O princes.

F14   1 I weep here, I grieve, I the singer, for I won't be taking our flowers with
me. Would that I might go adorned with these to the place where all
are shorn. I am sad.

7 They're just like the flowers on earth. Briefly we borrow these pleasure
flowers.[119] Be entertained! I am sad.

13 Where we live here on earth is not our home. Just this: just briefly do we
borrow them. Adorn yourselves, princes.

18 Only here can our hearts be content. Briefly we're friends. We're

F14v   borrowers. Our eternal home is not this earth. Where are the
flowers?[120] Adorn yourselves, princes.

XIV[121]

6 Princes, I've been hearing good songs in His home.[122] O Coacuech, the
trogons are strewn as gold, as flower banners: here on earth adorn
yourself with these.[123]

14 Song flowers lie beyond in His home. O lord, O chief,[124] O

F15   Chalchiuhtlatonac, the trogons are strewn as gold, as flower banners:
on earth adorn yourself with these.

---

119. *Zan cuel achic* 'just briefly'.
120. Read *yn cāni xocha*, i.e., *in canin xochitl*. Or *yn cāni ixocha*, i.e., *in canin ixochiuh* 'where are their flowers?'
121. Gloss: 'of Chalco's Tlacamazatl'. Stanzas 3–4 of this song also appear as stanza 33 of CM song 51 (CM 33:22–25).
122. Read *noconcac o yect[l]i huaya cuica[tl] i ye ichan i[n] tepilhuan* 'I've heard (a) good song(s) in His home, O princes'. Cf. CM 11:14 *noconcac on cuicatl nonithua xopan [...]* 'I've heard a song. I see him in Green Places [...]'. The unusual vocable *cohui* is attested at CM 17v:28, CM 19:5.
123. Read *amaxochitica*. And note the unusual *nepapanihui* (cf. DICT *nenepanihui* 'to be strewn').
124. *Cui[ca]tli* 'song'; *tlatquic* 'chief'.

3   ¶ ye tomoneltoca ya om ohuaye - teohua [4] oo yn cuateomtla ohuaya
ohuaya

5   ¶ yn ca ya mocuepa moyoollo / caauh[6]timaniz i cuātl ixpan i tlali
mo[7]cuepâya ylhuicâtl olini / ay câ [8] ye â·hualo chichimecâtl i
tlacâ[9]maçâtla ohuaya ohuaya

10   ¶ nocohuayn cacahuātl / quimati [11] noyool huiya çâ noconiliya ye [12]
yŷol / yn ipalnemohuâ/ni tlal[13]manalco y teômhuatzin i tla[14]oc a
melel i çô yazqui yaoyotl a ohua[15]ya ohuaya

16   ¶ y çô yazqui yehuâ ynchimalixo[17]chi omyohuâlo cuicâ yyehuāya [18]
dios ca - [1]

[folio 15v]

15

[1] çê - huitihui · ca pulihuitihui · yn [2] tlachinola ohuaya ohuaya

3   ¶ tomotlamachtia / yn ipalnemo[4]huani yn tomotlamachtia y /
ye[5]huaya Diosi [superscript:] *totecoyo* [line script:] yn çâ
cualehuatoc / tee[6]zi tecol tocoyachihua y chalco ye [7] omcâ tele
ilhuiçôli mochihuâ [8] yehuâ teotlatolli yatiuh ay q̂[9]manian i tele ma
yhui tele tichal[10]co / ohuaya ohuaya

11   ¶ y ye ylhuiçōlohuâ / ye tlalicui[12]lohua yehuaya diosy [superscript:]
totecoyo [line script:] tele yl[13]huiçōlo mochihua yehuâ teotla[14]tolli
yatiuh ay quemania[15]n i tele ma yhui tele tichal[16]ca oo / ohuaya
ohuaya

17   fin De la .I.

18   parte

3 And now you're believed, O priest, Cuateotl, that your hearts return. An eagle flood will lie outspread before His face.[125] The earth rolls over, the sky shakes. The Chichimec Tlacamazatl has been forsaken.[126]

10 I drink a cacao.[127] My heart enjoys it, and I give it to Life Giver's hearts to drink. O Teohuatzin of Tlalmanalco, may your agonies be off to war.

16 Oh, they'll be off. Their shield flowers, those bells, are making music, O God, they'll go and be extinguished, destroyed in the blaze.

15v

3 You're glad, Life Giver. You're glad, O God,[128] that they're rising up in battle.[129] You're creating grandmothers,[130] grandfathers there in Chalco. Well then, marvels are made, and holy words go off to the place unknown. "Well, let it be so. Well, we're Chalcans."

11 God makes marvels,[131] he paints the earth. Well then, these marvels are made, and holy words are off to the place unknown. "Well, let it be so. Well, we're Chalcans."

end of the first part

---

125. For *cuātl,* the better text in the CM variant has *quauhAtl* 'eagle flood'.
126. For *ā·hualo* CM has *cahualo* 'he is forsaken'.
127. Read *noconyain,* i.e., *noconi* 'I drink it', disregarding the vocable infix (*hua* written for *ya*) and the terminal *n.* Cf. CM 30:27 *xochincacahuatl* [...] *nocoyayc* 'A flower cacao [...] I did drink it'.
128. Superscript *totecoyo* 'Our Lord'.
129. Read *hualehuatoc.* For *cu* as a replacement for *hu* see GRAM 3.7. And see DICT hualehua 2, ehua 2 'to rise [against the enemy], to make war'.
130. *Tecih.*
131. Superscript *totecoyo* 'Our Lord'.

[folio 16]

16

+

1

2   ⸿   tlanec[superscript:]*h* [line script:] topehuaca · y yatocnihuā [3]
sopancala ytequi · çân itlatol ochia[4]lo · yn dios [superscript:] *totecoyo*
[line script:] aya · q̂ni quinequiz q̂ qui[5]manaz yn xochitl yn cuicatl a
[6] ohuaya ohuaya

7   ⸿   moch itlaocol ŷtechpâ ye huiz toco[8]huātlamati xopancalitequi · çâ[9]n
itlatol ochialo · yn dios [superscript:] *totecoyo* [line script:] aya q̂ni [10]
quinequiz que quimana y yn xo[11]chitl ŷ cuicatl a ohuaya ohuaya

12 ⸿   cuçâhuic xuchitla yyehuaya · [13] ye yzquixochitli · cacahuaxochi[14]tli ·
cacaloxochitl malitimaniya [15] a ca moxochihui yohuaya tios
[superscript:] *totecoyo* [line script:] a [16] ohuaya ohuaya

17 ⸿   yn tzan tictlanehuico moxochihuehue[18]uh - [1]

[folio 16v]

16

[1] mayacach oo · ye mocuico · a ca mo[2]xochihui · ehuaya dios
[superscript:] *totecoyo* [line script:] a ohuaya [3] ohuaya

4   ⸿   a nolyo quimati câhuayotl · yn icni[5]uhyotlim oo netlā o atocnihuani
[6] xochitl ahuiyac xahuiyacaa · ti[7]azque ocano ye ycha · anica
tine[8]mizque · ohuaya ohuaya ·

9   ⸿   ohua ma çē tonemizque · yca nicho[10]cay · ayôpâ tihuicê yn tlalticpâ
[11] xochitl ahuicac sahuicaa · tiyazque [12] ocano ye ycha mach nica
tinemiz [13] ohuaya ohuaya ·

14 ⸿   yz catq̂ tla yetetl [marginal gloss:] *ojo / 3 cabesas* [line script:] toxochio
ahuā[15]ye · yhuān i tocuic quipuluhua [16] telel ay totlacol iy ohuaya
[17] ohuaya

18 ⸿   y yatocnihuân aya · xonahuiyacani · [19] amochipâ tlalticpac çâ çên
oquiçaz [1]

[folio 17]

17

+

[1] yn icniuhyotl ahuaya ohuaya

F16   [XV] [Part 2, Song 1]

2 Now let us begin in this house of green places,[1] friends. God's words
are awaited.[2] What will he want? What will he give? Flowers! Songs![3]

7 All sorrows come from him. We call to him in this house of green
places.[4] God's words are awaited.[5] What will he want? What will he
give? Flowers! Songs!

12 Golden flowers, popcorn, cacao, and raven flowers are whirling. Oh,
God,[6] they're your flowers.

17 We can only borrow these flower drums,[7] these rattles of yours. Oh
F16V   God,[8] they're your songs, your flowers.

4 My heart enjoys these companions,[9] these comrades. Come, friends,[10]
be pleasured with these fragrant flowers.[11] We'll be off to His home.
We are not to live here.

9 Would that we might live forever. And so I weep. Not twice can we
come to earth. Be pleasured with these fragrant flowers.[12] We'll be off
to His home. Can we live here?

14 Behold! Let there be gems![13] Our flowers! These songs of ours destroy
our pain and sadness.

18 Friends, be pleasured. These are not forever on earth. These comrades
F17   are to pass away once and for all.

---

1. The glossator corrects *tlanec* to *tlaneh,* but the reading should no doubt be *tlanel* 'let it truly
be that [. . .]', where the copyist has misread a curled *l* as a *c.*
2. Superscript *totecoyo* 'Our Lord'.
3. GRAM 11.6 (sentence fragments introduced by *in*).
4. For *tocohuātlamati* read *toconhualmati* 'we call [*or* appeal] to him'.
5. Superscript 'Our Lord'.
6. Superscript 'Our Lord'.
7. For *tzan* read *zan* 'only'.
8. Superscript 'Our Lord'.
9. *A noyol quimati coayotl.*
10. Literally, 'Hey, you friends!' DICT netla.
11. Read *ahuiyac* 'fragrant'. Cf. the parallel passage at 16v:11. DICT ahhuiac.
12. Read *ahuiyac* 'fragrant'. Cf. 16v:6.
13. The glossator sees *tla yetetl* 'let there be three entities' and writes, 'Take notice: three capitals', imagining a reference to the kings of the Triple Alliance cities, or capitals, of Tenochtitlan,
Texcoco, and Tlacopan. For the use of *cabezas* in this sense, see IXT 2:92 (ch. 36). But the more
likely reading is *tla ye tetl* 'let there indeed be gems'.

2

3   ⸿ xochitl coliniya · cuicatl quitemo[4]huiya · mochan aya ·
    ypalnemo[5]hua · aztatotohuãy · xonahuiya [6] niquitohuâ ya nican · y
    ohuaya [7] ohuaya ·

8   ⸿ y mach oc mictlapã · y mach oquihual[9]matic ay tepilhua / çã
    chichime[10]ca yeyc no cahualo tlalticpac [11] aya xonahuiya niquitohua
    ye [12] nican i ohuaya ohuaya

13 ⸿ hualquiquixohua · hualalachia[14]loya · y xopâcalitequi · y
    hue[15]huetitlan ayyahue · çã cuel achica [16] ye onacazmaxochigeliuhtin
    emi[17]co tenoçêlotzin · cecepohualxochi[18]cozcahui moloco tlaltzinn i
    chi[1]

[folio 17v]

17

[1]yauhcohuaçin y y-n ayopã [2] nemohuâ · mach mocniuh[3]toliniɏa
ypalnemoya · tlal[4]ticpac a ye nicann - ohuaya [5] ohuaya

6   ⸿ ahu quineco xochitl · ahu q̂huã[7]lo cuicatl · cano ye yuhcâ i tete[8]cuitin
    ayyahue - çã yc onecape[9]huilo · cuauhpetlapâ ocelopetla[10]pân i
    xayacamachan i cohuâ[11]çin - tecuitliya - tlacomihuâtzin i [12] ayopâ
    nemohuâ mach mocniuh[13]toliniya - ypalnemohuani tlal[14]ticpâc oye
    nicann a ohuaya ohua[15]ya

16 ⸿ çãniyo yn xochitli tonecuiltol [17] huiya / ha ŷ mali ca titocnihuâ-[18]n
    aya yhuân i cuicatli yc telel [19] quiz huiya - ha ŷhuân i xochi[1]

[folio 18]

18

+

[1]cacahuatl i tacâyyexuchuh · tlal[2]ticpac tlamati toyolo yehuayâ - [3]
ma xomocuicatica - q̂ conequiz i[4]yolo yehuâ - ŷpaltiyanemi y
tlal[5]ticpac ohuaya ohuaya

[XVI] [Part 2, Song 2]

3 A master of egrets makes these flowers move, brings down these songs from your home, O Life Giver. Be pleasured. I say it here.

8 Princes, Chichimecs, call out to Him from Mictlan,[14] for they've been lost [in battle] here on earth.[15] Be pleasured. I say it here.

13 All are appearing, all are arriving in this house of green places beside the drum.[16] Briefly Tenocelotzin is scattered as ear and hand flowers. These become marigold jewels, these, your words, O Tlaltzin![17]

F17V   O Chiauhcoatzin! Not twice does one live. Does Life Giver have a craving for comrades here on earth?[18]

6 Well now! On this eagle mat, this jaguar mat where all are fanned,[19] all lords want flowers, lift songs.[20] O Xayacamach! Lord Coatzin! Tlacomihuatzin! Not twice does one live. Does Life Giver have a craving for comrades here on earth?

16 Our joy is only in these flowers,[21] these captured ones.[22] We're friends, together with these songs—and so our agonies come forth[23]—

F18   together with this flower cacao, our fragrant reed flowers![24] On earth our hearts are glad. Make music! What will Life Giver's heart require on earth?

14. For *oquihualmatic* read *onquihualmatih* 'they call out to him'. For the glottal stop, *h*, replaced by the velar stop, *c*, see GRAM 1.7, 2.5–6, 3.7.

15. For *cahua:te* 'to lose someone [in battle]' see FC 3:19:12, 25, 30; CM 73v:28, 74:3.

16. *Quiquixohua*, reduplicated *quixohua*; for *hualalachialo* read *huallalachiyalo* 'all are arriving', literally, 'all come looking hither'. DICT huallachiya, hualquiza 2, quixohua, quiza 9.

17. For the unanalyzable *moloco tlaltzin* read *motlatol tlaltzin*, 'your words, Tlaltzin'. Cf. 18v:11–12 *motlatol nopilçin* 'your words, my prince' and 18:9–10 *yehua tlalçin* 'it's Tlaltzin'. For equally corrupt text, see 21v:1, 23v:4–5. The alternate reading *molocotlaltzin* 'Molocotlaltzin' yields a name that is unattested and unanalyzable (though FC 2:194:21 has the remotely comparable *moloncoteuhoa* 'Keeper of the Gods of Molonco', incorporating a place name found also in CC).

18. *Mocniuhtolinia* 'he [honorific] has a craving with regard to comrades'. DICT tolina, tolinia:mo 2.

19. For *çâ yc* read *za ye*.

20. Literally, 'well now [*auh*], all want flowers, well now, all lift songs in this location, lords, just already [read *ça ye*], all are fanned, on eagle mat, on jaguar mat'.

21. *Tonecuiltonol* 'our joy'.

22. Read *yn malli* 'captured ones'. Alternate reading: *ynmal i* 'their captured one(s)' (treating the *i* as a vocable). Cf. CM 37:13 *nomal i* 'my captive(s)'.

23. Alternate translation: 'we are entertained [*lit.,* our pain goes away]'. DICT ellelli 4.

24. *Tacaiyexoch[i]uh* 'our reed incense-like flowers'. Cf. CM 35v:25 *tacaieuh* 'our reed incense'; CM 51:22 *acayetl* 'reed incense'. But RSNE 37:10 *tacayye[uh]* 'our smokes [smoking tubes]'. DICT iyetl.

6   ꝗ ha ỹhuan i totlaneuh / chimali a [7] xochitli · yn tlachinolxochitli · me
     [8] ya y moxochihui / ma xomocui[9]catia · titlatqui tecuitli · çâ yehua
     [10] tlalçin huiya · ycnopiloticâ · qui[11]malina xochitli · ayocuatzin[12]n i
     tecuitli yehuâ/n amechoonal[13]huiltiya o · ynqui nochan ipaltiyanemi y
     tlalticpac ohuayo o[14]huaya
15   ꝗ au ya y aneli nemohua yehuâya / o[16]puliz xochitli tla yehuâ y / tomac
     [17] omaniya no yhui titocnihuâa [1]

[folio 18v]

18

     [1] ■ tiyapupuliuh yn tlalticpac/qui ya [2] oohuiya
3   ꝗ mee moxochiuh · yz câ yn tocuic · y [4] titepiltzin tenôcelotl ycan
     ti[5]mapamna ĝçâloxochitlo - hui[6]molihui ya mocpacxochiuh
     ti[7]yazque ■ cano ye ychan an ohua[8]ya ohuaya -

3   *de Neçahualcoyotzin*

10   ꝗ xochipetlatipâni · tocoyaỹcui[11]lohuâ y mocuiqu i motlatol
  I no[12]pilçin oo - tinetzahualcoyotzin-[13]n ahuâyyahui yya yye ahuayya
     [14] yya ohuaya ohuaya
15   ꝗ a ycuiliuh moyolo tlapâpalxo[16]chitlo yca tiquicuilohuâ yn
 II mo[17]cuicqu i motlatol nopilçin oo [1]

[folio 19]

                                                         19

                                +

     [1] tinetzahualcoyotzinn ahuayyahu [2] yya yye - ahuâyya yya ohuaya
     o[3]huaya
4   ꝗ yca xonahuiyacâa yhuiti xochitli · [5] tomac maniya ma
 III oteyaquilo to[6]xochicozqui yn toquipâcoxochiuh [7] tla çêlia xochitli ·
     cuepunia xochi[8]tli · onca nemi tototl chachalaca [9] tlatohuâ ha
     huyohualo quima[10]nan dios [superscript:] *teotl* [line script:] ychan an
     ohuaya ohua[11]ya ·
12   ꝗ çâniyo yn toxochhui y-ca tonaa[13]huiya - çâniyo y cuicatl aya ·
 IV yca o[14]pupulihui - yn amotlaocol iya - [15] tepilhuani · ya yehuâ amelel
     [16] oquiçâ ohuaya ohuaya

6 And ah! our borrowed ones are shield flowers, blaze flowers. Now let these flowers be yours![25] Make music, O chief, O lord—it's Tlaltzin! Grievingly Lord Ayocuantzin twirls flowers. And he pleasures you [here]. As if in your home,[26] O Life Giver. [Yet] it's [here], on earth.

15 But it isn't true that one lives. These flowers are to be destroyed.[27] I wish they would lie in our hands. That way we're each other's comrades:

F18V we're destroyed on earth.[28]

3 Let's have your flowers![29] Here they are! Our songs! You adorn yourself with plume flowers, Prince Tenocelotl. Your flower crowns are stirring, and we are off to His home.

[XVII] [Part 2, Song 3][30]

10 On this flower mat you paint your songs, your words, my prince, you, Nezahualcoyotzin.

15 Ah, your heart is painted.[31] As multicolored flowers you paint your

F19 songs, your words, my prince, you, Nezahualcoyotzin.

4 With these be pleasured. These intoxicating flowers lie in our hands. Let everyone wear these flower necklaces, these flower crowns of ours.[32] Let flowers sprout, let flowers open. Chattering, singing, the birds are alive beyond. These jingles. God spreads them out in his home.[33]

12 Only with flowers are we pleasured. Only with songs is your sadness destroyed, O princes: you're entertained.

---

25. For *me ya y moxochihui* read *ma ye i moxochiuh i* 'let there be already your flowers!' *Me* written for *ma* recurs at 18v:3 and 24v:4. Cf. CM 16v:23 *ma ye xochitl* 'let there be already flowers'.

26. For *ynqui nochan* read *yuhquin mochan* 'as if in your home'.

27. Read *ompolihuiz*.

28. Read *tiyapopolihuih*.

29. Read *ma moxochiuh*. See 18:7–8, above.

30. Gloss: 'of Nezahualcoyotzin'.

31. Alternate translation: 'your hearts are painted'.

32. Read *ma onneaquilo* 'let people adorn themselves (with)' as in CM 53:1; *tocpacxochiuh* (cf. CM 30:29 *moquipacxochiuh* 'your flower crown'—the first *i* is a vocable).

33. Superscript *teotl* 'god [or spirit power]'. For *huyohualo* read *oyohualo*, i.e., *oyohualli* '[jingle] bells'.

17 ¶ quiyocoya ya · yn ipalnemohua ye[1]
 V

[folio 19v]

19

   [1]huâ · quiyahualtemohuiya mo[2]yocoyaçin y y-n a
   yahahuiloxo[3]chitli - y yca yehua hamelel oqui[4]çâ ohuaya ohuaya
 5 ¶ titoquimilohua o · titecuiltono[6]huâ · xoochitica cuicatica ya
 VI ye[7]huâya · xopan i xochitli yca tita[8]pāna ha y tlalticpac ye nicani [9]
   oo ha yahui yya ohayahui ooha[10]yya ohuaya ohuaya
11 ¶ q̂n oc câ tlamatiya noyolo yehuâ [12] nicaqui ya cuicatli ·
 VII niquita y xo[13]chitli · maca y cuetlahuiya ooo/ha [14] y tlaticpac
   oohayahui yya ohaya[15]hui oohayya ohuaya ohuaya

             4   *a lo divino gentilico*

17 ¶ çâ toteycneliya ■ / aca çâ tlahucoya / [18]
 VIII ynpalnemohuâni / yn cuix nelli [1]

[folio 20]

                                          20

             +

   [1] cuix no amo nelli / q̂ni conito[2]hua ŷ / maoc onetlamati yn
   to[3]yolo / yehuâ ohuaya ohuaya
 4 ¶ q̂xquich i ye neli quilhuiya · / yn · [5] amo nello - /çân
 IX omonenequin i[6]palnemohuani - / maoc onetla[7]mati y toyolo /
   yehuâ ohuaya [8] ohuaya
 9 ¶ çâ yehuâ dios · ypalnemohuâ / y - [10] ninetlamatia / / aca
 X çô · ayc yz ꞔô [11] ohuaya - / aca çô ayc nonahuiye [12] y tenehuaca /
   ohuaya ohuaya
13 ¶ yn çâ tictlaçōcêcêlohua o - ohua[14]ye - yn motechpâ ye huiz / y
 XI mone[15]cuilitonol / - ypalnemohuâ / yn iz[16]quixochitli -
   cacahuaxochitli / [17] çâ noconelehuiya - / çâ ninetla[18]matia / ohuaya
   ohuaya

17 Life Giver creates them. He, Self Maker, brings them down. And with
F19V these pleasure flowers you're entertained.

5 We adorn ourselves, enrich ourselves with flowers,[34] with songs. With
flowers from Green Places we adorn ourselves on earth.

11 How glad my heart is![35] I hear songs, I see flowers. I wish they wouldn't
wither on earth.

[XVIII] [Part 2, Song 4][36]

17 Are You obliging? Is Life Giver in a mournful mood[37]? Yes or no? What
F20 does he say? Let our hearts keep sorrowing.[38]

4 How many does he "yes" and "no"! This Life Giver is intractable. [But]
let our hearts keep sorrowing.

9 O God, O Life Giver, I'm in sorrow: will it never be?[39] Will I never have
the pleasure of One's company?[40]

13 You strew them as loved ones,[41] and ah! they come from you, your
riches, O Life Giver! They're the popcorn flowers, the cacao flowers,
that I crave in sorrowing.

34. Literally, 'enrich people with flowers'—unless the nonspecific object *te* 'people' has been
accidentally written for *to* 'ourselves'.

35. Read *quen oc çan tlamatiya noyollo*. DICT quen 4, quen oc 2.

36. Gloss: 'to the pagan divinity'. The song also appears as CM song 69, canto F (62:
23–62v:14).

37. Read *anca zan tlaocoya*. Cf. CM 62:23.

38. CM 62:24–25 *maoc onnentlamati in toyollo*.

39. CM 62:28 *anca ço aic yez* 'perchance indeed never will it be'.

40. CM 62:29 *tenahuac*.

41. CM 62:30 *In çan tictlaçotzetzeloa*.

[folio 20v]

20

1   ¶ acan chalchihuitli / - ậçāli patla[2]huac · moyolo motlatol /
XII totatzin [3] oo ehuaya dios [superscript:] *totecoyo* [line script:] y - /
     toteycnoytâ [4] toteycnopilita - / yn çâ cuel achic[5]çincâ - / yn motloc
     monahuac â / [6] ohuaya ohuaya
7   ¶ chalchiuhyzmolini - / moxochiuh y[8]palnemohuâ · / ye
XIII xochimimi[9]lihui / xiuhquecholquepûti[10]maniya - / yn çâ quel
     achic[11]çincâ / - yn motloc monahua[12]c a - / ohuaya ohuaya
13 ¶ yyoya·huee - / oyahui xahue / anahui[14]ya o / -
XIV anihuelamatin / tlalticpac o [15] ye nicâ - / ohuaya ohuaya
16 ¶ aca yuhcâ ye niyol / yuhcan nitla[17]cat / a ycnopilotli · / çã
XV   nicmatico [18] ye nican y tenahuâc â - ohuaya [19] ohuaya

[folio 21]

21

+

1   ¶ maoc netlatlaneo nicâ - / y yatocni[2]huãn i · / çâniyo nican · /
XVI ay tlalticpac a [3] ohuaya ohuaya
4   ¶ ya moztla huiptla / que conequiz y[5]yolo / ypalnemohuâ / toyazậ
XVII ye [6] yncha·/n atocnihuâ maoc tonaha[7]ahuiyacan / ohuaya ohuaya

5
de Neçahualcoyotzin quando andaba uyêdo del Rey de Azca putzalco

9   ¶ one notlacat aa - yyahue - one no[10]quiçaco dios [superscript:]
     1 *totecoyo* [line script:] ichani - y tlalticpac[11]qui ninotolinia ohuaya
     o[12]huaya ·
13 ¶ y ma o nel noquiz y ma o notlacat a [14] niquitohua yyeehuâya
     2 · tlee [15] nayçiz onnohuaco tepilhua[16]no ateyxco ninemi ậ huel
     xi[17]mimatiya ohuaya ohuaya
18 ¶ ye ya nonehuataz yn tlaltic[19]paqui yeyatla nolhuil çã
     3 ni[1]

[folio 21v]

21

[1]n/atliniya toonehuâ çã noyolo [2] tinocniuh yn ayaxcana yn
tlal[3]ticpac ya nican a ohuaya ohua[4]ya

F20V   1 It seems your hearts and words are jades,[42] broad plumes, O father,
         O God.[43] You're merciful, compassionate. Yet briefly are they near
         you and in your presence.

    7 Your flowers are greening as jades, O Life Giver. They flower-sprout,
         they're blossoming as turquoise swans. But briefly are they near you
         and in your presence.

  13 Alas, I have no pleasure here, no happiness on earth.

  16 Is this my lot? Is this my fate?[44] Ah, bereavement is all I've come to
         know in this company here.

F21   1 Let there be borrowing,[45] O friends. And only here. On earth!

    4 What will Life Giver's heart be requiring one of these days? We must
         travel to his home, O friends. Then let us be pleasured!

[XIX] [Part 2, Song 5][46]

    9 I'm born in vain, come forth in vain from God's home.[47] On earth I'm
         poor.

  13 Let me not come forth! Let me not be born! I say, what will befall me?[48]
         All the princes have come to be assembled.[49] I give no offense. Take
         care!

  18 Oh yes, I'm to go away ascending from my seat on earth, my lot,[50] I who
F21V   am poor.[51] My heart is suffering, friend. This earth is hardship.

42. For *acan* read *ancan*, i.e., *anca* 'it seems'.
43. Superscript 'Our Lord'.
44. Literally, 'perchance [*anca*] thus already I was brought to life, thus I was born?'
45. *Maoc netlatlanehuilo* 'let people borrow things'. DICT tlanehuia:mo-tla.
46. Gloss: 'of Nezahualcoyotzin when he was fleeing from the king of Azcapotzalco'. The song also appears as CM 13:14–13v:2 (song 18, stanzas 17–22), with RSNE stanzas 1–3, 4, 5, 6, 7, and 8 corresponding to CM stanzas 17, 18, 21, 22, 19, and 20, respectively.
47. Superscript 'Our Lord'.
48. CM 13:15 *tle naiz* 'what will befall me?' (literally, 'what will I do?'). DICT ayi:tla.
49. Read *onohuaco* 'all have come to assemble'. DICT o 5.
50. The better text in CM 13:17 has *ye noyehuataz yeyantli nolhuil* 'Indeed, I'm to go away ascending [to the] seat [which is] my reward [i.e., heaven]'. Cf. DICT -yeyan.
51. CM 13:17 *ninotolinia* 'I am poor'.

5 ℂ q̃ni nemohua yaa · yn tenahua[6]qui · mach ilihuiz tiyanemia [7]

4 tehuic teyxco niyanemi çã[8]n ihuiyaa çân i çêmele - yn [9] çã
   nonopechtecâ çã nitoloti[10]nemi aŷ tenahuac a · ohua[11]ya ohuaya ·

12 ℂ çã yeŷca nichoca yeehuaya · nic[13]notla-mati yeehuaya ·

5 nonic[14]nocahualoc · qui tenahua[15]qui tlalticpaqui · q̃ cone[16]qui
   moyolo yehua · ypalne[17]mohuani · maoc melel onquiçâ / [18] a
   ycnopilotl huiya · maoc oti[1]

[folio 22]

22

+

[1]malihui · monahuaqui titeotl ye[2]hua Dios [superscript:] *in totecoyo*
[line script:] · a tinnechmiquitlani [3] ohuaya ohuaya

4 ℂ açômo ye neli tipaquitiyane[5]mi tlalticpâqui · aca çã

6 titoc[6]nihuân inic hualpâquihuâ tlal[7]ticpaqui aca nnoch ihui
   titoto[8]liniya - aca noch ihui teopohui [9] tenahuac ya nican â /
   ohua[10]ya ohuaya

11 ℂ ma xicnotlamati noyolo yehua [12] macaoc tle xicyocoya

7 yeehua[13]ya / ye nelin ayaxcâ·n icnopil[14]tihuâ y tlalticpaqui · ye neli
   cococ [15] ye otimalihui oo y motloc mona[16]huâ y · ynpalnemohuâ
   yyao yya[17]hue · ahuayya oohuiya

18 ℂ çâ niquitemohuaya - niquimil[1]

8

[folio 22v]

22

[1]namiqui · yn tocnihuâ cuix o[2]cẽpa huiçẽ y cuix oc nemiqui[3]hui çâ
cê tiyapulihuia çã cê ye [4] nican i / yn tlalticpaqui · ma[5]ca cocoya
yyolo · ytloc ynahua[6]qui ynpalnemohua yya o · [7] yyahue · ahuayya
oohuiya -

6

9 ℂ çâ nopehua nocuica yaacohui y - ye [10] noconehua yn · çâ ca

9 ye ycuic yy / [11] yn ipalnemohuâ - yehuaya Dios a [12] ohuaya ohuaya

13 ℂ cuicaylhuiçolmana Dios · y ecoc [14] hualaçiz - y

10 moyocoyaçin ii · ante[15]pilhuan ma onnetlanehuilo yn [16]
   cacahuaxochitlii · ahuayyo ayy · [17] ohuaya ohuaya

5 How does one live in company? We're inconsiderate of others, and I
give offense. Just gently! Serenely![52] I just bend down, I just go
bowing in the presence of others.[53]

12 For this I weep. I grieve. I'm bereft in this company here on earth.
What does your heart require, O Life Giver? Be entertained! Let

F22   bereavement suppurate near you, O Spirit! O God,[54] you want me
dead!

4 Aren't we truly happy on earth? It seems we're each other's comrades.[55]
So there is happiness on earth. It seems to be that way with all of us
who are poor. It seems to be that way with every sufferer here in this
company.

11 Grieve, my heart! Make nothing![56] True, there's hardship, there's
bereavement on earth. And true, this wound would suppurate near
you and in your presence,[57] O Life Giver.

18 I seek comrades, I recall them. [But] do they come again? do they come

F22V   to life again? We die forever and utterly here on earth. Let no one's
heart be wounded near and in the presence of Life Giver.[58]

[XX] [Part 2, Song 6][59]

9 I strike up a song, singing the songs of God Life Giver.

13 God has arrived,[60] spreading song marvels. Self Maker is coming here,
you princes. Let these cacao flowers be borrowed.

---

52. *Cemelle* 'serenely'. But the variant (CM 13:20) has the better reading: *can ycel nelli* 'indeed
it's the only truth!'

53. Alternate translation: 'in the presence of Someone [i.e., God]'.

54. Superscript 'O Our Lord!'

55. For *aca* read *anca* 'it seems'.

56. The better text (CM 13:22) has *Maca xicnotlamati noyollo macaoc tle xicyocoya* 'Do not
grieve, O my heart! Do not create anything!' Alternate translation: 'Do not grieve, O my hearts!
[...]'.

57. CM 13:23 *monahuac*.

58. Literally, 'let not his [i.e., one's] heart be wounded'. On the impersonal 'he' see GN 4.3. But
the better reading is in CM 13:26–27: *macac cocoya yiollo* 'let no one's heart be wounded'.

59. The song also appears as CM song 73 (64:3–24) and again as CM song 82, canto D
(69v:10–28), but in both cases stanzas 3 and 4 of the RSNE version are placed at the end; and
CM song 82 lacks RSNE stanza 8.

60. Literally, 'God, who has arrived [*Dios y[n] e[h]coc*], he spreads song marvels [*cuicaylhuiçolmana*]'. But following the variants in CM (64:6 and 69v:13) the reading would be 'God

18   ¶ yyaquiyacohui - yyo huijahue - huiya [19] q̂
11   nocochihuaz i ma xochitica · ye[1]

[folio 23]

23

+

[1]huāya · mayc ninapātihui niya[2]patlaniz i · ninotoliniya · yca
ni[3]choca yn · ohuaya ohuaya
4   ¶ cuel achic monahuac yeehuâya, y[5]palnemohuani, y ye neli
12   toteycui[6]lohua acaa toteycnomati ay tlal[7]ticpâqui ohuaya ohuaya
8   ¶ nepâpa cua·huizhuayoticac ŷ mo[9]huehue yn ipalnemohua
13   yehua[10]ya Dios y xochitica çêlizticac aa-[11]yyahue yca miçônaahuiltia
/ ay te[12]pilhua ahuiya ohu ach i ye yuhcaa [13] cuicaxochitl huel
imanicâ ohua[14]ya ohuaya
15   ¶ y queçâlizquixochitl · omcueputoc [16] ye ocâ huiya · ycahuaca
14   otlato[17]hua yeehuaya · yn q̂çâlayacach[18]tototl ypalnemohuani ·
teocui[19]tlaxochitl aya cuepuntimania [1]

[folio 23v]

23

[1] ohu ach i ye yuhcaa cuicanxochit[2]hual imanicâ ohuaya ohuaya
3   ¶ çâ zinizcān i çâcua ye tlauhq̂chol yc â [4] tictlatlapalpuohua
15   ye mocuic ŷ■■[5]opoo çâ tiquimoq̂çaltiya ŷ mocni[6]huan i y cuauhtin
oçêlo yc tiquime[7]lacuahua ohuaya ohuaya
8   ¶ aqu icnopill in ac onacitiuh ŷn oca [9] piltihua mahuiztihua
16   yeehua[10]ya y mocnihuan i ŷ cuauhtin o[11]çêlo yc tiquimelacuahua
ohua[12]ya ohuaya

7

14   ¶ niqueçâ tohuehueuh niquinechi[15]cohua ya tocnihuan
1   oo ynme[16]lel quiçā niquicuicatia tiyaz[17]que yeuhca
17   xq̂lnamiquica xi[18]moquimiloca xiyamocuiltono[19]ca [1]

[folio 24]

24

+

[1] y yatocnihuan a ohuaya ohuaya

18 What's to befall me?[61] Let it be with flowers, let it be with these that I
F23   adorn myself, flying away, I that am poor. And for this I weep.

4 Brief is your presence, Life Giver. [But] yes, it's true: you paint us, it
seems you show us mercy [here] on earth.

8 This multitude, your drums, stand leafing out as eagles, O Life Giver,
O God. They're sprouting as flowers. With these the princes give you
pleasure. So it would seem in this patio of flower song.[62]

15 Plumelike popcorn flowers are blossoming where Life Giver shrills,
sings, as a plumelike rattle bird. Golden flowers are blossoming.
F23V   Ah, so it would seem in this patio of flower song.

3 Life Giver,[63] you're reciting your songs in colors—as trogons, troupials,
roseate swans. And you're taking these comrades of yours to be your
plumes, these eagles, these jaguars. Yes,[64] you're spurring them on.

8 Who'll be fortunate?[65] Who'll go where there's nobility and fame?[66]
Your comrades! These eagles, these jaguars! Yes, you spur them on.

[XXI] [Part 2, Song 7][67]

14 I stand up the drum, I gather our friends, and their cares are put aside:
I give them songs. We're off to that place [beyond].[68] Recall them.
F24   Adorn yourselves and rejoice, friends.

[who is] Necoc [*Dios yn necoc*] spreads song marvels'. Cf. CM 64:6–7: *cuicailhuiçolpan ỹ necoc hualacic y iehuā Tiox antépilhuā ma onnetlanehuilo yectli ya xochitl* 'from this Place of Song Marvels, Necoc has come, it is God. Princes! Let these holy blooms be borrowed'. The term "Necoc" ('On Both Sides') appears as *necoc iautl* ('Enemy on Both Sides') in a list of epithets—including *moiocoiatzi[n]* ('Self Maker')—applied to the supreme deity, Tezcatlipoca, at FC 3:12:19. Cf. CC 17:22–23 *àmo yn necol* [for *necoc*, the copyist reading a *c* for a curled *l*?] *ca yn diablo yn quichihuaya* 'Was it not Necoc, the Devil, who did it?'

61. The stanza opens with the vocables *yyahuiyacohui yyo huixahue huiya*. Apparently the copyist has misread a descending *h* as a *q*; and note the unusual *j* written for *x*. Cf. 6:5 and 38v:8.

62. CM 64:10 *cuicaxochithuall imanican* 'where song-flower patio lies'.

63. For the corrupt *ỹ■■opoo* read *ypalnemohuani* 'Life Giver', as in CM 64:15–16.

64. *Yc* 'thus'. CM 64:17 *ye* 'already' or 'indeed'.

65. If the reading is *aqu icnopilli* [. . .], as in CM 64:18, the translation becomes 'Who [will] be orphaned?' DICT icnopilli.

66. For *oca* read *oncan* as in CM 64:18.

67. Stanzas 1, 2b, 7, and 8 of this song appear also as stanzas 9, 10b, 11a, and 11b, respectively, in CM song 64 (52v:30–31, 53:2–7).

68. *Ye iuhcan.* Cf. 29v:6–7.

2 ⸿ yn cuix uc no yhuiya · cano yeuhcaan aya [3] cuix oc uo
~~18~~ yhuiya cano ximohua[4]ya ▪oohuyeo aye · oo
2 = = = = =

5 [⸿] *hu*aye // ma tihuiyacan i yecē ye nican i xo[6]chinahuatilo
3 yeçē ye nican i cuica[7]nahuatilo tlalticpâc u ohuaye
~~19~~ ximo[8]quimiloca xiyamocuiltonocâ - y ya[9]tocnihuan an ohuaya
ohuaya -
=

10 ⸿ tzinizcaxuchitla yhua quimalinan [11] yectli ya cuicatla · yc
4 toteyapânaco ti[12]cuicanitli huiya - yc totequimilohua
~~20~~ [13] nepapâ xuchitli - mayc xonahui[14]yacann atepilhuan a ohuaya [15]
ohuaya

16 ⸿ y cuix oɋ uh nemohua cano ye yuh [17] q̂nonamicani cani cuix
5 ohui va[18]huiyalo aca çâniyo nican i tlal[1]
~~21~~

[folio 24v]

24

[1]ticpaqui xochitica ya hualyaiy[2]ximacho cuicatica yye onetlanehu [3]
titocnihuan an ohuaya ohuaya
4 ⸿ me moxochiuh yca ximapana y tla[5]uhquechoxoochitl
6 aya - tonatima[6]niya y cacaloxochitli · ma ya yca [7] titoquimiloca
tlalticpac ye nica ye[8]çē ye nican i ohuaya ohuaya
9 ⸿ y çâ achiçinca y ma yhui cuel achic[10]c
7 onetlanehuilo yxochi oo aye ya o[11]huiya a ytquihuaz ye ychan i dios
aya[12]a yhua ximohuacan o ye ychani auh in a[13]moo çân ic opolihui y
telell oo ay totlao[14]col i ohuaya ohuaya
15 ⸿ tixiuhtotootl titlauhquechool tiyapa[16]tlatinemi moyocoya
8 ypalnemo[17]huâ timohuihuixohua ya timo[18]çêçêlohua nicani /
moquinochaa [19] moquinocala ymacan a ohuaya ohua[20]ya

[folio 25]

25

+

1 ⸿ monecuiltonol moteycnelil hue[2]lo nemohuaya ypalnemohua
9 y · y tlal[3]ticpâque y timohuihuixohua ya ti[4]moçêçêlohua nicani i
moquinocha[5]a moquinocal a ymacan â ohuaya [6] ohuaya

2 Is it just the same in that place? Is it just the same in the place where all are shorn? Let us be pleasured.[69] It's here that they're summoned with flowers, here on earth that they're summoned with songs.[70] Adorn yourselves and rejoice, friends.

10 He's whirling trogon flowers. And with these good songs you decorate, singer. You adorn with flowers of different kinds.[71] And so be pleasured, princes.

16 Is life the same in the Place Unknown?[72] Is there pleasure?[73] Perhaps only here on earth. Through these flowers their acquaintance is made,

F24V through these songs all are borrowed,[74] and we are comrades.

4 Let's have these flowers of yours.[75] Be adorned with these. Roseate swan flowers, raven flowers are shining. Let us adorn ourselves with these here on earth. Right here.

9 For a moment let it be so. For just a moment all his flowers are borrowed. They'll be carried off to God's home—and his home is the place where all are shorn. Well, isn't this the way our pain and sadness are destroyed?

15 O Cotinga, O Roseate Swan, O you that soar, Self Maker, Life Giver, you shake yourself, you scatter yourself here in your humble home, in your humble house.[76]

F25 1 All your riches, your favors are alive, O Life Giver, O Earth Owner. You shake yourself, you scatter yourself here in your humble home, in your humble house.

69. Read *ma tahuiyacan* as at 11v:4–5.

70. Alternate translation: 'summoned as flowers [. . .] summoned as songs'.

71. Alternate translation: 'you adorn with all the flowers'. DICT nepapan.

72. *Y cuix oqu iuh nemohua cano[n] ye iuh[can] quenonamican i* for *Yn cuix oc iuh nemohua [. . .]*. Cf. 24:2–3, also CM 61:12–13: *Ma yuh nemohua ȳ mach oc tiqualmati otiyaque ye ichan* 'Would that life were as it is! Do we still implore Him [when] we've traveled to His home?'

73. Disregarding the vocables *ohui v-* (for *ohui hu-*), read *cuix ahuiyalo*.

74. Read *onnetlanehuilo* as at 24v:10.

75. Read *ma moxochiuh* 'let there be your flowers'. Cf. 18:7–8, 18v:3.

76. Read *moicnochan moicnocal imancan*. Cf. CM 53:5 *moicnochan moicnocal*.

8

8   ⸿   maquizcuepuni oohuaye y moxo[9]chihu aya chalchimimilihui
10   xo[10]chiyzhuayo y tomac omaniya [11] q̂çâliyexochitl yeçê
tonequimi[12]lol hatepilhua huiya yyayya [13] çâ tictotlanehuiya y
tlalticpâc a [14] ohuaya ohuaya
15   ⸿   ma yzquixochitli ma cacahuaxo[16]chitli neneliuhtimaniya
11   to[17]mac omaniya q̂çâliyexochi[18]tli yeçê tonequimilol âtepil[19]hua
ahuiya yya ye çâ tictotlane[1]

[folio 25v]

25

[1]huiya y tlalticpâc a ohuaya ohuaya
2   ⸿   çâ nihuallaocoya çâ nitiçâhua[3]çi huiya cano tihui ye ychano
12   ayoc [4] hualnecuepâlo ayoc hualyloti[5]hua yeehuaya çê tihui ocano
ti[6]hui ohuaya ohuaya
7   ⸿   ma ytquihuan i ychano xochitli [8] cuicatli ma ye ninapâtihu i
13   teocui[9]tlacacaloxochitli queçâlizqui[10]xochitli yn tomac omania ayoc
[11] hualylotihua yehuaya çê tihui [12] oocano tihui ohuaya ohuaya
13   ⸿   titotoliniyan in anica tochan tima[14]çêhualti cano ximohua
14   yehuaya [15] cano ye ycha huiya yoyahue huia[16]hue çâ achica
onetlalcahuilo nica[17]n an ohuaya ohuaya
18   ⸿   çâ totla■■nehuipâni y tinemi ye ni[19]caa timacehualti cano
15   ximohua ye[20]huaya cano ye ycha huiya oyahue [1]

[folio 26]

26

+

[1] huixahue çâ achica onetlalcahui[2]lo nican an ohuaya ohuaya
3   ⸿   ohu aca çân iuh ye noyaz çân iuhqui [4] noyaz y cano ye
16   ychâ haca opâ oquiz[5]taz ycnopilootl huiya aca nnocotla[6]mitaz yn
icococa yn iteopuuhca tlatic[7]pâc oo ninotolinia ohuaya ohuaya
8   ⸿   y çâ one one nonemico ninoteopuhuaco [9] tenahuaq̂ aca
17   nocotlamitaz yn ico[10]coca yn iteopuuhca tlalticpac oo ni[11]notoliniyâ
ohuaya ohuaya

[XXII] [Part 2, Song 8]

8 Your flowers blossom as bracelets, swelling as jades, the petals
abounding, they lie in our hands. These fragrant plume flowers are
our adornment, you princes. Aya! We only borrow them on earth.

15 Let the popcorn flowers, the raven flowers be scattered, and fragrant
plume flowers lie in our hands. They are our adornment, you princes.

F25V Aya! We only borrow them on earth.

2 I, Tizahuatzin, am grieving here. Where are we to go? To His home!
There can be no coming back, there can be no return. We go away
forever. Beyond is where we go.[77]

7 Let these flowers, these songs be carried from his home. And would that
I might go away adorned. Gold raven flowers, plume popcorn flowers
lie in our hands. There can be no return. We go away forever. Beyond
is where we go.

13 We underlings are miserable, for our home is not here. It's where all are
shorn, and that place is His home. Alas, the abandoning comes soon.

18 We underlings, we who live here, are merely borrowed.[78] Where all are

F26 shorn, that place, is His home. Alas, the abandoning comes soon.

3 And so I must go, must go to His home.[79] Will there be a second
misery?[80] And when I've gone, will I have put an end to this pain and
suffering? On earth I am miserable.

8 In vain, in vain I came to live. I came to suffer in the presence of others.
When I've gone, will I have put an end to this pain and suffering?[81]
On earth I am miserable.

77. DICT *oncanon* 'there [beyond]'.

78. *Totla∎∎nehuipâni,* with its imperfectly copied sixth and seventh characters, could be made
out as *totlalanehuipâni,* which would be difficult to analyze. But if a *y* has been miscopied as a *p,*
and if the two dubious characters are an inserted vocable (*ya?*), the reading would be *totlayane-
huiyan i,* or, removing the vocables, *totlanehuiya,* for *titotlanehuia* 'we are borrowed'. On the loss
of the subject prefix see 2:13, above, and the accompanying note.

79. Literally, 'alas [*o*] it seems [*anca*] it is just thus indeed that I am to go, just thus that I am
to go where indeed is his home'.

80. Literally, 'perchance [*anca*] twice it will go issuing, this grief'.

81. Read *yni cococ a yni teohpouhca* for *inin cococ a inin teohpouhqui* 'this pain, ah! this
suffering'.

9   *de quaquauhtzin s^r de tepex*
      pan

13 ❡ quinenequi xochitl çâ noyolo yehua[14]ya çã nomac omaniya - çã
   nicui[15]canetlamati çã nicuicayeyecohua [16] y tlalticpaqui ye
   nicuacuauhçin[17]ni noconequi xochitl çã noma[18]c omani y
   ninetlamatia yo aye yo ahuayya [19] ohuia

      [folio 26v]

26

1 ❡ canelpâ toyazque yn ayc timiquiz[2]q̃ maçâ nichalchihuitl
   niteocui[3]tlatl o çâ ye o nipiçâloz nimamali[4]huaz i tlatilan o çã noyoli
   yo çã ye [5] nicuacuauhtzin çã ninentlama[6]tia yo aye yo ahuayo ohuiya
7 ❡ mochalchiuhteponaz moxiuhq̂[8]choliquiquiçin tocoyapiçâya çã ye [9]
   tiyoyotzinni oyahualaçic a oya [10] moqueçãco ya ŷ cuicanitla yyohuiya
11 ❡ cuelça xonahuiyacani ma ya hualmo[12]q̂çâ a yyolo nicococohua çã
   nique[13]hua cuicatli oyahualaçic a oya [14] moq̂çãco ya y cuicanitla
   yyohui[15]ya
16 ❡ y ma ya moyolo motoma y ma ya [17] moyolo ma açintinemiya
   tine[18]chcocoliya tinechmiquitlani [19] ŷn onoya ye ychân in
   onopulihui [1]

      [folio 27]

        27

     +

[1] aca çã yoquic oo noca tihualichocani [2] ~~nonopolihui~~ noca
tihualycnotla[3]mati çâ tinocni o çã ye niyao çã ye [4] niyauh ye ychan
ohuaya ohuaya
5 ❡ çâ quitohua noyolo ayoc çẽpâ ye [6] nihuiç ãya ayoc çẽpa
   niquiçâ[7]quiuh y ye yeçâ y tlalticpâc o çã ye ni[8]ya o çã ye niyauh ye
   ychâ ohuaya ohua[9]ya

[XXIII] [Part 2, Song 9]⁸²

13 My heart is greatly wanting flowers that lie in my hand. Yes, I song-
grieve, making songs on earth,⁸³ I, Cuacuauhtzin, wanting flowers
that lie in my hand. I grieve.

F26v 1 "Where might we go, so as never to die? Though I be jade, or gold, I'll
be smelted, or drilled on the mound."⁸⁴ Ah! I'm born, I,
Cuacuauhtzin, and I grieve.

7 Your precious log drums! You blow your conch for turquoise swans,
you, Yoyontzin.⁸⁵ The singer arrives, he appears.

11 It's time!⁸⁶ Be pleasured! And they shall appear! I wound their hearts.⁸⁷
I'm lifting songs. The singer arrives, he appears.

16 "Let your hearts be set free, let your hearts come forth.⁸⁸ You loathe
me, and you want me dead. When I've gone to His home, when I've

F27 perished, then perhaps you'll weep for me, you'll grieve for me,
O friend. I go, I'm off to His home.

5 "My heart says never again do I come, never again will I be born in the
good place, earth,⁸⁹ I go, I'm off to His home."

82. Spanish gloss: *de Cuacuauhtzin, señor de Tepechpan* 'of Cuacuauhtzin, lord of Tepechpan'.
The song also appears as CM song 43 (26:19–26v:12) and again as CM song 62, canto C (49v:11–
50:2), but in both cases stanzas 1 and 2 of the RSNE version are placed between CM stanzas 4
and 7. The *s* in the textual *sʳ*, for *señor*, is a descender, shaped like a shepherd's crook, quite unlike
the modern serpentine *s*. Comparison with the *s* at 1:1, 1:2, and elsewhere in the manuscript will
confirm that the character here is *s*.
83. Alternate translation: 'trying or sampling songs on earth'. DICT yecoa:tla.
84. Alternate translation: 'Let me be jade, gold; I'll be smelted and drilled in Mound Town'. Tla-
tillan 'Mound Town', a play on Tlatilolco (= Tlatelolco) 'Mound Place'. DICT -tlan, tlatelolli.
85. Alternate translation: 'These precious log drums of yours, these turquoise-swan conch
horns of yours, you forge them [i.e., you create them as a goldsmith crafts jewelry], you, Yoyontzin'. But CM 26:19–20 has *Nochalchiuhteponaz noxiuhquecholinquiquici nocoyapitzaya ça ye ni-
quahquauhtzin huiya onihualacic a ononiquetzacoya nicuicanitl ayio huiya* 'O my precious log
drums! I blow my conch for turquoise swans, I, Cuacuauhtzin'. Or: 'These precious log drums of
mine, these turquoise-swan conch horns of mine, I forge them, I, Cuacuauhtzin'.
86. CM 49v:14 *cuelcan* for *cualcan* 'now is the time' (CARO 103v, DICT cualcan, cuelcan).
87. Read *niccocoa* as at CM 26:21.
88. *Ma ya moyollo ma ahcitinemi ya* 'Let your heart(s), let them be arriving'.
89. Literally, 'Indeed my heart says never again will I come to issue forth (as a newborn)
indeed in the good place the earth' (for *yeçâ* read *yeccan* 'good place' as in CM 49v:20). DICT
quiza 8.

10 ꟓ çâne tequitl i xonahuiyaca huiya xo[11]nahuiyacan atocnihua huiya
ha[12]t amonahuiyazq̂ hat ahuellama[13]tizque tocnihuan oohuaye ca
ni[14]cuiç in yectla xochitli yectli ya cui[15]catli hahuayya oo ahuayya
yya [16] ha yyahuiya

17 ꟓ ayquin o xopann i quichihua ye [18] nican çâ ninotolinia çã ye nicua[1]

[folio 27v]

27

[1]cuauhtzin huiya hat amonahui[2]yazq̂ hat ahuelamatizq̂ tocni[3]huan
oohuaye ca nicuiç in yeitla [4] xochitli yectli ya cuicatli hahua[5]yya
oohahuayya yyaha yyohuiya

10

7 ꟓ maoc onicniuhtihua yehuaya [8] maoc totiyximatica xochitl [9] yca y -
onehualoz yn cuicatlo ti[10]yaq̂ ye ychâ / çã totlatolo yn o[11]nemi çē
nicân i tlalticpaca o[12]huaya ohuaya

13 ꟓ çã ye tococauhtihui ohuaye ŷ to[14]tlaocol i tocuic o çã ye
onixima[15]choz oneloz y cuicatl o tiyaq̂ ye y[16]châ çâ totlatolo yn
onemi çē [17] nicann i tlalticpâca ohuaya [18] ohuaya

19 ꟓ cuicatli quiçãq̂ y noyolo nicho[20]ca yehuaya ye nicnotlama[1]

[folio 28]

28

+

[1]tiya xochitica ticauhtehuazq̂ [2] tlalticpac ye nican i çã
tictotlane[3]huiya o tiyazq̂ ye ychân ohua[4]ya ohuaya

5 ꟓ ma nicnocozcati nepapâ xochitl [6] ma nomac omaniya ma
noc[7]pacxochihui ticauhtehuaz[8]q̂ - tlalticpac ye nican i çã
ticto[9]tlanehuiya o tiyazq̂ ye ynchân o[10]huaya ohuaya

11 ꟓ ohu aca ç iuhqui chalchihuitl ohua[12]ye y tocopepena y yectli ya
mo[13]cuic ypalnemohuani çã no y[14]uhqui yn icniuhyotl aya
tocoçequi[15]xtiya tlalticpac ye nican ohuaya [16] ohuaya

10 Be pleasured, greatly pleasured, oh but scarcely,⁹⁰ friends! And will you
    go be pleasured and content, O friends?⁹¹ Indeed, I'll pluck these
    holy flowers, these holy songs.

17 These never make Green Places here, and I am poor, I, Cuacuauhtzin.

F27V   Will you go be pleasured and content, O friends? Indeed, I'll pluck
    these holy flowers, these holy songs.

[XXIV] [Part 2, Song 10]⁹²

7 Let there be comrades, acquaintance with flowers. Songs shall be raised,
   [then] we're off to His home.⁹³ It's just our songs that live right here
   on earth.⁹⁴

13 We're leaving our songs, our creations. Their acquaintance shall be
    made: the songs shall be raised.⁹⁵ [Then] we're off to His home. It's
    just our songs that live right here on earth.

19 My heart hears songs, and I weep, I grieve, on account of these flowers.

F28   We're to go away and leave them here on earth. We merely borrow
    them, and we're off to His home.

5 Let me take this multitude of flowers as my necklace. Let me have them
   in my hand. Let them be my flower crown. We're to go away and
   leave them here on earth. We merely borrow them, and we're off to
   His home.

11 Life Giver, you're gathering up your good songs as though they were
    jades!⁹⁶ [So] this is how you bring together comrades here on earth.

---

90. *Zannen tequitl* 'just barely', as in CM 26v:6, 33v:7, 49v:28. DICT zannen, zan tequitl. And
in line 11 read *xonahahuiyacan* 'be greatly pleasured' as in CM 26v:6.

91. DICT at (as question marker).

92. The song also appears as CM song 82, canto C (69:16–69v:9).

93. Or, 'we will have gone to his home'. The CM 69:23 variant has *tiazq̂ ye ichan*, i.e., *tiazque
ye ichan* 'we will go to his home'.

94. *Çē* for *cen* is here translated as an intensifier, comparable to *yecen*. Thus *cen nican* 'right
here'. One would have expected *zan nican* 'right here', as in CM 32:16, 33v:26, 35v:28, 72v:25
(DICT zannican). *Zan cen ye nican* would be 'forever here', as at 42:7.

95. *Totlaocol* could be translated 'our sadness' instead of 'our creations' (see DICT tlaocolli,
tlayocolli). For *oneloz* read *onehualoz*, as in line 9.

96. Read *o anca ço iuhqui chalchihuitl* 'oh, it seems indeed they are like jades'.

17   ꟼ yc notlaocoya nicuicanitli yca [18] nichoca yn aytquihua xochitl [1]

[folio 28v]

28

[1] cono ye ychann i haytquihuaz [2] yectlo cuicatl ye çê nemiz ye
nica[3]n i tlalticpaqui mooquic too[4]nahuiyacan i antocnihuan i [5]
ohuaya ohuaya

6   ꟼ y macayac ycnotlamati ye nica[7]n atocnihuan i acan çô hayac hue[8]l
ichān i tlalticpaqui ayac mo[9]cahuaz q̂çāli ya puztequi ya ye[10]huaya y
tlacuiloli ya çâ oopupuli[11]hui xochitl ocuetlahuiya ye[12]hua yxquich
opan yahu i cano ye y[13]chann a ohuaya ohuaya

14   ꟼ y çā no yhui tinemi çā cuel achic [15] yn motloc monahuaqu in
ipal[16]nemohuanin i hualneyxima[17]cho tlalticpac ye nicani ayac
mo[18]cahuaz q̂çāli ya puztequi ya ye[19]huaya y tlacuiloli ya çān
oopupuli[20]hui xoochitl ocuetlahuiya yehua [1]

[folio 29]

29

+

[1] yxquich opa yahu i cano ye ychan[2]n â ohuaya ohuaya

11

4   ꟼ xiyahuelipehua ticuicanitl hui[5]ya maoc xocoçôçõna
moxochi[6]huehueuh mayc xiquimaha[7]huiltiya yn tepilhuani ŷ
cuauhti[8]n oçêlo · cuee◼l ach tiquitotlane[9]huiya ohuaya ohuaya

10   ꟼ y çān iyolo ya quinequi yn ipalne[11]mohuani cozcatli yn queçāli y[12]qu
i puztequiç ô ocaan i quimonequiz [13] quimotepehuatiuh yn tepilhuani
ŷ [14] cuauhtin oçelo cuel achic tiquito[15]tlanehuiya ohuaya ohuaya

16   ꟼ q̂xquich i cozcâtli q̂xquich i q̂çā[17]li tlatilo oo acâ chalchihuitli acâ [18]
teocuitlatl yn ma ye yca oo xoha[19]hahuiyaca ma ye yncâ o y ma [1]

[folio 29v]

29

[1] opupulihui ay totlaocoli ante[2]pilhuan a ohuaya ohuaya

17 I sing in sadness, weeping that these flowers, these good songs, can't be
F28V   carried to His home.⁹⁷ They'll just be alive here on earth.⁹⁸ So let's be
         pleasured,⁹⁹ friends.

6   Friends, let no one grieve here. It would seem that no one's home is
    earth. No one can remain.¹⁰⁰ Plumes splinter, paintings ruin, flowers
    wither. All are headed for His home.¹⁰¹

14 Such is life. People get to know each other briefly here on earth near you
    and in your presence, Life Giver. No one can remain. Plumes splinter,
F29   paintings ruin, flowers wither. All are headed for his home.

[XXV] [Part 2, Song 11]

4   Strike it up beautifully, singer. Beat your flower drum and pleasure the
    princes, the eagles, the jaguars. For a moment we borrow them.¹⁰²

10 Life Giver's heart requires these jewels, these plumes. And so they'll be
    splintered. He'll need them beyond. He'll strew these princes, these
    eagles, these jaguars. For a moment we borrow them.

16 So many jewels, so many plumes are done away with! It seems they're
    jades, it seems they're gold.¹⁰³ Be pleasured with these. With these,
F29V   you princes, let our sadness be destroyed.

97. Literally, 'therefore I am sad, I the singer, thus I weep that the flowers are not carried to his home [*canon ye ichan*], that the good songs are not carried'.

98. *Yecen nemiz* 'absolutely they are to live'. If the reading were *ye cen nemiz*, the translation would be 'indeed forever they are to live'.

99. CM 69v:1 *Maoquic tonahuiacan*.

100. Or, 'no one is to be left alive'. Cf. FC 3:26:17 *in oqujxqujchtin mocauhque* 'the few who were left [alive]' or 'those few who remained'.

101. For *opan yahu* read *ompa yauh*.

102. *Cuel achic* 'for a moment', as in line 14.

103. For *acâ* read *anca* 'perchance' or 'it seems', as at 22:5, 26:5, etc.

3 ¶ ahu i tocuic ahu in i toxochihu a[4]ya yn tonequimilol
xonahahui[5]yacan yc maliticac yn cuauhyo[6]tl oçeloyotla yca tiyzq̃ ỹ
cano yeuh[7]cann a ohuaya ohuaya

8 ¶ çâniyo o ye nica titocnihuan i [9] tlalticpâqui çâ cuel achica
to[10]tiyximati çâ titotlanehui[11]co o ye nicân ohuaya ohuaya

12 ¶ y maoc opâpaqui y toyolo ye[13]hua y tlalticpacqui çâ cuel achi[14]ca
totiyximati çâ titotlane[15]huico o ye nicann ahuaya ohuaya

16 ¶ maca xitlaocoyacan atepilhua[17]ni ayac ayac mocauhtaz yn tlal[1]

[folio 30]

30

+

[1]ticpac a ohuaya ohuaya

2 ¶ ohu aca çâ cuel achic yn inahuaqu i[3]n ipalnemohuani çâ
tocontlane[4]huico ychimalixochihui a yxtla[5]huaq̃tec a ohuaya ohuaya

12

7 ¶ onizmolitimani cuahuixochitl i[8]n izhuayo patlahuac aya aca [9]
yncuepucan çâ chimali xochitl i [10] moxochihu aya moyocoyan
i[11]palnemohua ahuayo ohuaya

12 ¶ y tlacochtli xochitl yelihui oo chal[13]chiuhcuepunia moxochihu aya
mo[14]yocoyan ipalnemohua ohua[15]ya ohuaya

16 ¶ xochitica yehua aca ye yhuitlo ye [17] moçêçêlohuaya ao can ixpan[1]

[folio 30v]

30

[1]ni y cacãmatlo ay huiziztepetl a [2] ohuaya ohuaya

3 ¶ y cuauhtli çãzi ya ozelotl chocâ a[4]o com ixpani y cacamatlo ay
hui[5]ziztepetl a ohuaya ohuaya

6 ¶ xochitl çeçêliuhticac oohuaye [7] cuapupuyahuatimani oo
moya[8]oxochihu i oçêloxochitla ỹn ocã [9] maniya yxtlahuaquiteca
o[10]huaya ohuaya

11 ¶ neli mach i motlaçô y moxochi[12]oo yn dios a ya
cuapupuyahu[13]timani oo moyaoxochihui o[14]cêloxochitli yn oca
mani ya [15] yxtlahuaquitec a ohuaya [16] ohuaya

3 Well, these songs of ours, these flowers of ours are our adornments.
Be pleasured. And so the eagles, the jaguars are spinning. And so
we're off to that place [beyond].[104]

8 Only here can we be comrades. Only for a moment do we know each
other on earth. We only come here to be borrowed.

12 Let our hearts be glad. Only for a moment do we know each other on
earth. We only come here to be borrowed.

F30 16 Princes, don't be sad. No one, no one will be left behind on earth.

2 Ah, just briefly near Life Giver. We merely come to borrow his shield
flowers on the field.

[XXVI] [Part 2, Song 12]

7 Eagle flowers, broad leafy ones, are sprouting. This seems to be their
blossoming place, and these are shield flowers, your flowers, Self
Maker, Life Giver.

12 The spear flowers scatter.[105] These are your flowers. They blossom as
jades, Self Maker, Life Giver.

16 As flowers, it seems, these feathers are scattered before Cacamatl at
F30V Thorn Knife Town.[106]

3 The eagle screams,[107] the jaguar roars before Cacamatl at Thorn Knife
Town.

6 Flowers sprinkle down. Your war flowers, jaguar flowers, are shining as
eagles. There they are: on the field.

11 Yes, these are your loved ones, your flowers, God. Your war flowers,
jaguar flowers, are shining as eagles. And there they are: on the field.

---

104. *Tiyazque yn canon ye iuhcan* 'we will go to that place [i.e., the other world]'. Cf. 23v:16.
DICT iuhcan 2.

105. *Xelihui*. The copyist may have mistaken a *g* for a *y* (cf. the *g* in the same verb at 17:16).

106. Alternately, read *huitzi[l]tepetl* or *huitzi[t]z[il]tepetl* 'hummingbird town', i.e., the warrior's paradise (DICT huitziltepetl 2). *Hui[t]zi[t]ztepetl* 'thorn knife town', unattested unless here, might carry the same figurative meaning but would more likely refer to the battlefield in the present context. DICT huitztli 2, itztli, tepetl 4.

107. *Tzatzi* 'screams'. DICT tzahtzi.

17 ⁊ aztatototl pâtlatinemiyan i[18]palnemohuani ậçâlaxochitli [1]

[folio 31]

31

+

[1] yn tlachinolmilinia quihualçê[2]çelohua yn izquixochitl a ohua[3]ya
ohuaya

4 ⁊ achi yn iuhca tiyanemi o yn ipal[5]nemohua queçâlaxochitli - y [6]
tlachinoli milinia quihualçê[7]çelohua yn izquixochitl a ohua[8]ya
ohuaya

13   *de Motecçumatzin •2• quâdo*
          lo de los huexutzincas

10 ⁊ tlachinolpuctli omchimalcoco[11]moca ye ehuaya /
oyohualte[12]uhtlehuaya a / onenehuihuix[13]toc ŷ moxochiuh dios o
ycahuaca [14] ye oca nepâpani cuauhtli yn o[15]zelotla ohuaya ohuaya

16 ⁊ yn çâ temocniuhtia oo / çâ te[17]ycnomati tlachinolmilini te[1]

[folio 31v]

31

[1]uhtli coçâhuiyan a acachotli ŷçâ[2]huaçeçelihui a
ohuehueuhti[3]moma ohuaya ohuaya

4 ⁊ yaomiquixoo·chatlapāno ohuaya [5] chimalpâpalocali maca huiya [6] a
ocan i tlacochitica quipuhua co[7]tlatlazticac yậçâlaxochiya[8]moxtlacuil
ol yn motecuizoma[9]çin huiya · a ocân i mexico quica[10]huaton
acaxochtli ahua yyao o i o[11]huaya ohuaya

12 ⁊ xochitl i cueputoc ye ocaa / o tlato[13]hua ye ehuaya / a ocan i
tlacoch[14]tica quipuhua cotlatlazticac ŷque[15]çâlaxochiyamoxtlacuilol
yn [16] motecuizomaçin huiya / a ocâ[17]n i mexico ậcahuaton
aca[18]xochitl ahua yyaoo ohuaya ohua[19]ya

17 The soaring Egret Bird Life Giver scatters blaze-stirring plume flood
F31   flowers, popcorn flowers.

4 Here where we live, Life Giver briefly scatters blaze-stirring plume flood
flowers, popcorn flowers.

[XXVII] [Part 2, Song 13][108]

10 A shield-roaring blaze-smoke rises up. Ah, and rising up as bell dust it's
equated with your flowers, God.[109] In the distance shrills a multitude
of eagles, jaguars.

16 He befriends and He shows mercy. In a blaze the dust is stirring: reed
F31V   flowers turn gold,[110] rain down as a blade-mist,[111] becoming great.[112]

4 In War-death Flower Flood Land, at the House of Butterfly Shields,[113]
Montezuma using javelins recites, tossing off plume-flood-flower
picture paintings. He's gone to that distant Mexico, leaving reed
flowers behind.[114]

12 Flowers are blossoming. Yonder he sings. This Montezuma using javelins
recites, tossing off plume-flood-flower picture paintings. He's gone to
that distant Mexico, leaving reed flowers behind.[115]

---

108. The song also appears as CM song 69, canto D (61v:9–33). Gloss: 'of Montezuma II, when
[there was] that matter concerning the Huexotzincans'.

109. In place of *dios* 'God' the CM version (at 61v:11) has *yaotzin,* a name applicable to either
Tezcatlipoca or Huitzilopochtli. DICT yaotl. CM 61v:10–11 *onnenehuixtoc* 'it is equal' (the unusual
reduplicative -*nenehuihuix*- may be a copyist's error).

110. CM 61v:14 *Acaxochitl* 'reed flowers'.

111. CM 61v:14 *ytzahuatztzetzelihui* 'they drizzle down as a blade mist'.

112. *Ohueheuhtimoma* is here treated as *onhuehueyatimoman* or *onhuehueixtimoman* 'they have
become great, settling down as a group'. The parallel passage at CM 61v:14 has *ōcuecuep[on]timan
a* 'they have blossomed over an area'.

113. Read *chimalpapalocalli imancan* 'where shield-butterfly-house lies'.

114. Literally, 'there [beyond] in Mexico he has gone in order to leave behind the reed
flower(s)'.

115. Here and in the matching stanza, above, in place of 'he's gone to that distant Mexico,
leaving reed flowers behind', CM 61v:17 has: *oncan in Mexico quipatlan tonacatiçatl* 'in that distant
Mexico he's bartering with sun chalk', that is, exchanging for equal value (cf. stanza 1: 'equated
with your flowers').

[folio 32]

32

+

1   ¶ motlauhquechol payatioo a yn ica to[2]ya yn titepilzin/n ay tlacahuepaa
    - [3] mopupuyauhtoc y yaqui yacohui [4] mitzhualixima in yehuaya dios
    ŷ / a[5]hua ŷyaaoo / ohuaya ohuaya
6   ¶ çâ topan iya ye oca / milini mozo[7]ni ye ehuaŷa / y tlachinoli oo / y
    co[8]comocatimani yc tomotlatiya [9] nicaa / teocuitlaxochitl
    momo[10]yahua ye oca nopilçin oo - titlaca[11]huepaçinn ahua yyahoo
    ohua[12]ya
13 ¶ ahuaye o ohuaye ninetlamatiya [14] ycnoyohua a noyolo yehuaya / [15] y
    noconitan icnopili mihuiçêçē[16]lohuaya y çā ca ye ocaa yhua[17]ya yyo
    yacohui ohuaya ohuaya
18 ¶ çâ ye çen iya ye ocan xoochitla ya / [1]

[folio 32v]

32

[1] yc oneyapanalo o / yn a tepilhu[2]a huiya ŷ a noconitan icnopili
mi[3]huiçēçēlohuaya y çā ca ye ocaa [4] yhuaya · yyo yacohui ohuaya
ohu[5]ya

14   *canto de Neçahualco*
          yotzin Acordandose de
          quauhtzin y de teçoçomoctzin

7   ¶ çâniyo y xochitli tonequimilo [8] çâniyo yn cuicatl yc huehuee[9]zin
    telel ŷ nepapan xochitl o[10]huaya ya ohuaya
11 ¶ y mach noca opulihuiz yq̂ cohua[12]yootl mach noca opulihuiz y[13]n ic
    niuhyo[superscript:]o[line script:]tl yn onoya ye yuh[14]cā ye niyoyoçi
    yn oohuaye o cui[15]catilano yehuaya Dios a ohuaya [16] ohuaya
17 ¶ tinezahualcoyotzin motecuizoma[18]zin maoc xonahuiyacan xonan[...]

[folio 33 missing]

F32   1   Your roseate swan's gone away shining.[116] And so you've departed, Prince Tlacahuepan. It's shining, it's gone. God comes to shear you.[117]

      6   In our home beyond, the blaze is stirring, seething,[118] roaring. You've been done away with, here [on earth. Now] the golden flowers are dispersed beyond, O prince, O Tlacahuepantzin.

    13   I grieve, my heart is in misery. This orphaned one is what I see, scattered as a feather there beyond.

    18   Yonder, together, all the princes are adorned with flowers. And ah!

F32V   this orphaned one is what I see, scattered as a feather there beyond.

[XXVIII] [Part 2, Song 14][119]

    7   Flowers are our only adornment. Only through songs does this pain of ours, this flower multitude, come falling down.[120]

   11   "Will companions be lost to me,[121] comrades lost to me, when I, Yoyontzin, have gone to the Singing Place, to God?"

   17   O Nezahualcoyotl, O Montezuma, be pleasured [. . .][122]

116. For *payatioo* read *poyauhtiuh* 'it goes away shining [as one that is illustrious]'. The expected form would be *mopoyauhtiuh* (cf. line 3).

117. In place of *dios* 'God', CM 61v:22–23 has *Xippilli Quauhtlehuanitl* 'the Turquoise Prince, Ascending Eagle [i.e., the sun]'. See DICT, CMSA p. 39.

118. For *mozoni* read *pozoni*, as at CM 61v:24.

119. Gloss: 'song of Nezahualcoyotzin recalling Cuauhtzin and Tezozomoctzin'. The song also appears in CM as 40 (25:8–25v:1) and as 5 (3v:1–17), where 40 has Nezahualcoyotl and Montezuma recalling Tezozomoc and Cuacuauhtzin, not Tezozomoc and Cuauhtzin, and 5 has Nezahualcoyotl, unaccompanied, recalling Tezozomoc only.

CM song 40 is given in full, below, enclosed in square brackets, to substitute for RSNE XVIII, here broken off after the first few lines (on account of the manuscript's missing folio).

120. As in the parallel passages in CM the verb *huetzi* 'to fall' is reduplicated, *huehuetzi*. But here the singer understands it differently, supplementing *[i]n tel[l]el* 'this pain of ours' with *in nepapan xochitl* 'this multitude of flowers', prompting the literal translation 'fall [down]' rather than 'fall(s) [away]' or 'subside(s)'.

121. For *yq̃ cohuayootl* read *in cohuayotl* as in CM.

122. Folio 33 is missing from the manuscript.

[*Cantares Mexicanos* song 40 (25:8–25v:1):

Çanyo in xochitl in tonequimilol çanyo in cuicatl ic huehuetzin telel a in
  tlp̈c a ohuaya ohuaya.
Ỹ mach noca ompolihuiz in cohuayotl mach noca ompolihuiz yn
  icniuhyotl yn onoya yehua niyoyontzin ohuaye on cuicatillanō yn
  ipalnemoani ohuaya ohuaya
Tineçahualcoyotzin Moteucçomatzin maoc xonahahuiacā xocōahuilticā
  Dios ypalnemoani ohuaya ohuaya.
A yç ac onmatia ompa tonyazque o ye ichano çanio o ye nicā in tinemico
  tlalticpac a ohuaya ohuaya.
Ma xiuhquecholxochitla o çan tzinitzcā in malintoc oo in
  mocpacxochiuh ça ye tonmoquimiloa çan titlatoaniya
  tineçahualcoyotl a ohuaya.
Yn ma ya moyol iuh quimati antepilhuā o anquauht amocelo a'mochipā
  titocnihuan a can cuel achic nican timochi toçazque o y ye ichan o
  ohuaya
Nitlayocoyay nicnotlamatiya çā nitepiltzin nineçahualcoyotl huiya
  xochitica yeehuā cuicatica niquimilnamiqui tepilhuāo a yn oyaque
  yehua teçoçomoctzino yehuā qua'quauhtzin a ohuaya ohuaya
Oc nellin nemoan quenonamican ma ya niquintoca inin tepilhuā huiya
  ma ya niquimonitquili toxochiuh aya ma ic ytech nonaci yectli yan
  cuicatli teçoçomoctzin etcᵃ
O ayc ompolihuiz in moteyo nopiltzin titeçoçomoctzin anca ça ye in
  mocuic oa yca nihualchoca ỹ çan nihualicnotlamati conon tiya ehua
  ohuaya ohuaya
Çan nihualayocoya o nicnotlamatia ayoquic oo ayoc quēmanian
  titechyaitaquiuh in tlap̈c y canon tiya yehua ohuaya ohuaya]

[Fin de la 2 parte]

[*Cantares Mexicanos* song 40:[123]

Flowers are our only adornment. Only through songs does our pain
on earth subside.
"Will companions be lost to me, comrades lost to me, when I,
Yoyontzin, have gone to the Singing Place and to Life Giver?"
O Nezahualcoyotl, O Montezuma, be pleased! Give pleasure to
God Life Giver.
"Ah, who here knows where we're to go [*or* where] His home is? It's
only here on earth that we're alive."
Let's have these turquoise-swanlike flowers! These are trogons that
are spinning—your crown of flowers! You array yourself, O king,
O Nezahualcoyotl!
"Let your hearts know this, O princes, O eagles, O jaguars: not forever
are we comrades. Only for a moment here, and all will be departing
for His home.
"I suffer and grieve, I, Prince Nezahualcoyotl. With flowers, with songs,
I recall the departed Princes Tezozomoc and Cuacuauhtzin.
"Do we truly live in the Place Unknown? Let me follow these princes.
Let me bring them our flowers. With good songs let me touch this
Tezozomoc, etc. [i.e., this Tezozomoc and this Cuacuauhtzin].
"Your fame will never be destroyed, O prince, O Tezozomoc. This would
seem to be your song. And so I'm weeping, suffering. Where have you
gone?
"I suffer. I grieve. You'll come to earth and find us nevermore, never
again. Where have you gone?"]

[end of the second part]

---

123. The corresponding RSNE text, broken off in the middle of the third stanza, may have a
total of only eight stanzas, not the ten of CM song 40, since the missing folio could hardly accommodate more than eight. A further variant, CM song 5 (3v:1–7), has only six stanzas, lacking
stanzas 3–4 and 7–8 of CM 40.

[1]

[...]

[folio 34]

34

+

1　¶ tlaca hayopâ tihuiçē tlalticpac a[2]tocnihua ahuiya quitohua yyollo [3]
　　motecuizomaçin çitlalcohuazin[4]n i cahualtzin huiya y nia
　　honahui[5]alo ma onetotilo âtepilhua aoççôn / [6] yuhca cano ye
　　yuhcan aya oo ahua[7]y■o

8　¶ mitec onemiya ~~nipalnemohuani~~ mitec oya tlacuilo[9]hua tlaocoyan
　　ipalnemohua ye[10]hua Dios huiya chichimecatli yn [11] tecpili yn
　　neçâhualcoyotla o[12]huaya ohuaya

13　¶ çâ huilaca tocohuini ye ohaye ylilili [14] cal haa calhuan o ohuayan tel
　　anelo [15] ticniuh yn ipalnemohua yehua [16] yoyoçin huiya tel anelo
　　tihueyo ye[17]hua Dios mane mane on aya mane [18] tlamachotoc yn
　　tonahuac onoq̂ [19] ohuaya ohuaya

20　¶ xochitla q̂mati yn amotlatoli a [1]

[folio 34v]

34

[1] comoolhuiya ŷ a comomamacâ[2]n a conitohua o ŷ / a comomama
[3] yn a conitihua o ŷn a comehua y[4]n a tepilhuan â ohuaya ohuaya

5　¶ çâ ye tiyoyotzin motecuizomatzin[6]n i cahualçin çintlalcohuatzinn [7]
　　cuauhtlahuatzinn amipilhua y[8]pan amanico ŷ tlatohuaniya / y[9]n
　　izcohuatla ohuaya ohuaya

10　¶ tamo cohuacale tamo xaquinale [11] ayao oya yye oya oo aya o ayao
　　ayhu[12]ya

13　¶ yzcohuatzi yn i tenochtitlani / hahua y[14]ya yyamo aye neçâhualcoyotl
　　[15] huiya ma yzquixochitli / ma ca[16]cahuaxochitli / ximilacaçô[17]can
　　ximomalinacan atepil[18]huan i huexoçicâ y xayacama[19]chan i
　　temayahuiçino ayao aya [1]

[folio 35]

35

+

[XXIX] [Part 3, Song 1]¹

[. . .]

F34   1 "Friends, let it not be 'never twice' that we come to earth," say the hearts of Montezuma, Citlalcoatzin, and Cahualtzin. "Let there be pleasure,² let there be dancing, princes. Nowhere is there such a place!"³

    8 God Life Giver lives within you. He paints, he creates, within you, O Chichimec prince, O Nezahualcoyotl.

  13 Just "huilaca-toco-huini-ye-ohaye-ililili-cal-haa-cal-huan-o-ohuaya."⁴ "But Yoyontzin, it is not true that you are Life Giver's friend. It is not true that you are God's great one. O comrades,⁵ beware, beware. Beware of rejoicing."

  20 These princes know flowers, your words. They say them to each other, to

F34v   each other, utter them. They give them to each other, utter them, sing them.⁶

    5 Yoyontzin, Montezuma, Cahualtzin, Citlalcoatzin, Cuauhtlatoatzin,⁷ you, his children, who have come to stand beside King Itzcoatl!⁸

  10 Tamo cohua-cale tamo xahui-nale aya o o yayye oya oo aya o aya o ay huia.⁹

  13 O Itzcoatzin of Tenochtitlan, O Nezahualcoyotl. Let there be popcorn flowers, cacao flowers. Spin! Whirl, you princes of Huexotzinco,

F35   Xayacamachan and Temaxahuitzin.

1. The missing first stanza would fall on the lost folio 33; and note that the last two stanzas are the same as the last two stanzas of song X in Part 1.

2. For *y nia* read *y ma* (the copyist has misread the three vertical strokes of the *m* as *ni*).

3. Read *aoccan yuhca canon ye yuhcan.*

4. Most of these vocables are standard. Cf. DICT pp. 729–36 (Concordance to Vocables).

5. DICT *tonahuac onoc* 'comrade'. Cf. 37:7 *y ma icniuhtlamacho* 'let there be comradeship' or 'may all have comrades'.

6. Read *conitohua o ŷ a conmomaca yn a conitohua o ŷn a conehua yn tepilhuan.*

7. Read *cuauhtlatohuatzin,* i.e., *cuauhtlatoatzin,* another of the sons of Itzcoatl (CC 36:25), along with Cahualtzin and Citlalcoatzin.

8. *Amanico* 'you [plural] have come to stand as a group [DICT mani 3]'. Alternate translation: 'you have come to lie outspread [as song flowers]'. Cf. CM 76:22–23 *niccaquia cuicatl onmanicoya ayao ay ha aya ayao haya* 'I hear the songs, they've come to lie outspread ayao-ay-ha-aya-ayao-haya'.

9. The stanza is all vocables except *tamo,* for Tamoanchan, the other world where human life is created. Cf. song X (in Part 1), stanza 7.

[1] ■ ay

2 ⸿ xochitica oo / totlatlacuilohua·n i[3]palnemohuani cuicatica oo ·
toco[4]tlapalaquiya tocotlapalpohua [5] y · nemitz i tlalticpacco yc
tictlatla[6]pana cuauhyotl · oçeloyotl · y mo[7]tlacuilolpani çā
tiyanemim ye ni[8]cani tp̄acca · ohuaya ohuaya

9 ⸿ yc tictlilania cohuayotl / a yn icni[10]uhyotl a y tecpilotl huiya
tocotla[11]palpuhua y nemitzi y tlalticpaco [12] yc tictlatlapana cuayotl ·
oçelo[13]yotl · y motlacuilolpani · çā tiya[14]nemi ye nican i tp̄aca
ohuaya [15] ohuaya

16 ⸿ ma çâ queçalpetlaqui · chalchiuh[17]petlacalco y · ma on tlatiloni · yn [18]
tepilhua ma tiyoq̄ timiquini ti[19]maçēhualti·n ahuin ahui yy timo[1]

[folio 35v]

35

[1]chin toyazq̄ / timochi tomiquizque · [2] yn tlalticpaca ohuaya ohuaya

3 ⸿ ca nicaqui ytopyo · ypetlacallo · ay te[4]pilhua ma tiyoq̄ timiquini
tima[5]çēhualtin ahuin ahui yy timochi [6] toyazq̄ timochi tomiquizq̄ y
tlaltic[7]pā a ohuaya ohuaya

8 ⸿ ayac chalchihuitl · ayac teocuitlal - [9] mocuepatzi y tp̄acqui tlatilo yo ■
[10] timochi toyazq̄ canin ye yuhcano · ayac [11] mocahuaz ça çê
tlapupulihuiz ti[12]yahui on ye yuhcâ · Dios ye ychan ohua[13]ya ohuaya

14 ⸿ çān iuhqui tlacuiloliya · yaa topupuli[15]hui · çān iuhqui xochitla ŷ a
tocue[16]tlahuiya · y tp̄c · o ohua yc quetzali ya [17] çācuan xiuhquecholi
y tlaquechol y[18]hua topopolihui tiyahui o ye yu■[19]câ dios ye ychan
ohuaya huaya

[folio 36]

36

+

1 ⸿ oh açico ye nicanini yelola ayya[2]hue a ŷtlaocol aya / ye nitec
onemi[3]ya / ma nechoquililo ŷ cuauhtla [4] oçēlotl · ohuaya nica · za
tipupuli·[5]huizq̄ · ayac mocahuatz iyo

[XXIX-A] [Part 3, Song 1-A][10]

2 You paint with flowers, with songs, Life Giver. You color the ones who'll
live on earth, you recite them in colors,[11] and so you're hatching
eagles,[12] jaguars, in your painting place. You're here on earth!

9 And so you're giving outline to these comrades, these companions, these
nobles. In colors you recite the ones who'll live on earth, and so
you're hatching eagles, jaguars, in your painting place. You're here on
earth!

16 "Let them be in plume mats, in a jade wickerwork. Let these princes be
done away with." Though we vassals are alive, we are mortal.[13] All of

F35V us are to pass away, all of us are to die on earth.

3 Princes, I understand this coffer, this wickerwork of His. Though we
vassals are alive, we are mortal. All of us are to pass away, all of us are
to die on earth.

8 No one will turn into jade, into gold: on earth he will be done away
with. All of us will pass away to that place. No one will be left. All will
be destroyed, forever. We're off to that place, God's home.

14 Like paintings we're destroyed, like flowers we wither on earth. As
plumes, the troupial, the green, the roseate swan, we're destroyed.
We're off to that place, God's home.

F36 1 Here! He's arrived.[14] His creations are alive inside me.[15] Let's have
weeping for eagles, for jaguars. We're to be destroyed here. No one
will be left.

---

10. Although this and the preceding song are run together by the copyist, the two are here
separated in order to preserve the usual eight-stanza form — a decision strengthened by the two-
stanza ending of the first song, since the same two stanzas serve as the finale of song X. In addition, note the thematic discontinuity between the two songs XXIX and XXIX-A. As implied in
the notes to song XXXI, the copyist evidently had trouble with the source for part 3.

11. Literally, 'with flowers you paint them, O Life Giver, with songs you color them, you color-
recite them who will live on earth'.

12. Literally, 'you're breaking eagles'. But the primary meaning is here taken to be 'breaking
open' or 'hatching' in the sense of giving birth. Cf. FC 11:53:20, 11:54:21; and 6:32:23 *titlapanj
titlacati in tlalticpac* 'you are hatched, you are born on earth'.

13. Read *ma tiyolque timiquini timaçehualtin* 'though we are living creatures, we habitually die,
we vassals'.

14. The unusual vocable *yelola* (a copyist's error for *yelolo*?) may be compared to the vocable
ololo (CM 39v:24, 40:10, 72:17, 73:8).

15. Alternate translation: 'his sadness is alive inside me'. DICT *tlaocolli, tlayocolli*.

6　¶ xicyocoyacaan atepilhua yya cuauh[7]ta in oçello · manel chalchihuitl ·
　　[8] manel teocuitlatl · no ye onpa ya - caa[9]noo ximohua yeehua / - çã
　　tipupu[10]lihuiq̂ ayac mocahuaz i /

2

12　¶ chalchitl o / ohuaye · ŷ teocuitlatl oo [13] y moxochiuh yehua - diosa
　　ahua[14]yyaoo aya ohuâya / ohuaya
15　¶ çã ye monecuiltonol ypalnemo[16]huani / ytzimiquixochitli /
　　yaomi[17]quiztla ya · hahua on oo aya a ohuâ[18]ya ohuâya

[folio 36v]

36

1　¶ yaomiquiztica yehuâya o hamo [2] miximati tiyaz
3　¶ yaotepân i tlachinolnahuac ami[4]yximati
5　¶ chimalteuhtli motecâ yehuâ tla[6]cochayahuitli çã moteca yehua
7　¶ y cuix oc neli ô neyximâchoya y [8] q̂nonamicãn iya ohuâ yehua[9]ya
　　ohuaya
10　¶ çâniyo yn teyotl / tocayotl aya yaô[11]micohua yehuâya achin i[12]huic
　　ximohuâ ô ay dios a ohua[13]ya ohuaya
14　¶ caahui xochiticâ yehuâya q̂çã

———　———　———

[folio 37]

37

+

3

1　¶ ximoq̂çã xicçona yn tohuehue[2]uh
3
4
5
6
7　¶ y ma ycniuhtlamacho maca ya qui[8]cuili yolo yehuâ çãniyo ni[9]caa
　　tocotlanehuicô çã[10]niyo tacayye oo yhuan [11] toxochihuâ · ohua ya
　　ohua[12]ya

6 Create these eagle-jaguars, you princes. Even jade, even gold must be off to the place where all are shorn. We're to be destroyed. No one will be left.

[XXX] [Part 3, Song 2]

12 Your flowers are jade, gold. O God!

15 Your riches. O Life Giver! The flower of knife death, war death.[16]

F36v 1 Through war death aren't they recognized? Oh, you must pass away![17]

3 In war,[18] in blaze aren't they recognized?

5 Shield dust is pouring down, spear mist,[19] pouring down.

7 Is it true that one is recognized in the Place Unknown?

10 Only for fame and renown does one die in war. In this way, and soon, one is shorn. O God!

14 As flowers it comes forth.[20]

[XXXI] [Part 3, Song 3][21]

F37 1 Come forth and play our drum.[22] […][23]

7 May all have comrades. Just take His hearts from Him.[24] Only here do we borrow them. Only our smokes and our flowers.[25]

---

16. Cf. FC 6:171:30 *aço mocnopiltiz, aço momâceoaltiz in jtzimjqujztli, in jtzimjqujzxuchitl* 'perchance your lot, your fate, will be knife death, the flower of knife death'. See also 42v:12–13, below.

17. "They" may refer to the "flowers" (i.e., warriors) of stanza 1. Cf. CM 20v:7–8: *ōmiximati oceloyotl* 'jaguars [i.e., warriors] are recognized'.

18. *Yaotempan* 'in war' or 'on the battlefield'. DICT tentli 6.

19. Or 'spear smoke'. DICT ayahuitl 1. *Moteca* 'it pours [as rain]' (CARO 50v; DICT teca: mo 4).

20. The vocable *caahui* may be compared to the vocables *cahue, cohui* (CM 17v:28, 19:5, 66v:2).

21. The copyist failed to leave room for the heading "3," squeezing it in as an afterthought; and probably to emphasize the break, therefore, three long dashes create a finis to the preceding song.

22. For *xicçona* read *xictzotzona*.

23. The copyist has left a blank space equivalent to four lines, apparently because the remainder of stanza 1 could not be read.

24. For *maca* read *maça*.

25. *Tacaiyeuh* […] *toxochiuh* 'our reed incense […] our flowers', here translated 'our smokes and our flowers', though the reference is presumably to incoming warriors, not smoking tubes and flowers per se. Cf. 18:1, above: *tacâyyexuchuh* for *tacaiyexochiuh* 'our reed incense-like flowers'. Cf. CM 35v:25 *tacaieuh* 'our reed incense'; CM 51:22 *acayetl* 'reed incense'. The interpretation 'smokes

13 ⟨ ximoq̃çā tinocniuh xoco[14]cui moxochiuh huehue[15]titla oo ma melel
      quiça yn[16]cā ximapana çā q̃çâlo[17]cô xochitli omac omani[18]ya çā
      teocuitlacacahua[1]

[folio 37v]

37

[1]xochitla ohuaya ohuaya

2   ⟨ hueli ya cuica ye nicâ xiuh[3]toto q̃chol tzinizcān iya q̃[4]chol atohuâ
      mocha quiyana[5]quiliya hayacachtlin hue[6]huetl ohuaya ohuaya

7   ⟨ oya nicua cacahuātl yc no[8]paquiya noyol ahuiya no[9]yol huelamatiya
      om ya[10]hue om hama ha yya a ohua[11]ya ohuaya

12 ⟨ ma ya nixoca y ma ya nicui[13]ca y yn i xomolco y caltech [14]
      ninonemitia yehuaya [15] dios y ya om yyahue om ha[16]ma ha yya
      ohuaya ohuaya

[folio 38]

38

+

1   ⟨ oya noconizqui cacahuaxo[2]chitl noyolo choca niquino[3]tlamati
      tlalticpac oo çā nino[4]toliniya oyahue ya yliya yye [5] ohuaya ohuaya

6   ⟨ çā moch niquilnamiqui ŷn a[7]nahuiya hanihuelamati [8] tlalticpâ oo çā
      ninotoliniya [9] oyahue ya yliya yye ohuaya [10] ohuaya

[3]4   *de Neçahualcoyotzin xo*
                              pâcuicatl

12 ⟨ amoxcalco pehua cuicayeye[13]cohua yehuaya dios i [superscript:] *in*
      totecoyo [line script:] quimo[14]yahua xochitl on ahuiya cui[15]catl o
      hama yyahue hahua[16]yya a oviya oviya

13 Arise,²⁶ friend, and get your flowers beside the drum. Be entertained. Adorn yourself with these. Flowers. They've all appeared,²⁷ they lie in
F37v   your hands.²⁸ They're gold cacao flowers.

2 Cotingas, swans, trogons sing beautifully here. The swan goes first,²⁹ and all the rattles and drums answer him.

7 I partake of this cacao, and I am happy. My heart is pleasured, my heart is glad.

12 "Let me weep,³⁰ let me sing. In the corner, against the wall I sustain myself,³¹ O God.

F38   1 "I have drunk cacao flowers,³² and my heart weeps. I grieve on earth. I am poor.

6 "I remember them all, I who am not pleasured, not happy on earth. I am poor."

[XXXII] [Part 3, Song 4]³³

12 In the house of pictures God starts making music,³⁴ scattering flowers, songs.³⁵

and flowers' derives from Durán, *Historia*, vol. 2, ch. 40, para. 39: *en el otro mundo ya no había de bailar, ni cantar, ni gozar del olor de las rosas y humazos* 'in the other world there was neither dancing nor singing nor enjoyment of roses and smokes [tobacco-filled smoking tubes]' (Durán 1967 2:310). The parallel passage in Tezozomoc's *Crónica mexicana*, ch. 59, gives *perfumaderos galanos* 'ornate incense burners' (Tezozomoc 1975:450). Both texts are Spanish versions of the missing Nahuatl *Crónica X*, which probably quotes a song text that had *acaiyetl* 'reed incense'. See DICT acatl, iyetl.

26. I.e., rise up and make war. DICT quetza:mo 1; cf. CM 6:14–19, 6v:12–18.

27. *Quiçaloc* 'all have issued forth'. DICT quiza 8.

28. Read *momac onmaniya* 'in your hands they lie', as at 39:16–17.

29. Read *attohua* 'he goes first'? SIM *attouia:nin (pour nino)* 'porter plainte le premier devant le juge'.

30. *Ma ya nichoca.*

31. I.e., I am homeless, or I am pitiable? Cf. MOL *xomulco caltech nemini* 'mostrenco [vagabond]'.

32. Read *noconiqui cacahuaxochitl*, i.e., *noconic in cacahuaxochitl* 'I have drunk cacao flowers'. If the text were allowed to stand as *noconizqui cacahuaxochitl* the translation would be 'I'm to drink cacao flowers'.

33. Gloss: 'of Nezahualcoyotzin, a song of green places'. The heading "4" is written boldly. Immediately to the left of it and a little higher is a smaller "3," as though the "3" were a preliminary or alternate heading. Cf. the note to the heading for the preceding song.

34. Superscript *in totecoyo* 'Our Lord'.

35. The vocable *ahuiya*, untranslated, also appears in CM (67v:4, 76:24, 77v:19).

[folio 38v]

38

1 ❡ ycahuaca cuicatl oyo·huale[2]huatihuiz çã · quinaquiliya [3]
toxochayacachi / quimoya[4]hua xochitli on ahuiya cui[5]catl o
hamayyahue hahua[6]yya o / oviya oviya

7 ❡ xochiticpac cuica y yectli coçx[8]coxi ye coyatotoma cujtl q̃o - ha [9]
ylili - yaha ylili y / o / huio hui [10] ohui ohuaya ohuaya

11 ❡ çã ye coyanaquiliya o - y nepâpa [12] q̃chol - yn yectli q̃chol · y hueli [13]
ya cuica y · o · ha ylili · yaha yli[14]li y · o · hui ohui ohui ohuaya [15]
ohuaya

16 ❡ amoxtlacuiloli y moyolo t■[17]cuicaticacô · yn ticçôçô ■■ [1]

[folio 39]

39

+

[1] ye mohuehueuh - yn ticuicanitli [2] xopancalayteco yn
toteya[3]ahuiltiya yao yli · yaha [4] ylili·li·li · yliya o hama ha[5]yya /
ohuaya ohuaya

6 ❡ tzan ticmoyahua oo - yn puyu[7]maxuchitla - y cacahuaxo[8]chitli - yn
ticuicanitli xopã[9]calayteco yn toteyaahuiltiya [10] yaolli · yaha ylililili ·
yliya [11] o hama hayya / ohuaya ohua[12]ya

13 ❡ xochitli ticyamanãya y nepã[14]pa xochitli yn câ toteyahuil[15]tiya -
titepilçinô tineçãhual[16]coyotzin - a noyol quimati mo[17]mac
onmaniya ticmocozcatiya / [1]

[folio 39v]

39

[1] xopân i xochitli·n o amaha [2] om hama hayyahu ohuaya [3] ohuaya

4 ❡ çã moch opã ye huiz a ommeyo[5]ca ylhuicatliteco ycã tote[6]yahuiltiya
titepilçi in oo ti[7]netzahualcoyotzin - a moyol [8] quimati momac
omaniya [9] ticmocozcatia xopân i [10] xochitlin o amaha ■m [11] hama
hayyaha ohuaya o[12]huaya

Fin de la 3 Parte

F38v   1   The songs are shrilling, they come sounding as bells. Our flower rattles answer him. He scatters flowers, songs.

     7   The good chachalaca sings over these flowers, setting free these songs.[36]

  11   A multitude of swans answer the Good Swan,[37] the true singer.[38]

  16   Your hearts are picture paintings. You're singing, you beat your drum.

F39   You, the singer, are giving pleasure in this house of green places.

     6   You scatter narcotic flowers,[39] cacao flowers. You, the singer, are giving pleasure in this house of green places.

  13   You're spreading flowers, a multitude of flowers. You're giving pleasure, Prince Nezahualcoyotzin. My heart enjoys them. They lie in your

F39v   hands, you take these green place flowers as your necklace.

     4   They all come from the Place of Duality, from Heaven.[40] With these you're giving pleasure, Prince Nezahualcoyotzin. Your heart enjoys them. They lie in your hands, you take these green place flowers as your necklace.

end of the third part

36. For *cujtl* read *cujcatl* 'song'. Though *j* is written for *x* at 22v:18, the *j* as *i* does not appear elsewhere in this manuscript. For the vocable *q̃o* read *ho*; here again, as at 10v:20, the copyist has misread a descending *h* as a *q* (see also 6.5)—and added a tilde.

37. Cf. CM 48:28 *iquecholhuā Dios* 'swans of God' and CM 17v:28 *in quechol yehuā Dios* 'the swan who is God'.

38. *I[n] hueli ya cuica* 'the one who actually sings'. Alternate translation: 'the one who sings well'. DICT huel.

39. Literally, 'you just [*tzan* for *zan*] scatter narcotic flowers [*poyomaxochitl*]'.

40. Cf. CC 4:42–47: *Auh motenehua mitoa ca ylhuicatl yytic yn tlatlatlauhtiaya yn moteotiaya [...] Auh ompa ontzatzia yuh quimatia ommeyocan chiucnauhnepaniuhcan ynic mani yn ilhuicatl* 'Now, it is told and related that it was to heaven that he [Topiltzin Quetzalcoatl] prayed, that he worshipped. [...] Well, as they knew, he was crying out to the Place of Duality, to the Nine Layers, which is how the sky is arranged'.

1   *xopâcuicatl de Neca*
                    valcoyotzin

15   ¶ xiyahuelipehua xiyahueli[1]

[folio 40]

40

+

[1]cuica / xochincalitequi · chichi[2]mecatl tecuitli - tacollihua[3]cinnā ·
ohuaya ohuaya

4   ¶ ma xahuiya · xipâqui ma melel [5] quiçā · ma tontlaocox i cuix ocçêpā [6]
tihuiçē y tp̄c·qui çā cuel achic hual[7]netlanehuilo · yxochihui · ŷcuic [8]
yehuaya dios a ohuaya

9   ¶ xochincâlco · pehua cuica xo[10]chinmecatlā momamalinâ · [11]
moyoliyo · ticuicanitli ŷya om[12]huiya

13   ¶ ticuicanitl xihualmoqueçā y - ti[14]cuicâtiya / tiquicozcatiya / yn
a[15]collihuâq̄ / oohuaya ya nelli ayc [16] tlamitz xochitl · ayc tlamitz
cuica[17]tli yo · ohuiya

[folio 40v]

40

1   ¶ xochipaquiya toyollon / çān a[2]chicâ ye nican yn tp̄c·qui · yo[3]huaya
yohuaya nenenemi[4]ya yectli ya toxochihui yohui[5]ya

6   ¶ ma xonahuiya ye nica / ticuicanitli / [7] xopacâlaytequi / yohuaya
yohua[8]ya nenenemiya yectli ya toxo[9]chihui yohuiya

10   ¶ hui toxochiuh yn tomacxochi[11]uh çā tocquipacxochiuh tpc [12] ye
nican yeçē ye nicā huiya y[13]lliya / ylliya ohuaya / o

14   ¶ ticahuazq̄ om tlallo ya tepetli - an[15]tepilhuâ / çā chichimeca ŷ -
anni[16]quitd̄z · xochitl · anniquitquiz oo [17] yectli ya cuicatli · tpc · ye
nica / ye[18]çē ye nicâ · huiya ylliya ylliya [19] ohuaya o

[folio 41]

41

+

[XXXIII] [Part 4, Song 1]¹

15 Begin in beauty, sing with beauty in this flower house,² O Chichimec
F40   Lord, O Acolhuatzin.
4 Be pleasured, be glad, be entertained. Don't be sad. Do we come to
   earth again? Only briefly are they borrowed here: these flowers of
   His, these songs of His: and He is God!
9 In this flower house He starts to sing: flower garlands are whirled, these
   hearts of yours, O singer!
13 Singer, come!³ You're giving songs,⁴ jewels to the Acolhuans. These
   flowers, will they truly be eternal? These songs, eternal?
F40v 1 Our hearts are glad with flowers. Just briefly here on earth. Our good
   flowers walk abroad!⁵
6 Be pleasured here, singer, in this house of green places. Our good
   flowers walk abroad!
10 Alas, these flowers are our hand flowers, our flower crowns here on
   earth, right here.
14 We're to leave this nation,⁶ you Chichimec princes. I'm not to carry off
   the flowers, not to carry off the good songs. Here on earth, right here.

1. Gloss: 'song of green places, of Nezahualcoyotzin'.
2. 'Begin with pleasure, sing with pleasure [...]' would be the translation if the text were interpreted as *xiahuilpehua xiahuilcuica [...]*, as in CM 16v:7.
3. Literally, 'Singer, appear [said of supernatural entities]'. DICT quetza:mo 3 and 4.
4. Read *tiquincuicatia*.
5. MOLS *passearse por las calles, plaças o huertas* 'ni,nenenemi. ni,quiquiztinemi. ni,quiça'. Cf.
FC 4:70:11, 12:97:5, and 12:104:22, where the verb *nenemi* means 'to move or march [in battle]'.
Although in the present context it may be tempting to translate *nenenemi* as 'live' or 'keep living',
such an interpretation is not provided for in early lexicography; and in the *netotiliztli, nenemi* and
its reduplicative form *nenenemi* always seem to mean 'move', or, better, 'march [in the military
sense]' (see RSNE 5v:11–12, 9v:16; for CM usages see DICT nehnehnemi, nehnemi).
6. DICT tlalli/tepetl.

1   ⸿ yllihuacanoo - geellihuacâna - [2] niqueçaco xochicuahuitla ·
    yqui[3]paqui tlapâni yectli ye nocuic [4] om · hama yye / ayahui ohuaya
    · o

5   ⸿ nicmoyahua yn tocuic gelihui [6] om o/ca tinemiya / titlaocoya y - [7]
    ma melel quitza macaoc tle qui[8]matin / moyolo yehuâ / cuicaticâ [9]
    tla - ximoquimilocan / om hama [10] yyee / ayahuiyo

2

12 ⸿ ach iuhqui xochitl · yn cuicâtl / yn [13] tonequimilol i antocnihuâ / yca
    [14] ye tonemico · yn tp̄c · ca ohuaya o

15 ⸿ yye neli yehua tocuic - ye neli ye [16] toxochi oo yectli ya cuicatli - [17] ŷ
    tlanel chalchihuitl · y teo[18]cuitlatl · yn q̂tzali patlahua / [1]

[folio 41v]

41

[1] tla noconomanili huehuetitla [2] ye nican · cuix neli can pulihuiz [3]
yn tomiquiz yn tp̄c·qui ha hu■ [4] nicuicani tla / yca hui ye yuhcan [5]
ohuaya o

6   ⸿ tocuicâpactia yoo ohaye / tito[7]xochinquimolohua nican ne[8]li mach
    in quimatin · toyolo ye[9]huâ / çã toconcauhtehua oohua[10]ye yncâ ye
    nichoca nicnotlama[11]tiya ohuaya o

12 ⸿ yn tlacã ye nellin ayac / ye cotlami[13]tehuaz monecuiltonol y
    moxochi[14]uh moyocoyatzin yehua ya dios i / [15] çã tococauhtehuâ
    oohuaye - yn[16]ca ye nichocâ - nicnotlamatiya [17] ohuaya o /

18 ⸿ xochitica ye nicân momalina[19]co tecpinlotl · ynn icniuhyotl - [20] ma
    yc xonahuiyacan / aya - [1]

[folio 42]

42

+

[1] y çe nican/n i tlalticpac a ohua[2]ya ohuaya

F41   1   I've come to set up the flower tree.⁷ Within it my good songs are
              bursting open.

       5   I scatter these songs of ours. They're parceled out where you are
              grieving.⁸ Be entertained. Don't let your heart be worried anymore.
              Be adorned with these songs.

[XXXIV] [Part 4, Song 2]

       12 Like flowers, songs are our adornment, friends. It's for this that we've
              come to live on earth.

       15 Truly our songs, truly our flowers are good songs. Let's have these jades,
              these gold ones, these broad plumes. Let me have them here beside
F41v   the drum. Can it be true that death for us would be vanquished here
              on earth? Singer that I am, oh would that it might be so.

       6   We are song-glad,⁹ adorned with flowers here. Yes, our hearts enjoy
              them. Alas, we go away and leave them, and so I weep, I grieve.

       12 If only it were not true: no one when he's gone will enjoy your riches,
              your flowers, God Self Maker. We go away and leave them, and so I
              weep, I grieve.

       18 As flowers here the nobles, the comrades come spinning?¹⁰ Be
F42   pleasured. Right here on earth.¹¹

----

7. The stanza opens with the vocables *yllihuacanoo yeellihuacâna* (cf. CM 17v:28 *ylihuâcano*), taking *geellihuacana* as a copyist's error. But if the *g* is a deliberate orthographic variant of *x* (as at 17:16 and 41:5), the vocable is *xeelihuacana,* reminiscent of the verb *xelihui* 'to be scattered or parceled out'.

8. Omitting the vocables, read: *xelihui oncan tinemi titlaocoya.* For *nemi* 'to be [doing something]' see DICT *nemi* 5.

9. Literally, 'we gladden ourselves with song' (*titocuicapacti*). On the omission of the subject prefix see the note to 2:14.

10. Alternate translation: 'By means of flowers here the nobles [read *tecpillotl*], the comrades become spun [*or* twisted]'. On purposive verbs see GN 2.5.

11. Read *cen nican* 'right here'. See 27v:11 and accompanying note.

3 ⸿ q̃nonamicân i câno ye yuhcân[4]ni · ayaoc no yuhcân i tp̃cqui - [5]
   xochitli · cuicantli · ŷ manē ye ni[6]cân an / ohuaya o
7 ⸿ çâ çê ye nican / ma nequimilo[8]lon / acon maho ye yuhcâ / aya[9]oc
   nellon / onnemohua yehuâya
10 ⸿ aya tlaomcoya · aya quilnamiqui / om[11]ya huixahue / annelli tochâ-no
   [12] tiyanemi ohuaya ohuaya

3

14 ⸿ ayquin o chimaltica yeehuaya ye [15] om çemilhuitiya / yn tepilhuan a
   o[16]huaya ohuaya
17   maha tlaocoxti hamo[. . .][1]

[folio 42v]

42

[1]yl / hamonecuiltonol / yao[2]yotl / yaqui yan cuantleco[3]huatzin a
quimatiya om ye[4]huaya dios a ohuaya ohuaya

4

6 ⸿ chalchihuitlo · huaya · y■ [7] xihuitlo · y motiçâyo ye [. . .][8]huiyon
   ipalnemohua ha[9]huayya oo ayye ohuaya ohua[10]ya
11 ⸿ yyeo necuiltonolo - a tepilhua[12]ni ytzimiquixochitl / yao[13]miquiztla
   ya / ahuaya oo a[14]yya ohuaya ohuaya

fin de los cantos -

144 fojas por todo

3 The Place Unknown, that [other] place, is not the same as earth. Flowers, songs lie here.[12]

7 Forever here! Let all be adorned. Who is known in that place?[13] It is not true that there is life.

10 He does not grieve,[14] He recalls no one.[15] It is not true that we live in Our Home.

[XXXV] [Part 4, Song 3]

14 "Never with shields do princes get through the day."[16]

17 Would that he might not pass away grieving,[17] "War is not your joy,[18] not

F42v   your wealth." Cuatlecoatzin, gone away,[19] knows God.

[XXXVI] [Part 4, Song 4]

6 Jade, turquoise: your chalk, [your] plumes,[20] O Life Giver.

11 All princes are rich with the flower of knife death, war death.[21]

end of the songs

144 folios in all[22]

12. For *manē* read *mani*. If *manē* is allowed to stand, the translation is: 'Flowers, songs — don't let them be here!'

13. Read *acon macho ye yuhcan* 'Who is known in that place?' (as suggested in Garibay 1964:99). Cf. CM 8:19 *quimatia ypalnemohuani* 'he knows Life Giver'; CM 9v:21 *anqui nelin ye quimatin ypalnemoa* 'it would seem indeed that he knows Life Giver'.

14. *Aya tlaocoya* 'not at all does he grieve'. DICT aya 3.

15. *Ayac quilnamiqui.*

16. "Get through the day" is an understatement meaning "to survive for a while," i.e., to stay alive. DICT cemilhuitia, cemilhuitillani:te, cemilhuitiltia:te.

17. Read *maca tlaocoxtiuh.*

18. Where the corner of the manuscript has been torn away, leaving *hamo[...]yl*, the likely reading is *hamonetlamachtyl* for *ahmonetlamachtil*, 'not your joy'. DICT netlamachtilli.

19. Alternate translation: 'Cuatlecoatzin, a warrior, knows God'. DICT yahqui.

20. A hole in the manuscript leaves the truncated *[...]huiyon*, which may be reconstructed as *mihuiyon* for *mihhuiyo* 'your plumes [plus the intrusive nasal *n*]'. DICT tizatl/ihhuitl, ihhuiyotl.

21. Cf. 36:16–17.

22. Counting the missing folio 33, the *Romances* manuscript has 42 folios (i.e., 84 sides, or pages), preceded by the 102 folios of Pomar's *Relación*.

Commentary

In the following notes repeated reference is made to the essay On the Translation of Aztec Poetry (TRAN), above, cited in most cases by section number only. Thus (6.2), for example, means TRAN section 6.2. Only song I has been provided with phrase-by-phrase annotation; the remaining songs may be similarly glossed, using the Guide to the Vocabulary, above. Information on the usage of the *netotiliztli* as a whole will be found in the *Cantares* dictionary-concordance (DICT), where the vocabulary is organized with documentation, textual citations, and cross-references to synonyms.

Previous translations of the *Romances* may be found in Garibay's *Poesía náhuatl I* (1964) and, for *Romances* songs XI and XXIII, in Karttunen and Lockhart, "La estructura de la poesía náhuatl vista por sus variantes" (1980). Selected readings are in León-Portilla, *Fifteen Poets of the Aztec World* (1992).

General comments. The overall purpose of the songs in the *Romances* is to promote warfare, especially between the Triple Alliance (Mexico, Texcoco, and Tlacopan), on one side, and, on the other, Huexotzinco, Tlaxcala, and Chalco (the Alliance's regular enemies through much of the 1400s and Cortés' enablers during the Conquest period, 1519–21). To this end warrior kings out of the past are summoned to earth along with their ghost legions, who enact imagined scenes of battle on the dance floor; or, a singer may simply issue a call to arms, praise the value of combat, or, frequently, deal with laggards and dissenters who require special encouragement.

It is assumed that all the songs—even if they borrow heavily from a pre-Conquest repertory—were put together in their present form in the mid-1500s, no later than 1582 (the date of Pomar's *Relación*, to which the lost *Romances* original seems to have been attached, as is the extant copy).

Overview of the thirty-six songs. (Part 1.) I. Mexica allies and enemy Tlaxcalans are called to battle. II. Ally Nezahualcoyotl arrives with warriors. III. Allies arrive, submit to the war ethic, giving their lives. IV. A pro-war singer refutes a doubter. V. A presumed doubter complains that he has been unfairly accused, offers his life. VI. A fearful warrior submits, asks to be united with the dead. VII. Warriors arrive for combat in Mexico, prepare to die. VIII. Chalcan enemies arrive, prepare for combat. IX. Tlaxcalan enemies are summoned to be defeated in combat. X. Tlaxcalans arrive to be sacrificed. XI. Mexica warriors arrive to reenact the final battle against Cortés. XII. Pro-Mexica leaders arrive, restoring Mexico's greatness. XIII. Warriors are brought to life, briefly, through music. XIV. Chalcan enemies are brought to life and defeated.

(Part 2.) XV. A musical call to arms. XVI. Past warrior-kings of Tlaxcala are summoned to be defeated. XVII. Warriors appear as "flowers," briefly, before they "wither." XVIII. A singer petitions the supreme spirit for fresh warriors. XIX. A doubter is heard among the incoming warriors. XX. Incoming warriors win "nobility and fame." XXI. The supreme spirit provides warriors from the sky world. XXII. A pro-Mexica warrior-king arrives, resolves doubts. XXIII. A Mexica warrior-king summons enemies to be defeated. XXIV. Sacrificed warriors will be reunited in the sky world. XXV. A warrior-singer is summoned, who summons additional warriors. XXVI. An allied warrior-king arrives, bringing further warriors. XXVII. Montezuma's warriors give their lives as fresh warriors descend from the sky world. XXVIII. A further exchange of dying warriors for incoming warriors.

(Part 3.) XXIX. Allied and enemy warriors arrive despite doubters' objections. XXIX-A. The supreme spirit descends, bringing warriors ready for battle. XXX. A singer promises to perpetuate a warrior's fame. XXXI. Allies are encouraged to capture incoming enemy warriors. XXXII. Incoming "flowers" are produced by Nezahualcoyotl and the supreme spirit.

(Part 4.) XXXIII. An ancestral warrior-king arrives, bringing fresh warriors. XXXIV. Against the voice of a doubter, warriors arrive, seeking fame. XXXV. Voices of doubt and encouragement. XXXVI. Affirming the doctrine, a singer promises that all warriors will be "rich" in the other world.

Part 1

Song I (1:3–2:17)

Historical figures. All persons named in the song were active during the Conquest period, 1519–21, except Tlacahuepan (d. ca. 1498), anachronistically summoned in stanza 3. These appear in three groups:

(1) Tecayehuatzin of Huextozinco, Xicotencatl of Tlaxcala, Temilo[tecatl?] of Tlaxcala, Cuitlizcatl of Tlaxcala.
(2) Tlacahuepan of Mexico Tenochtitlan.
(3) Temilotzin of Mexico Tlatelolco.

Synopsis. A pro-Mexica singer issues a call to arms and summons both enemy and allied ghost warriors to enact a Mexica (or Triple Alliance) victory against the enemy Tlaxcalans and Huexotzincans (TRAN 22.2).

Synopsis by stanza.
Let's go "sing" (make war) on the battlefield. Don't be cowardly, Mexica. Seek "flowers" (captives or comrades).
Tlaxcalan and Huexotzincan leaders "sing" (make war) against Mexico, producing warrior revenants as potential captives.
Mexican hero Tlacahuepan appears on the battlefield with "eagle" troops who pleasure themselves by taking captives.
Yes, these Mexican revenants arrive from the sky world, gladdening the supreme spirit with their war deeds.
God himself descends to the battlefield, bringing spirit warriors from the "house of troupials."
God "adorns" himself with "flowers" (captives or potential captives), "whirled" (i.e., twisted, crafted) as garlands.
Mexican hero Temilotzin descends from the sky bringing further warriors, recklessly courting death (since life is brief).
Yes, Temilotzin, sent by God, comes to reunite with battlefield friends (to defeat Tlaxcalan and Huexotzincan enemies).

Annotated English text.
Friends [i.e., comrades in arms (concrete noun) (TRAN 7.4, 11.2–3)], let us sing [*or* make war (9.9)], let us go sing in the house of sun flowers [i.e., the sky world or the battlefield (2.5, 5.1, 7.3)]. And who [among you will not be cowardly (12.9) and thus] will seek them [i.e., seek the

"flowers" (2.1–3), the incoming warriors from the sky world, either as
captives or allied comrades on the battlefield], who will meet them here
beside the drum [i.e., on the dance floor or on the battlefield (8.1, 9.9)]?
"[Intending to elicit God's pity (10.2–3)] I grieve in sadness for these
flowers [i.e., in order to bring forth these "flowers" (10.6–10)], I, your
poor [i.e., pitiable (10.6)] friend, Chichimec Lord Tecayehuatzin [of
Huexotzinco, Mexico's traditional enemy, at the time of the Spanish
Conquest (CONC)]. Who among us will [dare to be so cowardly as
to (12.9)] fail to entertain, to gladden God Self Maker [who will
pleasurably receive the sacrificed captives we obtain in battle (2.3)]?"
At flood's edge [i.e., the battlefield (2.1)] yonder in Tlaxcala [in league
with Huexotzinco (CONC)] let him [i.e., Tecayehuatzin] sing narcotic
flower songs [i.e., produce irresistible "flowers," i.e., warriors as
potential captives (13.1–4)]. Let Xicotencatl [Tlaxcalan ally of Cortés
(CONC)], Temilotzin [*read* Temilotecatl, a Tlaxcalan ruler in the time
of Cortés (CONC)], and Lord Cuitlizcatl [Tlaxcalan chieftain who
aided Cortés (CONC)] sing narcotic songs. Let us hear "ohuaya
ohuaya [i.e., mournful song-weeping that produces warriors from the
sky world (10.1–6)]."
In Eagle Tamoanchan [i.e., warriors' paradise or the battlefield (2.5, 18.3)],
the home of jaguar bells [i.e., warriors (9.7)], in Huexotzinco, where
the dying is, there's Dancer [alternate name for Tlacahuepan (CONC
Mahceuhcatzin)]. It's Tlacahuepan [of Mexico Tenochtitlan, heroic
brother of Montezuma II, died fighting in Huexotzinco a generation
before Cortés (CONC)]. His eagle flower princes [i.e., warriors under
his command] find their pleasure in that house of green places [i.e.,
take Huexotzincan captives on the battlefield (7.3), or give their lives in
battle and ascend to the paradisal Green Places (2.5)].
As cacao flowers [as incoming warriors from the sky world (2.2)] they
come sounding the dance cry [*or* war cry (9.5)], finding flower pleasure
[i.e., capturing "flowers," or potential victims for sacrifice] yonder in
the middle of the flood [i.e., on the battlefield (2.1)], come carrying
their gold shield hand-slings [i.e., weapons, or accompanying warriors
(4.4)], their fans [i.e., ornaments of the dance, or accompanying
warriors (9.7)]. "With flood-flower eagle sadness, with plume banners
we come entertaining [i.e., making war to gladden the supreme power]

in this house of green places [i.e., the battlefield as it resembles the other world (2.5)]."

Jade gongs [warriors (9.7)] shrill [give war whoops (8.1, 9.8)]. A drizzling rain of flowers [i.e., incoming "songs," the warriors (8.4)] falls to earth. From the house of troupials [i.e., the warriors' eternal home in the sky (2.1)], from the bosom of the [celestial] fields the Holy Spirit, God, descends.

From Green Places [i.e., paradise (2.5)] he descends. It's Life Giver. He provides himself with song petals, he adorns himself with flowers [i.e., captives offered to him as sacrificial victims (17.2n)] here beside the drum. They're whirled [i.e., crafted as garlands of twisted flower-ropes (15.5, 16.1)], they come from you, these drunken [i.e., insensate and therefore easily captured (13.1–4)] flowers [i.e., warriors (2.1–3)]. Be entertained [i.e., enjoy them, O Life Giver]!

"Friends, I've come [I, Temilotzin (see next stanza),] to string them as jewels (15.2), spread them out as trogons, make them stir as spirit swans [i.e., the warriors I produce (3.2, 3.5, 5.4–5)], twirl [i.e., create (16.1, 19.5)] them as gold, these comrades [of the sun (2.2–3)]. As plume-captives I'll snare them [in order to bring them down from the sky world]. I'll song-whirl [i.e., create as though songs (18.1, 19.1–5)] these companions, in this palace [i.e., the dance floor as it represents the battlefield (9.8)] I'll [i.e., I the singer-ritualist will] bring them forth. Ah, all of us, then in a moment all of us will have departed for the dead land. For we only come to borrow them.

"I come, I appear! Friends, I come created as a song, come fashioned as a song [i.e, as an incoming warrior (8.1–3)]. God sends me here. I have flowers [i.e., accompanying warriors], I am Temilotzin [of Mexico Tlatelolco, tragic hero of the Spanish Conquest (CONC)]. I've come to assemble a company of friends [i.e., I've come to forge an alliance of earthly warriors and spirit warriors (7.4)]."

Remarks. The overlapping of historical figures from the Conquest period (Cuitlizcatl, Temilotzin, etc.) with a figure out of the deeper past (Tlacahue-pan) recurs in the complex of song variants mentioned below in the commentary for song XX. The "Temilotzin" of stanza 2 is here read as a variant or error for Temilotecatl, following the rule described in "Rulers Named in the

Romances" in the Introduction. Note that "Temilotzin" would be an allow-able, apocopated variant of "Temilotecatl" (see GRAM 7.7a).

In the opening stanza the nonstandard *to[n]cuicatacan* 'let us go sing' may indicate that the singer is imitating the dialect of Tlaxcala (see DICT *yauh* 4). On the use of dialect in Mexica songs, see FC 8:45:13–23 but also CMSA pp. 93–94.

'Captives' in stanza 7 freely translates *huixto,* the combining form of *huixto-tli,* plural *huixtotin.* In a sixteenth-century sky diagram the level immediately above the sun, labeled *huixtutla* (i.e., *huixtotlan* 'place of the huixto[tin]'), has as its emblem a figure evidently representing the deity Huixtocihuatl or a sacrificial victim dressed as that deity (Códice Vaticano 3738 1964:9 [pl. 1] and Nicholson 1971: fig. 7 and table 2; cf. Códice Telleriano-Remensis 1964: pl. 1 or 1995: 1r and Quiñones Keber 1995:139–40). Sahagún mentions a Gulf Coast people called *Olmeca, vixtoti[n],* whose ruler was named *Olmecatl, vix-totli;* and these *vixtoti* were said to be *nonotzaleque* ['they who have entities that are prayed to', i.e., priests, magicians] (FC 10:192:28–30). By way of ex-planation the same author, elsewhere, writes of 'a certain class of people who were something like hired killers, called nonotzaleque, hardened profes-sionals who did the killing' (*vna gente que eran como asisinos los quales se lla-mauan nonotzaleque, era gente vsada y atreujda, para matar*) (CF lib. 11, cap. 1, para. 1, fol. 3v). Further, in the description of a sacrifice honoring the deity Huixtocihuatl, Sahagún's Nahuatl text designates the functionaries who per-form the sacrifice as *huixtoti[n]* (CF lib. 2, cap. 26, fol. 47v) —yet his accom-panying Spanish text has been repeatedly misread to mean that the captives themselves are the *huixtotin* (SIM 690; HG 1:173 [lib. 2, cap. 26, para. 11]; FC 2:88; Sahagún 1997:106n70; correctly read in Sahagún 1971:98). Thus, while Sahagún has it that the *huixtotin* were the officiants of sacrifice, not the sac-rificed captives, the Códice Vaticano diagram is ambiguous in this regard, allowing the pictorial figure to be read as either the deity or the dressed-up surrogate. The song text at hand, presumably, means captives or potential captives rather than officiants. However, although the *nicquetzalhuixtoylpiz* is clearly written (with a gap between *huixto* and *ylpiz*), the oddity of *huixto-,* even if plausibly analyzed, raises the possibility of corrupt transmission. By metathesis the *huixto-* might have sprung from *xitto-,* with an intrusive *hu* thrown in; and if a syllable were dropped (as often happens in this manu-script), the reading could be *nicquetzalxi[t]to[mon]ilpiz* 'I'll snare [or noose] them as plumes', conveying the same meaning as 'I'll snare them as plume captives' — bringing the text into conformity with CM. DICT xittomonil-pia:tla. On metathesis, see GRAM 4.3; on intrusive characters, GRAM 3.9. On dropped syllables, see the note to the Translation at 1:12.

Song II (2v:1–3v:12) (= CM XXV [18v:16–19:10], and stanzas 3–4 again at CM 69:28–32)

Historical figure. Nezahualcoyotl, ruled 1431–72 as king of Texcoco.

Synopsis. Nezahualcoyotl (i.e., Yoyontzin) arrives from the other world, bringing "flowers" (i.e., warriors) to the dance floor (as it represents the battlefield).

Song III (3v:14–4v:10)

Historical figures. All persons here summoned from the other world were active in the mid-1400s (see immediately below).

Synopsis. A singer-warrior summons Nezahualcoyotl and his brother Tzon-tecochatzin then summons Montezuma I and *his* brothers Citlalcoatzin and Cahualtzin. The revenants arrive with their comrades in arms and submit to the war ethic (TRAN 12), thus remaining only briefly on earth before returning to the other world, i.e., the "place where all are shorn, the place unknown" (CONC Quenamihcan, Ximohuacan).

Song IV (4v:12–5v:8)

Synopsis. Two voices are heard: a war enthusiast and a warrior who doubts. The doubter's points (enclosed by quotation marks in the translation): there is no paradise; no one can trust the supreme spirit (TRAN 12.12); there is no life in this world ("on earth"); life is brief; the supreme spirit clouds our minds ("makes us drunk") with false promises of an afterlife; no one can escape death.

The enthusiast's points: everyone makes "prayers and services," i.e., makes war (9.9); everyone wants glory on the battlefield; the music of war (10.1 [ohuaya]) has divine authority (8.1 [origin of music]); the supreme spirit enjoys music; there is life in this world ("on earth"); the supreme spirit does make us "drunk" with desire for war (13.1–4), does rule this world—therefore submit.

Remarks. Ideas expressed in song IV are more explicitly stated in the somewhat similar eight stanzas of the second half of CM song XXXI. The doubter's points, rejecting the old war ethic, are linked with the new values of Christianity in CM song VII: "It was thus in the old days. Here on earth he'd give you chalk wine and make you enter the place of danger. He'd order flood and blaze. He'd break you. He'd ruin you."

Song V (5v:10–6v:18)

Historical figures. The singer-ritualist invokes Cacamatl, nephew of Montezuma II and ruler of Texcoco, who attempted to save Mexico from the Spaniards in 1520 but was apprehended and executed (López de Gómara 1964 or 1968, ch. 91). Using Cacamatl as the "agent" for the supreme spirit Life Giver (TRAN 3.1–3), the singer summons Cacamatl's predecessors, Nezahualpilli and Nezahualcoyotl, who arrive on earth with their armies. (See the query about this Cacamatl in the Commentary for song XXVI.)

Synopsis. The ritualist quotes dissenters who scorn him for his adherence to the war ethic. Undaunted, he eagerly embraces combat, singing "ohuaye" (TRAN 10.1); and speaking as though he were Cacamatl, he summons ghost warriors from the other world ("swan feathers," "flower bells"), offering himself as the payment (20.1).

Remarks. In stanza 5 the ghost warriors are called "God's loved ones," a term that also designates the Christian saints (DICT tlazohtli). All warriors are *tlazotin* 'loved ones' (FC 6:12:26); a Christian saint is *itlaço in dios* 'God's loved one' (SPC 79:16); saints in heaven, or angels, are *yn itlaçohuā yn dios* 'God's loved ones' (Burkhart 2001:104). Here the inanimate plural, *itlaçô dioss* 'God's loved ones', is appropriate since the incoming warriors, metaphorically, are (inanimate) flowers.

Song VI (7:2–8:14) (= CM XLVIII)

Historical figure. The singer's inspiration, or "agent" (TRAN 3.1–3), is Tlaltecatzin (i.e., Totoquihuaztli), lord of Tlacopan (one of the cities allied with

Mexico in the so-called Triple Alliance) at the time of Cortés' arrival. (This is probably not Tlaltecatzin of fourteenth-century Cuauhchinanco as the CM glossator believes, writing "Song of Tlaltecatzin of Cuauhchinanco.")

Synopsis. As ghost warriors arrive, the singer (using the voice of Tlaltecatzin) fears that he will need to give his life in battle as their payment. Accepting the inevitability of his own death, he asks that these revenants be sacrificed so that he and they may be united in paradise (see CMSA pp. 450–51 for a detailed paraphrase).

Remarks. In stanza 3, Santa María, the "fragrant woman," is identified with the supreme power. From the *Santoral en mexicano,* an early-seventeenth-century Nahuatl manuscript, Burkhart translates *oraciones* addressed to Saint Mary that include the epithets *tzopelicachipahualizahuiacayocatzintle* 'oh fragrant one of sweet purity' (Burkhart 2001:54); *tzopelicatzintle ahui-acatzinei icnohuacatzintle* 'oh sweet one, oh fragrant one, oh merciful one' (ibid.:57); *àhuiacaichpochxochitzintle* 'oh fragrant and maidenly flower' (ibid.:90).

Drum cadence. Either the horizontal log drum, *teponaztli,* or the upright skin drum, *huehuetl,* can be used to perform the two-tone cadence; or the two can be "tuned," if they are played together. Various intervals such as a fifth or a minor third are possible, depending on the length of the slits in the log drum and the tautness of the skin drum, which is struck with the hands at the center of the head (to produce the lower tone) or near the rim (for the higher tone). The notation, based on the syllables *ti, to, ki,* and *ko,* has only two vowels, which may be taken to represent the higher and lower tones, since the *i* is pronounced high in the mouth; the *o,* low. On the analogy of modern woodwind tonguing, which produces notes in a series of t-t-t-t in moderate tempo and t-k-t-k in faster tempo, the cadence *tocoti tocoti,* etc., may be read: ♪♪ ♪♪♪♪, etc. (CMSA pp. 72–77).

Song VII (8:16–9:4)

Synopsis. Otherwordly warriors are summoned to combat in Mexico, also called *atlixco* 'water face' and *anahuac* 'next to the water' (DICT atlan 3, atlihtic 3, atlixco 2, anahuac 1—in reference to the Venice-like setting of

Tenochtitlan and Tlatelolco). The warriors prepare to take captives and to become captives themselves.

Song VIII (9:6–19)

Historical figure. "Chalco's *come* to fight" implies an imagined engagement in Mexico if the singer is there, as is most likely (TRAN 22.1–6), and the 'spirit-owner lord' (*teohua tecuitli*) of stanza 2 would therefore be a Chalcan leader (DICT teohuah 3, ACHIM passim) bringing hostile troops to the imperial seat. No more can be said with any certainty since the phraseology is formulaic. But listeners in the mid-1500s would undoubtedly have been reminded that Chalcans did come in 1521 to aid Cortés in the siege of Mexico, led by Chalcan lords including Omacatzin, *teohua tecuitli* of Chalco Tlalmanalco. Subsequently known as don Hernando de Guzmán (d. 1534), Omacatzin is the subject of CM song LXIII, composed after 1565, in which Cortés and his Chalcan allies are figuratively trounced and sent back to the other world; in that song the Chalcans are portrayed as "peepers," batrachians whose raucous croaking was said to produce headaches (CMSA pp. 301–13, 469–70; DICT guzman 2).

Synopsis. Chalcan warriors, summoned from the other world, prepare for combat "here" in God's "home" on earth, i.e., the battlefield (TRAN 2.5).

Song IX (9:21–10:4)

Historical figures. Two figures are named, Coatecatl and Iztac Coatl, both associated with the early history of Totomihuacan in the Tlaxcala-Huextozinco region (Totomihuacan is linked with Huexotzinco and Iztac Coyotl in CM 8v:9–14).

Synopsis. The (presumably pro-Mexica) singer, appealing directly to the supreme spirit, summons Huexotzincan and Tlaxcalan ghost warriors to be defeated in combat (presumably by Mexica warriors) and returned to the other world, concluding that this military action has been decreed by God (TRAN 12.11).

Remarks. In the final stanza God is identified with both Christ and Santa María (see "Dating the Songs" in the Introduction).

Song X (10:6–11:8)

Historical figures. Calmecahua, Matzin, and Temaxahuitzin, who aided Cortés in the Conquest of Mexico, are lords of various polities in the Huexotzinco-Tlaxcala region. They are joined by "Xayacamach," a name attached to at least half a dozen historical figures from the same region (see CONC). Anachronistically, Itzcoatl, king of Tenochtitlan, and his relative Nezahualcoyotl (also called Yoyontzin) are summoned from a deeper past to engage these foes in symbolic combat.

Synopsis. Identifying alternately with both sides, the singer-ritualist produces ghost warriors representing pro-Mexica forces as well as enemy forces from the region of Huexotzinco and Tlaxcala. The locale is Tenochtitlan, at the Eagle Gate on the south side of the main square (CONC Cuauhquiahuac). Revenants of both sides arrive from the Place of Duality (CONC Omeyocan), the Huexotzincans and Tlaxcalans to be defeated (i.e., to become "thrashed ones"), to be "chalked" for sacrifice.

Remarks. Note that Tenochtitlan is called "Huexotzinco" (CONC Huexotzinco 2) at the end of stanza 3. However, the "of Huexotzinco" in stanzas 2 and 8 and at the beginning of stanza 3 means Huexotzinco per se. In CM the Eagle Gate is named only in songs that overtly deal with the siege of Mexico, mentioning the *capitán* (i.e., Cortés), Malintzin (the interpreter for Cortés), and other unmistakable figures and incidents (CM songs LXVI, LXVIII, XCI).

Song XI (11:10–12:18) (= CM song LXIX, canto C)

Historical figure? The designations "Chichimec," "Tenitl" (freely, "Barbarian"), and "Arbiter" do not include a personal name and could refer to the supreme spirit or, more likely in this case, a fictional warrior king serving as the "agent" of supreme power (TRAN 3.1–3) — or, if "Teni(tl)" should be read as "Telitl," a fourteenth-century king connected to the Triple Alliance (see the note to line 11:13).

Synopsis. Warriors from the other world arrive on earth, ready for combat (against Cortés; see "Remarks," below).

Remarks. In CM this is merely the third canto in a six-canto song, which opens with the humiliations suffered by Mexico's fourteenth-century founders as compared with the suffering of the Mexica in 1519–21 ("Once again we're to be destroyed in our city"). The fourth canto is treated below, as RSNE song XXVII; the sixth and final canto, also below, as song XVIII. A detailed commentary of the entire song is in CMSA pp. 486–90.

Drum cadence. See commentary for song VI, above. Thus the cadence for song XI (*tototi tototi*) would read: ♪♪♩ ♪♪♩.

Song XII (12v:2–13v:2)

Historical figures. The three kings Axayacatl of Tenochtitlan, Chimalpopoca of Tlacopan, and Nezahualpilli of Texcoco were the Triple Alliance rulers in the 1470s.

Synopsis. Triple Alliance kings are summoned from the other world along with warriors destined to be "shattered" in battle. Once again provided with "mesquites," "ceibas," "cypresses," i.e., great leaders (TRAN 4.3), Mexico, itself like a protective tree, gloriously "spreads a crown of jade" (cf. 22.4).

Song XIII (13v:3–14v:4)

Synopsis. A singer-ritualist is assembling *icniuhyotl* 'comrades', *coayotl* 'companions', i.e., incoming warriors from the other world (note the abstract nouns and see TRAN 11); thus the dance floor, or "flower house," would become a place inhabited by "flowers," i.e., potential victims on the battlefield (TRAN 2.1–3). The ritualist has crafted (15.5), or "twirled" (19.5), these "flowers," these "garlands" (16.1–2). These "pleasure flowers," i.e., potential victims (cf. 7.3), are "just like the flowers on earth": we enjoy them, "adorn" ourselves with them (17.2n), only "briefly" (12.8). Soon we will be leaving for our "eternal home" (cf. 5.1), leaving our "flowers" behind. Weeping, grieving, the singer makes himself "sad," pitiable (10.8–9), implying that he deserves consideration (10.6).

Remarks. The ambiguous term *onnequechnahualo* 'there's mutual embracing' may refer to the grappling of warriors in combat, as apparently in CM 18:26–27–18v:8–9: *Quauhyotica oceloyotica ma onnequechnahualo antepilhuani ycahcahuāca yn chimallin cohua ma'limani [. . .] yxtlahuacā yaonahuac*

'Let there be mutual embracing of eagles, of jaguars, O princes. Shields, companions, are shrilling. Let them stand upon this flood [...] on the field of battle'. (For *ma'limani* read *ma ahlimani* = *ma atlimani* 'let them [i.e., the shields] stand as a group flood-wise'. DICT atl 2.)

Song XIV (14v:6–15v:16) (stanzas 3–4 = CM song LI, stanza 33,
i.e., CM folio 33, lines 22–25)

Historical figures? The five who are named in this song appear to be stereotypes applicable to Chalcans in general. Two of them, perhaps, are figures of opprobrium: Coacuech (Rattlesnake Rattle) and Tlacamazatl (Bestial Person). For details see CONC Chalchiuhtlatonac, Coacuech, Cuateotl, Teohuahtzin, Tlacamazatl.

Synopsis. A (presumably pro-Mexica) singer calls on departed Chalcan leaders to bring down their troops from the sky world (TRAN 3.1–3), the Chalcans imagining that their losses on the battlefield will produce further Chalcan revenants, i.e., that their "hearts" (4.5) will "return," thus relying on the doctrine of exchange (20.1). The Chalcans do "believe" this but are deceived (DICT neltoca:mo). Instead, as "the earth rolls over" and "the sky shakes," signaling the moment of exchange, or payment (20.3), the Chalcans (for example, Tlacamazatl) are simply "forsaken," i.e., lost in battle (DICT cahua:te), without producing further revenants of their own kind. The revenants who do arrive are Chalco's enemies (see Remarks, below). The Chalcans, now outnumbered, are "extinguished," overwhelmed by the enemies, who come created from the other world as "grandmothers, grandfathers" (16.2), as God "paints the earth" with these (presumably pro-Mexica) revenants who are Chalco's enemies (as in CM 32v:14, 67v:24, etc.).

Remarks. The song is a much abbreviated restatement of CM song LI, interpreting the fifteenth-century Chalcan War as a glorious victory for Mexico, more glorious than it actually was (CMSA pp. 235–41, 451–52). In that song the trickery of the unexpected exchange (see above) is spelled out with greater clarity, as the singer announces: *cequi yan quauhtlia ocelotl cequiya mexicatl acolhua tepanecatl o mochihua in chalca* 'Multiple eagles and jaguars, multiple Mexicans, Acolhuans, and Tepanecs, do the Chalcans become' (CM 33v:3–5). It may be supposed that mid-sixteenth-century Mexica audiences hearing either of these songs, CM LI or RSNE XIV, would be reminded more of the Conquest of 1519–21 (in which Chalco aided Cortés) than of the fifteenth-century Chalcan War. Cf. the Commentary for song VIII.

Part 2

Song XV (16:2–17:1) (pt. 2, song 1)

Synopsis. A musical call to arms. The theory of music (TRAN 8.1) and the theory of war death (2.2, 5.1–3) are constantly interchanged. Using the concrete term *antocnihuan* 'friends', the singer repeatedly addresses his fellow musician-ritualists, while referring to the incoming warriors by the abstract term *icniuhyotl*, translated 'comrades' (11.2).

In the "house of green places," i.e., the dance floor or the battlefield (2.5 and 9.1–9), the singers await God's "words," i.e., the incoming warriors. What does God want? Songs per se, as musical offerings, but also "songs," or "sorrows," that are war captives to be sacrificed as human offerings. What will God give? Songs per se, as a musical answer from the sky world (TRAN 8.1–3), but also incoming warriors returned to the battlefields of earth. These come "whirling" (17.5–7, 18.1, 19.1–4) as "flowers," "drums," "rattles" (9.7).

Our pleasure on the battlefield, or the dance floor, is brief (12.8). We'll enjoy these otherworldly comrades while we can (21.3).

Song XVI (17:3–18v:8) (pt. 2, song 2)

Historical figures. Rulers representing the traditional enemies of Mexico are named in four groups:

(1) Tenocelotzin of Huexotzinco (fl. before 1430), Tlaltzin (unidentified), Chiauhcoatzin of Huexotzinco (fl. before 1430?).
(2) Xayacamach of Huexotzinco (or Tlaxcala?), Coatzin of Tlaxcala, Tlacomihuatzin of Tlaxcala (14th or 15th century).
(3) Tlaltzin (again), Ayocuantzin (of Huexotzinco or Chalco?).
(4) Tenocelotl of Huexotzinco (again).

Synopsis. The (presumably Mexica) singer calls on past rulers of enemy nations, who bring down their armies from the sky world, knowing that they will be annihilated on the battlefield.

Remarks. On "ear and hand flowers," mentioned in the third stanza, see TRAN 4.5.

Song XVII (18v:10–19v:15) (pt. 2, song 3)

Historical figure. Nezahualcoyotl.

Synopsis. The singer appeals to Nezahualcoyotl, whom he envisions as creating, or "painting" (TRAN 15.1, 15.4), "flowers" (2.1–3). Nezahualcoyotl is only the surrogate, or agent. Actually it is God (3.1–3) who "brings down" the flowers (from the sky world) and "spreads them out" on the dance floor, i.e., the imagined battlefield (9.8). The "flowers," naturally, will soon "wither" (2.2, 12.8).

Remarks. On Nezahualcoyotl as putative author, see the Commentary for songs XIX and XXII.

Song XVIII (19v:17–21:7) (pt. 2, song 4)
(= CM song LXIX, canto F)

Synopsis. A singer petitions Life Giver for a distribution of incoming warriors, uncertain of success, since the supreme spirit is intractable (TRAN 12.12). Yet the "loved ones" do arrive as "flowers," "jades," "swans." Eventually, in exchange (20.1), we ourselves must die (in battle), as Life Giver "requires" (12.11).

Remarks. In CM this is the sixth and final canto in a six-canto song on the theme of the Spanish Conquest. The third canto is treated above, as RSNE song XI; the fourth canto, below, as RSNE song XXVII. See the Remarks for song XI. Regarding the "loved ones," see the Remarks for song V.

Song XIX (21:9–22v:7) (pt. 2, song 5)
(= CM song XVIII, stanzas 17–22)

Synopsis. The singer adopts the voice of a doubter among the incoming warriors.

Remarks. The passage at hand is only eight stanzas out of the 55-stanza song in CM, where the voice of doubt is eventually overwhelmed in the excitement of combat (TRAN 21.1–2). Not here, however. Yet the inner meaning may well be the unspoken reply (12.13), which would of course negate the doubter.

The glossator's idea that the eight-stanza passage in RSNE is "of Neza-hualcoyotzin when he was fleeing from the king of Azcapotzalco" finds no justification either in RSNE or in the full text in CM. A clue to the glossator's thinking lies in the numbering that he has added to the stanzas beginning on folio 18v, line 10 (first stanza of pt. 2, song 3), extending through folio 26, line 11 (the last stanza of pt. 2, song 8). Evidently he sees pt. 2, songs 3–8, as especially worthy of study, and perhaps he imagines that the entire group belongs to Nezahualcoyotl, taking the opening stanzas of song 3 (= song XVII), "your words, my prince, you, Nezahualcoyotzin," as a prefatory attribution. Coming to the passage that constitutes RSNE XIX, with its unrelieved negativity, the glossator links it with the major traumatic episode in Nezahualcoyotl's life as it has been portrayed in native annals: his flight from the henchmen of Azcapotzalco's king, who had hoped to have him murdered and did indeed drive him into exile. A version of the story is told in pictures on plate 9 of Codex Xolotl (Castillo 1972:87–103); another version, not in pictures but in words, is in Codex Chimalpopoca (CC 34:33–39:52) — a topic much rehearsed by Alva Ixtlilxóchitl (IXT passim).

The concluding song in the supposed Nezahualcoyotl group is XXII (pt. 2, song 8); but in order to read XXII as a composition of Nezahualcoyotl the glossator would have to interpret folio 25v, lines 2–3, not as 'I, Tizahuatzin, am grieving here' (*çâ nihuallaocoya çâ nitiçâhuaçi huiya*) but as something like 'I, the chalk owner, am grieving' (cf. Garibay 1964:65, 133). The name Tizahuatzin, however, is attested in the *netotiliztli* not only in RSNE song XXII but in CM 21:1–2: *ohuaye o ayyee xichoca oon Chimalpopo-catzin tacolmitzin oo titiçahuatzin* 'Weep, Chimalpopoca, and you, Acolmiz-tli, and you, Tizahuatzin'. Following his usual practice, the glossator, if he had noticed the name in the text, would probably have labeled the song "de Tizahuatzin."

Song XX (22v:9–23v:12) (pt. 2, song 6)

(= CM song LXXIII; also CM song LXXXII, canto D)

Synopsis. A singer identifies with Life Giver, who descends to earth bringing a distribution of "marvels" (TRAN 14.3), "cacao flowers" (2.2, 4.6, 13.1), and "swans" (5.5), spurring them on to combat. In battle these "eagles," these "jaguars," will win "nobility and fame," sacrificing their lives, as Life Giver "takes" them back to the sky world as his "comrades" (2.1–2).

Remarks. The RSNE version has been generalized. In the CM variants the sixth stanza names Mexica heroes (in place of Life Giver), who act as Life Giver's surrogates, or agents (TRAN 3.1–3), arriving on the scene with troops ready for action. In CM LXXXII the surrogates are Tlacotzin and Oquiztzin (who were captured by Cortés during the Conquest); in CM LXXIII they are Ixtlilcuechahuac and Tlacahuepan, brothers of Montezuma II and Mexica heroes par excellence (FC 6:13:2–3), killed in combat a generation before the Conquest. See DICT Tlacotzin, Oquiztzin, Ixtlilcuechahuac, Tlacahuepan.

Song XXI (23v:14–25:6) (pt. 2, song 7)
(= CM song LXIV, stanzas 9–11)

Synopsis. The supreme power, God, acting through the voice of the singer-ritualist, "shakes" down (TRAN 8.4) a distribution of sky warriors as "flowers" (2.1–3), "roseate swans" (5.5), "riches," "favors," destined to give their lives in battle.

Remarks. The first two and last two stanzas of this song recur together in the middle of a 20-stanza song in CM, where the city of Mexico, ultimately, is glorified ("lies shining") in a shower of incoming warriors called "angels," "mist," "new ones."

Song XXII (25:8–26:11) (pt. 2, song 8)

Historical figure. Tizahuatzin, fifteenth-century lord of Toltitlan (part of the Tepanec sphere) and son of King Itzcoatl of Tenochtitlan.

Synopsis. Adopting the voice of Tizahuatzin, the singer song-grieves (TRAN 10.9), producing warriors ready for combat (10.10). Raising the usual doubter's objections (cf. 12.7–8), he nevertheless concludes with the essential question, "When I've gone, will I have put an end to this [God's] pain and suffering?"—to which the answer, though unexpressed, must be yes (1.8, 12.1–6).

Remarks. This is the last in the series of six songs laboriously numbered and renumbered, stanza by stanza, by the pro-Texcoco glossator (see the transcription), who evidently believes that all six are compositions of the Texcocan king Nezahualcoyotl (see the Remarks for XIX).

Song XXIII (26:13–27v:5) (pt. 2, song 9)
(= CM song XLIII; CM song LXII, canto C)

Historical figure(s?). The only named figure is, or should be, "Cuacuauhtzin," presumably the Cuacuauhtzin (d. 1409?) who was the first king of Mexico Tlatelolco. In the third stanza the singer replaces this "Cuacuauhtzin" (so named in the two CM variants of the same stanza) with an unexpected "Yoyontzin" (alternate name for Nezahualcoyotl), suggesting that he is adapting a Mexica song to conform with an interest in Texcoco matters.

Synopsis. (The song makes better sense if the stanzas are rearranged according to the sequence in CM. Thus RSNE stanzas 1–8 should be ordered 3–6, 1, 2, 7, 8. And the "Yoyontzin" of stanza 3 should be replaced with "Cuacuauhtzin," as in CM.) The singer identifies with Cuacuauhtzin, who appears on earth as a warrior, blowing his "conch" to summon further warriors, evidently enemies. The enemies complain (TRAN 12.7–8, 21.1–2), but Cuacuauhtzin prevails, announcing his intention to "pluck" these "flowers" (2.3–4), inviting his comrades to seek the "Green Places" of paradise (2.5).

Or, following the RSNE author, Cuacuauhtzin is aided by Yoyontzin, both representing the Triple Alliance, as they summon enemy warriors, etc.

Remarks. The siege of Mexico, 1521, *ended* with a desperate battle in the borough of Tlatelolco, whereas the history of Tlatelolco *began* with the reign of old King Cuacuauhtzin. An irrelevant observation, seemingly. Yet the contrast between the heroic founding of Mexico and its tragic downfall forms the basis of the longest song in CM, the great *atequilizcuicatl* 'water-pouring song', which runs to 114 stanzas (CM song LXVIII). It is also the theme of another of the major songs in CM, the *xopancuicatl* 'song of green places' (CM song LXIX), running to 51 stanzas.

In CM the song at hand appears as the third canto in a suite of three cantos of obvious Mexica orientation. The *Romances* glossator, however, helped along by the singer's emendation (see above), thinks our song pertains to a Cuacuauhtzin who was lord of Tepechpan (a minor community under the control of Nezahualcoyotl, i.e., Yoyontzin, king of Texcoco). Probably the glossator has been influenced by the verb "grieve," which simply means "sing" or "make war" (TRAN 9.9, 10.9), imagining that Cuacuauhtzin has been aggrieved by "Yoyontzin." The matter is discussed in "The Texcoco Connection" in the Introduction.

The ambiguous second stanza apparently refers to Tlatelolco, literally 'mound place' (Códice Ramírez 1975:34 [*Tlatelulco,* que quiere dezir *lugar de terrapleno*]). The more benign reading of the second sentence would be: "Let me be jade, gold [i.e., a warrior (TRAN 15.2, 18.1, 20.2)]; I'll be smelted and drilled [i.e., created, brought to life (9.1, 15.2)] on The Mound or in Mound Town [i.e., in Tlatelolco]." But "smelted and drilled" can also be rendered "ignited [blown upon] and drilled [as with a fire drill]," suggesting dedicatory rites (CC 81:15–37) or a calendrical ceremony (FC 7:27:1–7:28:13) at the summit of a temple mound, where fire is drilled in the opened breast of a sacrificial victim.

Song XXIV (27v:7–29:2) (pt. 2, song 10)
(= CM song LXXXII, canto C)

Synopsis. A singer summons "comrades," "flowers," "songs," i.e., fellow warriors (TRAN 2.1–3, 8.1–3), from the sky world. As payment for their arrival (20.1), we on earth must depart, taking their place in the sky world—where eventually all will be reunited.

Remarks. In CM the song is the third in a four-canto sequence, of which the final canto is a variant of RSNE XX (see above). As noted in the commentary for XX, that final canto as it appears in CM describes the glorious, if momentary, return to earth of Tlacotzin and Oquiztzin, who had been captured by Cortés during the Conquest.

Song XXV (29:4–30:5) (pt. 2, song 11)

Synopsis. The singer summons an unnamed "singer" from the sky world (TRAN 3.1–3), who in turn produces "jewels," "plumes," "eagles," "jaguars," i.e., sky warriors (15.1–3, 2.1–2), who will be merely "borrowed" (12.7–8), on the "field," i.e., the battlefield (2.2, 2.5).

Song XXVI (30:7–31:8) (pt. 2, song 12)

Historical figure. Cacamatl, king of Texcoco, is clearly featured in this song as in song V (see above). Oddly, though he is worthy of being treated as a native hero of the Conquest (having been put to death by Cortés), he is not mentioned in CM. The term *cacamatl* 'baby maize ear' does appear in CM as a figure of speech designating the warrior newly returned from the sky world; and two or more historical figures named Cacamatl—among Mexico's traditional enemies, not as the ruler of Texcoco—also appear in CM. It may be asked whether the pro-Texcoco informant, or informants, who supplied the texts could have adapted Mexica material in putting together both V and XXVI, deliberately giving these pieces a Texcoco flavor.

Moreover, the passage *yhuitlo ye moçêçêlohuaya ao can ixpanni y cacāmatlo ay huiziztepetl* 'feathers are scattered before Cacamatl at Thorn Knife Town', while not impossible, is suspect. The CM usage, at least, is *huitziltepetl* 'Hummingbird Town [or Hummingbird Mountain]', evidently a name for the warrior's paradise, where the supreme spirit dwells (or a name for the battlefield or the dance floor as it represented that paradise); and *ixpan* is a stock term in CM, almost always and repeatedly meaning 'before [or in the presence of]' God. For example, *ixpan in Dios [...] nicyatzezeloa* 'before God I scatter them' (CM 22v:3–4); *quitzetzelohuaya [...] yxpani yn ipalnemohuani* 'he scatters them before Life Giver' (CM 68v:8–9). The singer would seem to have taken a phrase in which God, or Life Giver, is named and inexpertly substituted "Cacamatl" (DICT cacamatl, huitziltepetl, ixpan).

For other examples in which the RSNE singer has changed or suppressed names, see the Commentary for songs XX (suppressed) and XXIII (changed).

Synopsis. Using Cacamatl as agent for the supreme power (TRAN 3.1–3), the singer brings down a "scattering" (8.4), or "sprinkling," of incoming warriors from the sky world, destined to give their lives on the "field" of battle.

Song XXVII (31:10–32v:5) (pt. 2, song 13)
(= CM song LXIX, canto D)

Historical figures. Montezuma II and his brother, the proverbial war hero Tlacahuepan (see the Commentary for songs I and XX).

Synopsis. Warriors, called "shields" and "blaze-smoke," rise to the upper world as they are killed in battle, serving as the payment (TRAN 20.1) for an incoming multitude of sky warriors "raining down" as eagles and jaguars. It is Montezuma who makes this payment, "reciting" the incoming warriors as though they were songs (8.1–3), himself ascending to an apotheosized Mexico in the sky (22.4), leaving the new arrivals behind as "reed flowers." Among the Mexica warriors claimed by the sun is the past hero Tlacahuepan, or a substitute for Tlacahuepan, whom "God" comes to "shear." ("God" here replaces the sun, called "Ascending Eagle" and "Turquoise Prince" in the more unacculturated CM variant.)

Remarks. The glossator sees this as a song commemorating the war with Huexotzinco, ca. 1498, in which the hero Tlacahuepan was killed (or captured and sacrificed). However, the CM variant belongs to a larger song that clearly treats the siege of Mexico, 1521. The symbolic mention of "Tlacahuepan," who died a generation earlier, is a typical anachronism (see also RSNE song I), as is "Montezuma," who actually died before the siege and did not lead troops in battle against Cortés as implied here.

Song XXVIII (32v:7–?) (pt. 2, song 14)
(= CM song XL; CM V)

Historical figures. These are named in two groups:

(1) Nezahualcoyotl and Montezuma I, mid-fifteenth-century kings of Texcoco and Mexico Tenochtitlan, respectively.
(2) Tezozomoc and Cuacuauhtzin, fourteenth- through early-fifteenth-century kings of Azcapotzalco and Mexico Tlatelolco, respectively.

Synopsis. A singer states the doctrine of exchange (TRAN 20.1), by which an incoming distribution of "flowers," i.e., warriors (2.1–3), must be paid for by a sacrifice of equivalent "flowers," or "songs" (8.1–3), then assumes the role of Yoyontzin (i.e., Nezahualcoyotl), who voices a typical objection, lamenting that his time on earth will be brief (12.8, 21.3). The singer ignores the objection and directly summons both Nezahualcoyotl and Montezuma. Doubts are expressed by these two, whose "grieving" (10.9) has the wanted effect of producing further revenants, "turquoise-swanlike flowers," including Tezozomoc and Cuacuauhtzin.

Remarks. The glossator's "Cuauhtzin" probably picks up an error in the RSNE text, now incomplete on account of the missing folio. "Cuacuauh-tzin," as in CM, is the better reading, though "Cuauhtzin" (see CONC) is remotely possible in this context.

Attempts to square the song with old chronicles and legends portraying Tezozomoc as a despised tyrant and enemy of Nezahualcoyotl (and of Montezuma) would seem doomed to failure. All four figures mentioned in the song are merely symbols, here representing the glorious past of Mexico and its allies.

Part 3

Song XXIX (?–35:1) (pt. 3, song 1)

Historical figures. Montezuma I, Cahualtzin, Citlalcoatzin, and Cuauhtlah-toatzin are all sons of King Itzcoatl of Tenochtitlan, ca. 1430; and Nezahual-coyotl (also called Yoyontzin), said to be the nephew of Itzcoatl (IXT 1:404, cf. DHIST 73), is here also included among Itzcoatl's "children." On the other side are the indeterminate representatives of the enemy Tlaxcalans-Huexotzincans, Xayacamachan and Temaxahuitzin. It is here assumed that the textual "Temayahuitzin" is a variant of the "Temaxahuitzin" attested in Muñoz Camargo 1892:102 (lib. 1, cap. 12) as a Tlaxcalan captain who aided Cortés.

Synopsis. (The first stanza is missing.) A singer, using the voices of Monte-zuma and Citlalcoatzin, dismisses the often heard objection that our lives are "never twice [*lit.,* not twice]," proclaiming, "Let it not be 'never twice'" (TRAN 21.5). Thus Montezuma and the other ancestral Mexica (including Nezahualcoyotl) arrive on earth as part of an influx of "popcorn flowers, cacao flowers" (2.2, 4.6), despite continuing objections (12.7–8, 21.1–5). Arriving also, at last, are the enemy leaders Xayacamachan and Temaxahuitzin. The stage, then, is set for combat.

Remarks. Comparison shows that XXIX is a variant on the theme more clearly expressed in song X, with which it shares the same two final stanzas. As noted in the commentary for X, the mention of Eagle Gate in that song suggests the siege of Mexico, 1521. The anachronistic summoning of ances-tral Mexica ghosts out of a deeper past accords with the ritual technique already seen in previous songs (I, X, XXVII).

Here, as elsewhere, the theory of song production (TRAN 8.1–2) over-laps with the theory of resurrection (2.2, 5.1–6), allowing the piece to be read as though songs per se were being obtained from the sky world.

Song XXIX-A (35:2–36:10) (pt. 3, song 1-A)

Synopsis. Through his words the singer brings the supreme power to earth as a means of "hatching" (TRAN 2.1–2) eagles and jaguars (abstract form), i.e., producing warriors from the sky world (11.4), giving "outline" and "colors" (15.4) to these "companions" (abstract form); he issues a call to arms, urg-ing the incoming warriors to "create," or "weep for," further eagle-jaguars, i.e., further distributions of sky warriors ready to engage in combat, ready for death.

Remarks. To be hidden in a coffer or wickerwork evidently means to be killed. Cf. DICT petlacalco 1.

Song XXX (36:12–36v:14) (pt. 3, song 2)

Synopsis. The singer promises an unnamed warrior that his death in battle—or, if captured, by sacrifice ("knife death")—will result in songs that per-petuate his fame (TRAN 8.1–3, 12.10).

Remarks. "Flowers" that are "jade, gold" here seem to be songs per se. But throughout the *netotiliztli* "jade" and "gold" also denote the warrior himself. Accordingly, there is a suggestion in the first and last stanzas that warriors, or "flowers," from the sky world will "come forth" as "jade" and "gold" to replace the warrior(s) lost in battle. Cf. 7v:14 et seq.: "My flowers are gold […] these jades […]. Could they be my payment? It is thus that I'd be born in future time!" For similar allusions to "jade" and "gold" see 6v:13, 10v:16, 26v:2, 29:17–18, 36:7–8.

In the fifth stanza the imagined warriors come "pouring" out of the sky as "shield dust" or "spear mist" (TRAN 4.7, 8.4). In CM, 'dust' *teuhtli* is ap-parently a play on 'lord' *teuctli* (see DICT teuhtli).

"The *flower* of knife death" (second stanza), as also in song XXXVI, is "the *beauty* of knife death"—one of the rare *netotiliztli* usages in which the term "flower" does not denote either the song or the warrior. See the note to the translation at 36:16.

Song XXXI (37:1–38:10) (pt. 3, song 3)

Synopsis. A singer exhorts his comrades to "arise" (as warriors in battle) and take advantage of incoming "flowers," i.e., potential captives (TRAN 1.12, 2.1–3). A disconsolate voice is heard, grieving (in order to produce these revenants?) — see 10.2–9.

Song XXXII (38:11–39v:12) (pt. 3, song 4)

Historical figure. Nezahualcoyotl.

Synopsis. A singer addresses the supreme power, who produces songs that scatter down as "flowers" (TRAN 1.12, 2.1–3, 3.2, 8.4); addresses Nezahualcoyotl (3.3), who continues producing "flowers" that now "lie in our hands" (13.4), with which he "adorns" himself (17.2n). These "flowers" come from the Place of Duality, i.e., the other world where human life is created (14.2; CONC Omeyocan).

Remarks. The bird *coxcox* 'chachalaca' here seems to be identified with the supreme power as master musician, as are various other birds in the *netotiliztli*. See DICT coxcox, huitzilin, quechol. Cf. 30v:17 "the soaring Egret Bird Life Giver."

Part 4

Song XXXIII (39v:14–41:10) (pt. 4, song 1)

Historical figure. Acolhuatzin, a founding "prince" of the Acolhuan nation (see CONC).

Synopsis. A singer calls upon ancestral Acolhuatzin, who starts to sing, or "grieve" (TRAN 10.6–10), producing "flowers" (2.1–3), "hearts" (4.5), "flower garlands" (15.5–16.1), "jewels" (15.1–2), for his fellow Acolhuans. The "flowers" "walk abroad [*or* march along, i.e., as warriors (2.2)]," to be taken as captives, or "hand flowers," with which the Acolhuans will "entertain" themselves, "adorn" themselves, or "crown" themselves (17.2n).

Remarks. The glossator evidently thinks that Acolhuatzin is an alternate name for Nezahualcoyotl, perhaps because the latter is a Texcocan (i.e., Acolhuan); and he calls the song a *xopancuicatl* 'song of green places' prob-

ably because he sees 'house of green places' in the sixth stanza. The Nezahualcoyotl = Acolhuatzin might not be impossible, but it is unlikely and
unattested; the phrase "house of green places" by no means requires that
a song in which this term appears be called a *xopancuicatl* (cf. CM usages,
passim).

RSNE XXXIII does not have a surviving variant, but CM XX (and no
other) shares its opening phrases, *xiahuilompehua xiahuiloncuica* 'begin in
pleasure, sing with pleasure' (treating the *om* or *on* as a vocable), and the
two songs have a few other locutions in common: "in this flower house,"
"be pleasured," "borrow," "flower tree," "scatter," "parcel out"—not enough,
and not distinctive enough, to demand comparison, although the opening phrases might catch one's attention. CM XX is the first in a group of
twenty-four songs said by the CM glossator to be "plain songs [*melahuac
cuicatl*]" that are "of three kinds: flower songs [*xochicuicatl*], eagle songs
[*cuauhcuicatl*], and bereavement songs [*icnocuicatl*] all run together" (CM
16v:4–6). CM XX includes the names of Nezahualcoyotl and Montezuma
("I, Prince Nezahualcoyotl"; "your words, O princes, O Nezahualcoyotl,
O Montezuma").

Songs XXXIV, XXXV, XXXVI
(41:12–42v:14) (pt. 4, songs 2–4)

Historical figure. Cuatlecoatzin of Mexico Tenochtitlan, rewarded by King
Itzcoatl for services in the Tepanec War, ca. 1430.

Synopsis. (These last three songs may be considered together, though in the
manuscript there is no indication that they form a suite, as do many groups
of three or more songs in CM.)

In XXXIV a singer summons "jades" and "gold", i.e., warriors (TRAN
15.2, 18.1, 20.2) from the other world. They arrive as proof that death is vanquished here on earth, that the warrior's fame—the warrior himself—lives
on through the power of music. We warriors are to "adorn" (17.2n) ourselves
with these "flowers," we're to "enjoy" them, i.e., we're to take them as captives in battle. But the voice of a doubter is heard, arguing (contrary to the
doctrine) that there is no lasting enjoyment, no life in the hereafter ("Our
Home"), no supreme spirit who can be "known" there.

Song XXXV, as if bridging XXXIV and XXXVI, continues with the doubter's objection ("War is not your joy"), then abruptly contradicts it, asserting that the long-deceased war leader Cuatlecoatzin "knows God" (despite the doubter in XXXIV who suggests that a supreme spirit cannot be "known" in the hereafter).

Song XXXVI, as if a triumphant finale, affirms the doctrine in terms that are most shocking to Western sensibilities, offering the supreme spirit his "chalk" and "plumes" (i.e., sacrificial victims) (5.1, 20.1), promising all warriors that the "flower of knife death" (i.e., death on the stone of sacrifice) will make them "rich" (12.1).

Remarks. In XXXIV the singer, after apparently giving the doctrine a fair hearing, goes on to express an even more contemptuous negativity than in the seemingly despairing XIX (but see TRAN 12.13). Songs are merely songs, he now says, and never mind the false promise of resurrection for warriors who sacrifice their lives. In the last two stanzas he rejects the notion that a supreme spirit can be "known" in "that place" (i.e., the warrior's paradise most probably, not the heaven of Christianity); rejects the idea that this spirit, or any spirit, can "recall" dead warriors to life; rejects the dogma of perpetual or continued life in "Our Home" (here again most probably the warrior's paradise, though in the sixteenth century the term "Our Home" had come to mean the hereafter of Christianity). Here again, as in XIX, the inner meaning may be the unspoken reply (TRAN 12.13).

(Song XXXIV could be reinterpreted as a dialogue between a voice of doubt and a voice of affirmation, using quotation marks as was done with song IV. In that case the opening sentence in the fifth stanza would be assigned to the affirmative voice and the question mark removed.)

The two final songs, which bring us back to the native—or, more precisely, nativistic—doctrine are curiously terse. But the three-stanza song VIII may be compared; also two songs in CM, the three-stanza XLIX and the one-stanza LIV-A.

Concordance to Proper Nouns

All names of persons mentioned in the *Romances,* whether historical or supernatural, as well as all names of nations, national groups, and places (real or mythical), are entered in this Concordance with a complete list of occurrences. Main entries are written with glottal stops, shown by an H (as distinguished from the HU, which indicates the sound /w/), so that these entries, for comparison, can be more readily located in *A Nahuatl-English Dictionary and Concordance to the Cantares Mexicanos* (DICT). References to the *Romances* are by folio and line number: for example, 39v:17 (folio 39 verso, line 17). If the item is also found in the *Cantares,* a CM appears. In addition to definitions, in some cases, "key words" are given, meaning words or phrases used in the Translation in place of cumbersome glosses, where a particular Nahuatl term has no satisfactory English equivalent. Abbreviations are as follows.

cap., capítulo (chapter)
ch., chapter
d., died
fig., figuratively
g.n., group name (e.g. Huexotzincatl, Chichimecatl)
lib., libro (book)
lit., literally
para., paragraph
pc.n., place name, geographical name
p.n., personal name (male unless "female" is specified)
pl., plural
poss., possessive form
sec(s)., section(s)
Span., Spanish

syn., synonym(s)
var(s)., variant(s)

ACOLHUA or ACOLHUATZIN or ACOLIHUATZIN, p.n.

1. Acolhuatzin, one of the founding "príncipes" of Acolhuacan, "del nombre común de la nación" (Clavijero 1958–59 1:160), whose name is usually recorded as "Aculhua" (see García Granados 1952–53 1:23–25), eleventh-century Acolhuan prince, who received Azcapotzalco as his province and became first ruler of the Tepanecs (IXT 1:298–99), d. 1239 (IXT 1:318). 40:2–3.
2. Figurative use? See 12:16 and accompanying note, CM.
3. Spurious interpretation? The glossator at 39v:14 sees a reference to NEZAHUALCOYOTL of Acolhuacan (cf. 40:2–3).

ACOLHUAH, var. ACOLIHUAH, pl. ACOLHUAHQUEH or ACOLIHUAHQUEH, g.n., Acolhuan(s), inhabitant(s) of Acolhuacan. 40:14–15, CM.

ANAHUAC, pc.n.

1. At the riverside or the seashore (CARO 20v).
2. Refers to MEXIHCO? Mexico nican [. . .] anahuac 'here in Mexico [. . .] beside the waters', CM 22v:26–29. 8v:12, 8v:16. Syn. MEXIHCO.
3. At the shores of paradise (see TEZ 402–3).
4. New Spain (Motolinía 1971b cap. 1), the known world before Cortés (ibid.: tierra grande cercada y rodeada de agua), Anahuac, the world. CM.

ATLIXCO or ATL IXCO, pc.n.

1. On water, on the face or surface of the water (MOL).
2. Fig., Mexico (cf. DICT atlan 3, atlihtic 3). Key word: Water Face (CM 60:10). 8:17. Syn. MEXIHCO.
3. Fig., battlefield (see DICT atl 2, atlihtic 5, atlixco 3). CM 24v:27.
4. Town in the Puebla region, associated with Huexotzinco, where Mexica customarily obtained victims in battle (DHIST cap. 29 and passim). 8:15 gloss, CM.

AXAYACATL or AXAYACATZIN, p.n.

1. Ruler of Tenochtitlan, d. 1481 (CC 57:36). 12v:1 gloss, 13:4, 13:12, CM.

2. Axayacatzin Xicotencatl, Tlaxcalan commander, d. 1521 (Gibson 1967:25–26). CM.

AYOCUAN or AYOCUANTZIN (18:11 ayocuatzin).
  1. A woodland bird (FC 11:2:4–8).
  2. Agami heron (?, see HG lib. 11 p. 236).
  3. One of the leaders of the Mexicans prior to the founding of Tenochtitlan (UAH sec. 1).
  4. Ayocuan the elder, ruler of Amaquemecan Itztlacozauhcan, Chalco, 1411–65 (CHIM 87 and 102). CM.
  5. Ayocuan the younger, ruler of Amaquemecan Itztlacozauhcan, d. 1511 at age 20 (CHIM 44 and 232).
  6. Name of one or more persons mentioned in the Annals of Cuauhtinchan, a town in the Tlaxcala-Puebla region (KHTC secs. 327 and 404), son of "Quetzpal" (KHTC sec. 366).
  7. Unidentified; associated with Huexotzinco (?), CM (coupled with Cuetzpal at CM 9v:20 and 14v:13). 18:11 (ayocuatzin).

AZCAPOTZALCO, pc.n., town immediately northwest of Mexico, seat of the Tepanec realm and its powerful ruler TEZOZOMOC 1 until ca. 1426 (UAH) or 1430 (CC 47:35–36). 21:8 gloss.

CACAMATL or CACAMATZIN, p.n.
  1. Ruler of Acolhuacan in 1519 (MEX), among the nobles who stood with Montezuma when Cortés arrived in Tenochtitlan, 1519 (FC 12:43:10), imprisoned by Cortés (López de Gómara 1964 or 1988 ch. 91), secretly murdered by order of Cortés (TORQ 1:469–71). 5v:9 gloss, 6v:6–7, 30v:1, 30v:4.
  2. Unidentified. CM.

CAHUALTZIN, p.n.
  1. A Mexican leader in the Chalcan War (TEZ cap. 26). Coupled with Chimalpopoca, CM 18:22, with Montezuma, CM 20v:10. 4:15, 34:4, 34v:6.
  2. Son-in-law of CHIMALPOPOCA 1 (MEX 98 and 105 or ACHIM 1:125 and 1:129). Same as 1, above?
  3. Contemporary of MOTEUCZOMAH 1 (DHIST cap. 11 p. 99), brother of MOTEUCZOMAH 1 (CC 36:23). Same as 1, above?

CALMECAHUA, p.n., Tlaxcalan lord who greeted Cortés in Tlaxcala in 1519 (IXT 2:212), commiserated with him after his retreat from Mexico in 1520 (IXT 2:232), accompanied him in the siege of Mexico, 1521 (Muñoz Camargo 1892 lib. 1 cap. 12 p. 102). 10:13.

CHALCATL, pl. CHALCAH, g.n., native(s) of CHALCO. 15v:9–10, 15v:15–16, CM.

CHALCHIUHTLATONAC, p.n.
1. A founder of the Chalcan nation (IXT 2:17–19).
2. Fourteenth-century Chalcan leader (CHIM 172–73).
3. Fifteenth-century Chalcan leader (CHIM 199–200).
4. Indeterminate Chalcan leader. 14v:16, CM.

CHALCO, pc.n.
1. A province dominated by the city of Tlalmanalco (CMSA p. 56, Motolinía 1971b:206). 9:7, 14v:5 gloss, 15v:6, CM.
2. Chalcan lakeside town, formerly Chalco Atenco, now Chalco (TORQ 1:116).

CHANTLI, see TOCHAN.

CHIAUHCOATL or CHIAUHCOATZIN, see CHIYAUHCOATL.

CHICHIMECATL, pl. CHICHIMECAH, g.n.
1. Chichimec, an aborigine of the central highlands, a barbarian (for extended discussion see FC 10: ch. 29; for usages see CC 12:43–49 and 39:35–50). 15:8?
2. A rude tribesman of the northern part of the central highlands, a desert dweller (FC 11:256).
3. One who claims Chichimec ancestry (*sensu* 2, above) or who lives in Chichimec territory (*sensu* 1, above), i.e., an Aztec (Nahua), as opposed to Mixtecs, Zapotecs, Huaxtecs, etc. (DHIST cap. 59 p. 449 para. 9, FC 10:196–97), especially an Aztec nobleman or warrior, often used as a title. See 11:12 and accompanying note; 12:14, 17:9, 34:10–11 (chichimecatli yn tecpili), 40v:15, CM. See CHICHIMECATL TEUCTLI.

CHICHIMECATL TEUCTLI, vars. CHICHIMECATEUCTLI (CHIM 138), CHICHIMECATECUITLI (1:9), Chichimec Lord.

1. Title used by certain kings. With Tecayehuatzin, 1:9 (chichimecatecuitli), 10v:1; with Acolhuatzin, 40:1–2 (chichimecatl tecuitli); CM 10:8.
2. By extension, the supreme spirit, God. CM 31v:17, CM 61:21.

CHIMALPOPOCA or CHIMALPOPOCATZIN, p.n.
1. Ruler of Tenochtitlan, d. 1426 (CHIM 190). CM.
2. Ruler of Tlacopan, installed 1470 (CHIM 208), d. 1489 (IXT 2:157). 12v:1 gloss, 13:7–8, CM.

CHIYAUHCOATL or CHIYAUHCOATZIN or CHIAUHCOATL, p.n.
1. Chiyauhcohuatzin, one of the principal lords of Huexotzinco, along with TENOCELOTZIN, XAYACAMACHAN, and Texochimatitzin, before 1430 (TORQ 1:138), same as 2? 17:18.
2. Chiauhcoatl, lord of Tepeyacac (in the Puebla region) in 1441 and 1467, allied with TENOCELOTL of Huexotzinco in 1441 (CC 51:4, 53:38, cf. TEZ 306 and 309), same as 1?
3. Chiyauhcohuatzin, lord of Chiyauhtzinco in Huexotzinco, d. 1498 (CHIM 225); Chiauhcoatl, cuckolded NEZAHUALPILLI, d. 1498 (CC 59:17).

CITLALCOATL or CITLALCOATZIN, p.n.
1. Son of ITZCOATL and brother of MOTEUCZOMAH 1 (CC 36:24), served as *tlacochcalcatl* (a high official) under MOTEUCZOMAH 1 (CC 50:23–24). 4:14, 34:3, 34v:6.
2. Ruler of Toltitlan, a town in the Tepanec region (CC), at the time the Spaniards arrived (CC 31:29).

COACUECHTLI
1. Rattle of rattlesnake (MOL).
2. Coacuech, a rude Chichimec chieftain of the eleventh century, associated with the prehistory of Acolhuacan (IXT 2:22).
3. Coacuech, fourteenth-century governor of Tepeyacac, a town in the Puebla region (DHIST cap. 18 para. 51 p. 162).
4. Unidentified. 14v:8.

COATECATL, p.n.
1. Ancestral figure in the history of Totomihuacan (a town in the Tlaxcala-Puebla region) (KHTC secs. 288 and 294). 9v:17?

2. Ruler of Xiuhtepec, fourteenth-century (IXT 1:324).

3. Ruler of Tlatelolco, fourteenth-century (IXT 1:313).

4. Messenger sent by ITZCOATL (TEZ 278–79).

5. *Gobernador* of Tlacopan, ca. 1526 (IXT 1:494).

COATZIN, p.n.

1. Coatzin *teuctli* 'Lord Coatzin', a pre-Conquest lord of Quiahuiztlan, one of the four towns of Tlaxcala (Gibson 1967:200). 17v:10–11, CM.

2. Lord of Tepetlixpan Xochimilco, fl. 1459–65 (CHIM 203–4). CM.

CUAHCUAUHTZIN, p.n.

1. The first ruler of Tlatelolco (UAH sec. 218). See note to 32v:6, CM.

2. Lord of Tepechpan, whose beautiful wife was taken by NEZAHUALCOYOTL after causing Cuacuauhtzin's death in battle (dubious story told in IXT 2:117–20 [cap. 43]). 26:12 gloss.

3. Same as 1? 26:16, 26v:5, 27v:1, CM.

CUATEOTL, p.n.

1. The elder, fourteenth-century ruler of the borough of Itzcahuacan in Tlalmanalco Chalco (CHIM 179).

2. The younger, fifteenth-century ruler of Itzcahuacan (CHIM 98, 102, and 195). CM.

3. Indeterminate Chalcan ruler. 15:4.

CUATLECOATL or CUATLECOATZIN, p.n., high official in MEXIHCO, rewarded by ITZCOATL for services in the war against AZCAPOTZALCO, ca. 1430 (TEZ 249 and 254, DHIST). 42v:2–3.

CUAUHQUIAHUAC, Eagle Gate, a portal with stone carvings on the south side of the main square, or temple compound, in Tenochtitlan (see FC 12:85:28–36, cf. FC 12 front matter: map). 10:19–20, CM.

CUAUHTLAHTOATZIN, p.n., son of ITZCOATL and brother of MOTEUCZOMAH 1 (CC 36:25), 34v:7 (cuauhtlahuatzinn).

CUAUHTLAHUATZIN, see CUAUHTLAHTOATZIN.

CUAUHTZIN, p.n.

1. Fictitious name, Eagle, meaning any warrior? CM 76v:7.

2. Actual name of at least ten pre-Conquest nobles or warriors (see García Granados 1952–53).

3. Tenth- or eleventh-century ruler of Azcapotzalco (TORQ 1:253, cf. UAH for dates). 32v:6 gloss?

CUITLIZCATL, p.n., Tlaxcalan chieftain who aided Cortés in the siege of Mexico (IXT 2:256). Cuitlitzcaltecuitli = Lord Cuitlizcatl, 1:15.

DIOS, vars. DIYOS (8:4), TIOS (16:15), p.n., Span., *dios,* i.e., God. 1:12, 1v:15, 2:15, 3:8, 4v:13, 4v:17, 6:8, 6:15, 7:4, 7:9, 8:4, 9:9, 9:12, 9:18, 9v:17, 10:4, 10:7, 10v:8, 12:8, 12v:4, 12v:8, 12v:12, 12v:18, 15:18, 15v:5, 15v:12, 16:4, 16:9, 16:15, 16v:2, 19:10, 20:9, 20v:3, 22:2, 22v:11, 22v:13, 23:10, 24v:11, 30v:12, 31:13, 32:4, 32v:15, 34:10, 34:17, 35v:12, 35v:19, 36:13, 36v:12, 37v:15, 38:13, 40:8, 41v:14, 42v:4, CM. Syn. ESPIRITU SANTO; IPALNEMOHUA 2; MOYOCOYA 2; see TAHTLI; TEOTL; see TEUCTLI; see TEUCYOTL; TLALTICPAQUEH; see TONATIUH 3.

ESPIRITU SANTO, p.n., Span., *espíritu santo,* i.e., the Holy Spirit, the Holy Ghost. 1v:15, CM (spiritu santo). Syn. DIOS.

HUEXOTZINCATL, pl. HUEXOTZINCAH, g.n., Huexotzincan(s), inhabitant(s) of HUEXOTZINCO 1. 31:9 gloss (Span. pl. *Huexotzincas*), CM.

HUEXOTZINCO, pc.n.
1. City or nation in the Puebla region often allied with TLAXCALLAN against Mexico, sometimes mingled with TLAXCALLAN in song texts. 1:17, 10:5 gloss, 10:12, 10v:2, 11:6, 34v:18, CM.
2. Huexotzinco, 'Willow Place', i.e., Mexico (see CMSA 29–30: Identification with the enemy). CM 63:27 (mexico nican huiya no yhui huexotzinco = 'here in Mexico which is the same as Huexotzinco'), CM 82:16 (huexotzinco mexico). 10v:4–5.

ILHUICATLIHTIC or ILHUICATLIHTEC, pc.n., within the sky (CARO 21v); warrior's paradise, home of the sun (FC 6:15:11); heaven (of Christianity) (MOLS parayso celestial). 39v:5, CM. Cf. OMEYOCAN, TAMOANCHAN.

IPALNEMOHUA, vars. IPALNEMOHUANI, IPALTINEMI (18:4, 18:13), p.n., lit., 'he by whom one lives'.
1. Refers to Tezcatlipoca (Ponce 1984:211, FC 3:11:13).

2. Refers to God (CARO 17: Dios se llama *ipalnemoani* por quien se viue, el que da vida), i.e., Life Giver. 1v:17–18, 5:4, 5:12–13, 5:19, 6:11, 8:20, 12v:12, 15:12, 15v:3–4, 17:4, 17v:3, 17v:13, 18:4, 18:13, 19:17, 19v:18, 20:6, 20:9, 20v:8, 21:5, 21v:16–17, 22:16, 22v:6, 22v:11, 23:5, 23:9, 23:18, 24v:15–16, 25:2, 28:13, 28v:15–16, 29:10–11, 30:3, 30:11, 30:14, 30v:17–18, 31:4–5, 34:9, 34:15, 35:3, 36:15–16, 42v:8, CM. Syn. DIOS, MOYOCOYA, TLALTICPAQUEH.

ITZCOATL or ITZCOATZIN, p.n., ruler of Tenochtitlan, d. 1440 (MEX 109 or ACHIM 1:131). 11:2, 34v:9, 34v:13.

IZTAC COYOTL, p.n.
   1. Early-fifteenth-century lord of Totomihuacan (a town in the Puebla-Tlaxcala region) (UAH secs. 86, 255, and 270). 9v:18? CM.
   2. Iztaccoyotzin, a high official in the borough of Acxotlan in Tlalmanalco Chalco, fl. 1465 (CHIM 110, CHIM 204). CM.

MAHCEUHCATZIN or MAHCEUHQUI (CM), p.n., Dancer (MOL maceuhqui 'baylador o dançador'), alternate name for TLACAHUEPAN 3. *In Maceuhcatzin, in Tlacavepantzin,* FC 6:13:2. 1:18, CM.

MARIA, see SANTA MARIA.

MATZIN, p.n., Tlaxcalan chieftain (*caudillo tlaxcalteca*) who led troops in support of Cortés in the siege of Mexico (IXT 2:215). 10:13.

MEXIHCO, pc.n., Mexico, city state comprising the twin boroughs of Tenochtitlan and Tlatelolco, site of present Mexico City. 8v:6, 12v:1 gloss, 13:14, 13v:1, 31v:9, 31v:17, CM. Syn. ANAHUAC 2, ATLIXCO 2, TENOCHTITLAN.

MICTLAN, pc.n., lit., dead land, i.e., the underworld (FC 3:39:6–30), hell (CARO 53v), warrior's paradise in the sky (FC 6:11:21). 17:8, CM. Cf. QUENAMIHCAN, TOCHAN, XIMOHUACAN.

MOTEUCZOMAH or MOTEUCZOMAHTZIN, var. MOTECUIZOMAHTZIN, p.n.
   1. Montezuma the elder, ruler of Tenochtitlan 1440–68 (MEX 110–11 or ACHIM 1:133), d. 1468 (MEX 111 or ACHIM 1:133). 4:15, 32v:17, 34:3, 34v:5, CM.

2. Montezuma the younger, ruler of Tenochtitlan 1502–20, d. 1520
(MEX 148–49 or ACHIM 1:157–59). 31:9 gloss, 31v:8, 31v:16, CM.

MOYOCOYA or MOYOCOYATZIN, p.n., Self Maker, i.e., the supreme
spirit.
1. Tezcatlipoca (FC 3:12:19, FC 6:11:12).
2. God. Moyoco(ya)(tzin), 1:11–12, 4v:12, 4v:16–17, 19v:1–2, 22v:14,
24v:16. 30:10, 30:13–14, 41v:14. Syn. DIOS.

NANTLI, mother.
1. Tinan (should be *tenan* 'one's mother' as at CM 60:6), title applied
to an unidentified goddess, possibly St. Cecilia (CM 30:29). 7:12
(applied to St. Mary?).
2. Monantzin 'your mother' applied to St. Mary (CM 46v:16).

NEZAHUALCOYOTL or NEZAHUALCOYOTZIN, p.n., ruler of
Acolhuacan 1431–72, d. 1472 (CC 47:39 and 55:11). 2v:6–7
(necāhualcoyotl tecuitli = Lord Nezahualcoyotl), 3v:8, 3v:19, 4:16,
6v:10, 11:3, 18v:9 gloss, 18v:12, 19:1, 21:8 gloss, 32v:6 gloss, 32v:17, 34:11,
34v:14, 38:11 gloss, 39:15–16, 39v:7, CM. Syn. YOHYONTZIN.

NEZAHUALPILLI or NEZAHUALPILTZINTLI, p.n., ruler of
Acolhuacan 1472–1515, d. 1515 (CC 55:13 and 61:42). 6v:8, 12v:1 gloss,
13:8, CM.

OMEYOCAN, pc.n., Place of Duality, otherworldly abode of
supernaturals (CC 4:46), where human life originates (FC 6:175:21).
Cf. CM 35v:27 *ome ycac* 'he [God] is as two'. Cf. FC 6:141:25–26,
6:168:11, 6:175:20: *in vme tecutli, in vme cioatl* 'Two Lord, Two Woman
[the creators of human life]'. 10v:14. Cf. ILHUICATLIHTIC,
TAMOANCHAN.

PILLI, see TEPILTZIN.

POPOCATZIN, see 12:15 and accompanying note.

QUENAMIHCAN, attested in RSNE and CM only as the var.
QUENONAMIHCAN. Some kind of place, how-is-it place, fig., the
hereafter, the Place Unknown (FC 3:39:31). 24:17, 36v:8, 42:3, CM.
Syn. MICTLAN, XIMOHUACAN.

SANTA MARIA, female p.n., Span. Santa María, i.e., Saint Mary. S maria, 10:2, CM (santa maria).

TAHTLI, father. Totatzin = Our Father, i.e., God, 3:8, 6:7, 20v:2, CM. Syn. DIOS.

TAMOANCHAN, pc.n.
1. Mythical place where human beings were created (CC 76:51–77:32). Note: of unknown derivation (Andrews 2003:503), the word appears to mean 'home of Tamoan' (CM 24:18 tamoan ychan, cf. Muñoz Camargo 1892:155 [lib. 1, cap. 19]), with the indicated thing or person variously called Tamin (CM 78v:28), Taminchon (CM 78v:30), or Tamo (CM 15:5); presumed Nahuatl and even Mayan etymologies are summarized in Lehmann 1974:334–37 and Davies 1977:101–4. 11:19–20, 11v:6–7 (tamohuānichan), CM. Cf. ILHUICATLIHTIC, OMEYOCAN.
2. Extended or figurative usages. Tamo (vocable suggesting Tamoanchan), 10v:20, 34v:10; cf. CM 15:5. Cuauhtamiyohuanchan = Eagle Tamoanchan (figurative name for the battlefield?), 1:16.

-TEC, see TEUCTLI.

TECAYEHUATZIN, p.n., lord of Huexotzinco during the reign of MOTEUCZOMAH 2 (Muñoz Camargo 1892:113–15, TEZ 638–39 ["Tecuanhehuatzin" "Tecuan ehuatl"], TEZ 646 ["Tecuan ehuatl"], DHIST 454–57, TORQ 1:200). 1:9, CM.

TECUITLI, see TEUCTLI.

TEMAXAHUITZIN, p.n., one of the Tlaxcalan captains who aided Cortés in the siege of Mexico (Muñoz Camargo 1892:102 [lib. 1, cap. 12]). Written *temayahuitzin* at 10:14, 11:7–8, and 34v:19; *tenmayahuitzin* at 10v:8.

TEMAYAHUITZIN, see TEMAXAHUITZIN.

TEMILOTECATL, p.n., ruler of one of the four boroughs of Tlaxcala at the time of Cortés' arrival (TORQ 1:416). See TEMILOTZIN 3.

TEMILOTZIN, p.n.
1. Son of the Huitzilihuitl who ruled Tenochtitlan until 1417 (IXT 2:37, cf. CC 32:6–8).

2. Styled *tlacateccatl* 'commanding general' in the siege of Mexico (FC 12:112:15), baptized as Pedro Temilo, served as *tlatoani* 'ruler' of Tlatelolco 1522–27(?) (FC 8:7:30). 2:16, CM.

3. Shortened form of TEMILOTECATL? On the apocopation of personal names in song texts, see GRAM 7.7. 1:14.

TENITL, p.n., see 11:13 (teni) and accompanying note.

TENOCELOTL or TENOCELOTZIN, p.n.
1. Ruler of Huexotzinco in 1362, son of XAYACAMACHAN 4 (CC 27:8).
2. One of the principal lords of Huexotzinco, along with XAYACAMACHAN 5, CHIYAUHCOATZIN, and Texochimatitzin, before 1430 (TORQ 1:138), ruler of Huexotzinco in 1430 and 1441 (CC 43:24 and 51:3). 17:17, 18v:4.

TENOCHTITLAN, pc.n., one of the twin boroughs of MEXIHCO, the principal borough, also called "México," called "San Francisco de México" after the Conquest (Motolinía 1971a:180–81 [tratado 3 cap. 7]). 11:2, 34v:13, CM.

TEOHUAH, lit., spirit owner.
1. Title of a priest who signaled the arrival of gods from the other world (FC 2:119:15–22).
2. Title held by certain Chalcan leaders (cf. TEOHUAH TEUCTLI). Key word: priest. 15:3, CM. See also TEOHUAHTZIN 2.

TEOHUAH TEUCTLI or TEOHUAH TECUITLI, spirit-owner lord, title held by various Chalcan leaders (ZCHIM 1:57:22: *teohua teuhctli* 'spirit-owner lord'; CHIM 158, 173, and 184). 9:14, CM.

TEOHUAHTZIN, p.n.
1. Teohua, ruler of Calpan (CC 64:1), a "borough" of Huexotzinco (Muñoz Camargo 1892:51 [lib. 1 cap. 6]), in 1519 (CC).
2. Name for any Chalcan leader? Cf. TEOHUAH 2, TEOHUAH TEUCTLI. 15:13.

TEOTL, p.n. God (MOLS Dios 'teotl'), spirit (DICT). 2:15 gloss, 19:10 gloss, 22:1, CM. Syn. DIOS.

TEPECHPAN, var. TEPEXPAN, pc.n., a town within the realm of TEXCOCO, i.e., within the realm of Acolhuacan (CC 64:34). 26:12 gloss.

TEPILTZIN, lit., 'someone's prince (or noble)', apparently used as a title (CM 79v:7). 10:8, 13:3–4; cf. 10v:13, 13:11, 18v:4, 39:15, 39v:6.

TETZCOHCO, see TEXCOCO.

TEUCTLI, vars. TECUITLI, TECUITZINTLI, poss. -tec (CM) or -tecui (CM) or -teuc (CM). Nobleman (MOL tecutli), lord (DICT). Tecuitzintli = lord, 13:11–12. Notec = my Lord, i.e., God (cf. CM 79v:13 *notec* 'my lord'), 8:3. Tecuitli = lord, 2v:7, 14v:15, 18:9, 18:12. See CHICHIMECATL TEUCTLI, CUITLIZCATL, NEZAHUALCOYOTL, TEOHUAH TECUITLI. Cf. TLATQUIC.

TEUCYOTL, abstract form of TEUCTLI, lordship, lord. Totecoyo (*for* toteucyo *or* totecuyo) = Our Lord, i.e., God, glosses at 2:17 (item 4), 3:8, 4v:13, 4v:17, 12:8, 12v:4, 12v:8, 12v:12, 12v:18, 15v:5, 15v:12, 16:4, 16:9, 16:15, 16v:2, 20v:3, 21:10, 22:2, 38:13, CM (totecuyo). Tocuiyc (*copyist's error for* totecuiyo) = Our Lord, i.e., Christ, 10:1, CM (totecuiyo). Syn. DIOS.

TEXCOCO, vars. TEZCOCO, TETZCOHCO (CARO 56 and 97), pc.n., city state, seat of Acolhuacan (SIM). 5v:9 gloss (tezcuco), 12v:1 gloss (tezcuco).

TEZOZOMOC or TEZOZOMOCTLI or TEZOZOMOCTZIN, p.n.
   1. Tezozomoc the elder, king of the Tepanecs 1343–1426, d. 1426 (UAH secs. 214 and 258, MEX 100 or ACHIM 1:127 Huehue Teçoçomoctli), or d. ca. 1430 (see CC 39:48 et seq.). 32v:6 gloss, CM.
   2. Tezozomoc the younger, lord of Azcapotzalco ca. 1474–99, d. ca. 1499 (TORQ 1:254).
   3. Son of ITZCOATL and father of AXAYACATL 1, never reigned (MEX 114 or ACHIM 1:135, TORQ 1:162).
   4. Son of AXAYACATL 1 (TEZ 572, MEX 164 or ACHIM I:169). CM?
   5. Ruler of Colhuacan when the Spaniards arrived (CC 63:52).

TIOS, see DIOS.

TIZAHUATZIN, p.n., lord of Toltitlan (UAH sec. 254), a town in the Tepanec region (CC), son of ITZCOATL (UAH). 25v:2–3, CM.

TLACAHUEPAN or TLACAHUEPANTZIN, p.n.
   1. A god whose surrogate was sacrificed at the feast of Toxcatl (FC

2:73:8); name of a god identified with Huitzilopochtli (FC 3:25:6–8).
2. Brother of MOTEUCZOMAH 1, killed in the Chalcan War, mid-1400s (DHIST 145 [cap. 17, para. 4]).
3. Brother of MOTEUCZOMAH 2, died fighting in Huexotzinco in 1495 (CC 59:9) or ca. 1498 (AUB 49, MEX 135 or ACHIM 1:149) (see Brundage 1972:323). 1:18–19, 32:2, 32:10–11, CM. Syn. MAHCEUHCATZIN.

TLACAMAZATL
1. A bestial person (MOLS bestial hombre 'tlacamaçatl'), CM. Cf. DICT *mazatl/tochin* 'beast/wanton, an immoral person'.
2. Fictitious p.n., term of opprobrium? 14v:5 gloss, 15:8–9, CM.

TLACOMIHUATZIN, p.n., fourteenth- or fifteenth-century lord of the Tlaxcalan town of Ocotelolco (Muñoz Camargo 1892:74–79 and 95 [lib. 1 caps. 7, 8, and 11]). 17v:11, CM.

TLACOPAN, pc.n., Tepanec town near the western lakeshore just opposite Mexico, seat of the Tepanecs after 1428 (IXT 1:444–45), now called Tacuba (CARO 56v). 12v:1 gloss.

TLAHTOANI, ruler, king (of a pre-Conquest city state) (see HG 2:283–86 [lib. 8 cap. 1 paras. 1–19 and paras. 20–25], cf. FC 8:1:9–8:5:12). 34v:8, CM.

TLAILOTLAC, var. TLAILOTLAQUI, title held by various kings and officials in Mexico (MEX 115 or ACHIM 1:137, TEZ 352 Tlailotlatl), in Chalco (MEX 72 or ACHIM 1:107, CHIM 138–39), and in Tlaxcala? (see Muñoz Camargo 1892:73 [lib. 1 cap. 7 "Tlatlatactetzpantzin" = Tlaylotlactetzpantzin?]); magistrate, arbiter (title of a high judge, or judge's advisor, in Mexico) (see TORQ 2:352). Key word: arbiter. 11v:3, 12:15, CM.

TLALMANALCO, pc.n., Chalcan capital (DHIST 22 [cap. 2 para. 8]). 15:12–13.

TLALTECATZIN (should be TLALTECCATZIN with var. TLALTEUCTLI, see DICT), p.n.

1. Fourteenth-century ruler of Cuauhchinanco (IXT 1:321). 7:1 gloss, CM.
2. Title or alternate name applied to Totoquihuaztli (TEZ 629, 634, 639), ruler of Tlacopan and lord of the Tepanecs when Cortés arrived in 1519 (CC 63:53), d. 1519 (IXT 2:236). 7:5, CM.

TLALTICPAQUEH, p.n., earth owner, world owner.
1. Refers to Tezcatlipoca (FC 6:4:33, Ruiz de Alarcón 1984:49).
2. Refers to God (CARO 7). 25:2–3, CM. Syn. DIOS.

TLALTZIN, p.n.
1. Tlaltzinteuctli 'Lord Tlaltzin', a ruler of Chalco, inaugurated 1441, d. 1465 (CC 51:7 and 53:12).
2. Same as 1? 17:18, 18:10 ('O chief, O lord—it's Tlaltzin!').

TLATQUIC, lit., carrier or burden bearer, title used by Chalcan rulers (see CHIM 176, 202, and 264). Key word: chief. 14v:16, 18:9, CM.

TLAXCALLAN, pc.n., Tlaxcala, often allied with HUEXOTZINCO against Mexico. Note: the four principal cities of Tlaxcala province were regarded as boroughs of a single "city," or "capital," also called Tlaxcala (see DHIST 23 [cap. 2 para. 15] and cf. Heyden and Horcasitas in Durán 1964:348). 1:13, CM.

TOCHAN, pc.n., our home, the hereafter (FC 6:21:9). 42:11, CM. Cf. ILHUICATLIHTIC, MICTLAN, QUENAMIHCAN, XIMOHUACAN.

TONATIUH
1. Sun (MOL). CM.
2. Day, i.e., 24-hour period (DICT). CM.
3. p.n., Jesus (see 10:1 and accompanying note). CM.

TOTAHTZIN, see TAHTLI.

TZONTECOCHATZIN, p.n., elder brother of NEZAHUALCOYOTL (CC 35:31). 4:1.

XAYACAMACH or XAYACAMACHAN, p.n.
1. Early ruler of Tizatlan (the principal Tlaxcalan town) (Muñoz Camargo 1892:99–100 [lib. 1 cap. 12]), same as 3 or 4? CM.

2. A later ruler of Tizatlan (Muñoz Camargo 1892:100), same as 4 or 5?
3. A ruler of Huexotzinco in 1257 (CC 18:2).
4. A ruler of Huexotzinco in 1339 (CC 24:9).
5. Fifteenth-century ruler of Huexotzinco (TORQ 1:138, TEZ 476, DHIST 337 [cap. 43 para. 21]). CM.
6. Visitor to Mexico from Huexotzinco, 1515–18, assassinated by command of MOTEUCZOMAH 2 (CC 61:47, CC 63:26–36).
7. Indeterminate lord of Huexotzinco or Tlaxcala. A "prince" of Huexotzinco associated with CALMECAHUA, MATZIN, and TEMAXAHUITZIN, 10:12–13, 10v:9, 11:7. A Tlaxcalan (?) lord associated with COATZIN and TLACOMIHUATZIN, 17v:10.

XICOTENCATL, p.n.

1. Xicotencatl the elder, ruler of the Tlaxcalan borough of Tizatlan and of all Tlaxcala at the time of Cortés' arrival, baptized as Lorenzo Xicotencatl (CC 63:57, Muñoz Camargo 1892:84 [lib. 1 cap. 9]). CM.
2. Axayacatzin Xicotencatl, son of 1 (Muñoz Camargo 1892:84 [lib. 1 cap 9]).
3. Motenehuatzin Xicotencatl, son of 1 and brother of 2 (Muñoz Camargo 1892:92 [lib. 1 cap. 9]). CM (Motenehuatzin).
4. Rodrigo de Castañeda, a soldier in Cortés' army (CDHM 1:432), called "Castañeda Xicotencatl" (FC 12:95:26). CM.
5. Indeterminate Tlaxcalan warrior or leader. 1:14.

XIMOHUACAN, var. XIMOHUAYAN (CM), place where all are shorn, i.e., the dead land, the hereafter (TEZ 436 [cap. 55], FC 3:39:31, DICT). Note that the form *ximohuacan* would be disallowed by Andrews (2003:498). 24v:12. Cf. MICTLAN, QUENAMIHCAN, TOCHAN.

YOHYONTZIN, p.n.

1. Alternate name for NEZAHUALCOYOTL (CHIM 195). 2v:1, 2v:7, 2v:17, 3:10–11, 4:5, 10:8, 26v:9, 32v:14, 34:16, 34v:5, CM.
2. Don Jorge Alvarado Yoyontzin, youngest son of NEZAHUALPILLI and grandson of NEZAHUALCOYOTL, served as *tlatoani* of Acolhuacan for one year ca. 1531 (ACHIM 2:211–15, IXT 2:152, FC 8:10:26, Gibson 1964:170). CM.

Verbs, Particles, and Common Nouns

Romances vocabulary not entered here will be found either in the Concordance to Proper Nouns or in the *Cantares* dictionary (DICT). Single-object transitive verbs are entered with the indefinite form of the (direct) object, TE (human) or TLA (general), e.g., HUIMOLOA:TLA. Definitions are presented in the Translation and accompanying notes.

AHAHUILLOTL, 19v:2.

AHMANA:TE, 5v:4.

AOCCAN, 34:5.

ATTOHUA, 37v:4.

AYATL, see note to 6v:16.

CALTECH, see XOMOLCO CALTECH.

CEN NICAN, 27v:11, 27v:16–17, 42:1.

CHIMALMATLATL, see TEOCUITLACHIMALMATLATL.

COCOLLI, see TEOAXOCHICUAUHCOCOLLI.

COCOLLOTL, 5v:12.

CUALANYOTL, 5v:12.

CUAUHTIN, 8v:8–9, 23v:6, 23v:10, cf. 9:2.

CUAUHTLI, see CUAUHTIN, TEOAXOCHICUAUHCOCOLLI,
XOCHICUAPPILLI.

CUEPONCAN, 30:9.

HUALLALACHIYA, 17:13.

HUALQUIQUIZA, 17:13 (*hualquiquixohua*).

HUEHUEIYA or HUEHUEYA, see note to 31v:2–3.

HUELMATI:TLA, 12v:17.

Appendix 1

Two Versions of the Myth of the Origin of Music

Musical performance is an act of reciprocity between the earthly musician and a sky spirit who may be identified as the supreme deity Tezcatlipoca, the sun, or the Christian *dios* 'God'. As repeatedly stated in the songs themselves, the music "entertains" the earthly lords and princes who hear it, just as it "entertains" the supreme spirit. Occasionally there may be a suggestion that the supernatural source initiates the song, which the human musician "answers," as in *Romances* 37v:2–6: "The swan goes first, and all the rattles and drums answer him." But the usual idea is that the singer 'begins' or 'strikes up' (*pehua*), and the supernatural source 'answers' (*nanquilia*), as in *Cantares* 3:19: *teoquecholme nechnananquilia in nicuicani* 'the spirit swans are answering me the singer'. ("Swans" are companions of the sun; see TRAN 2.1, 5.5, 16.1.) Or *Cantares* 35v:14: *noncuicapehua nicanaya ye'coya moxochiuh ipalnemoani* 'here I strike up a song, and your flowers arrive, O Life Giver'. Thus the act of "beginning," or "striking up," initiates the musical process (see *Romances* songs VIII, XV, XX, XXV, and XXXIII), as set forth in a sixteenth-century myth of origin, the two surviving versions of which are as follows.

1

Now, it's time to be apprised of who this *Tezcatlipuca* is—whom the Indians consider of great importance, being the reason we've spoken of him so frequently. The name is composed of three [terms:] *tezcatl*, which means 'mirror'; *tlepuca*, which in turn is made up of *tletl*, meaning 'light', and *puctli*, 'smoke'; and together they form this name Tezcatlipuca, because it is said he always carries a very bright mirror with him and gives off smoke on account of the incense and other aromatic things he carries. It is also said that this same god created the wind, who appeared as a black figure with a great spine all bloody, a sign of sacrifice, to whom the god *Tezcatlipuca* said: "Come here, go beyond the ocean to the house of the sun, who has many musicians and trumpeters with him that serve him and sing; among whom are some with three feet, others with ears so large they cover their whole body; and, when you get to the edge of the water, call to my nieces *Esacapachtli*, which is a turtle, and to *Acilmatl*, which is half woman, half fish, and to *Altcipatli*, which is the whale, and tell them to form a bridge for you to cross over; and bring me back from the sun's house those musicians with their instruments so you can honor me," and having said this much he took off and was seen no more. Then the wind god went to the edge of the water and called to the ones who have been mentioned, and they came right away and made a bridge, over which he crossed. Seeing him approach, the sun said to his musicians: "Here comes the trickster [*le meschant*]; nobody answer him, for whoever answers him will go with him." These aforesaid musicians were dressed in four colors: white, red, yellow, and green. As soon as he arrived, the wind god called out to them, singing; and one of them answered immediately and went off with him and brought the music that they use at the present time in their dances in honor of their gods, the way we do on the pipe organ.

—translated from the French of André Thévet
(Jonghe 1905:32–33), a mid-sixteenth-century version
of a lost Spanish original (of 1543 per ibid.: 6)

2

[Book II,] Chapter II. *Of how the sun was created and of the death of the gods.*
So, when men had been created and had multiplied, each of the gods took with him, or had with him, certain men as devotees and servants. And since for some years, it is said, there was no sun, the gods got together at a pueblo called Teutiuacan, which is six leagues from Mexico, and built a great fire; and, stationing themselves on four sides of it, these gods told their devotees that whichever one of them was quickest in dashing into the fire would have the honor of being created as the sun; that is, the first one to throw himself into the fire would come out as the sun; and [it is said] that one of them, the bravest, rushed forward and jumped into the fire; and he descended to the infernal regions; and it is said that as they waited to see where he would

come out, they put down quail, locusts, butterflies, and snakes, some of them here, some of them there, as they could not determine which way he would come forth; and finally, unable to guess, they consigned all of these to be sacrificed, which in later times was to become a very prevalent custom in front of their idols; and finally the sun did come forth where it was supposed to; but it stopped and wouldn't go farther. And when the aforesaid gods saw that it wouldn't travel its course, they decided to send Tlotli ['falcon'] as their messenger, to tell him, or order him, to travel the course; and he answered that he would not move from the place where he was until they themselves had been put to death and destroyed; and at that reply, which frightened some and made others angry, one of them, named Citli ['hare'], took a bow and three arrows and shot at the sun, aiming to split his face: the sun ducked and was not hit: he shot another arrow, and the sun dodged, and the same thing happened the third time: and the sun, annoyed, took one of the arrows and shot it back at Citli and split his face [hence the origin of the hare's split lip?], causing his death. Seeing this, the other gods became discouraged, as it was apparent they could not prevail against the sun: and in despair they resigned themselves to being killed, and they all sacrificed each other by [opening] the breast; and the priest of this sacrifice was Xolotl, who opened their breasts with a large knife, killing them, and then killed himself, and each one bequeathed the clothes that they wore, which were mantles, to their devotees in memory of their devotion and friendship. And thus appeased, the sun ran its course. And these devotees, or servants, of the dead gods encased these mantles in certain pieces of wood, and making a slot or perforation in the wood, they inserted, for a heart, some little green stones and snakeskin and jaguar pelt, and this bundle they called *tlaquimilloli*, and each one labeled it with the name of the devil who had given him the mantle, and this was the principal idol that they held in great reverence, and they did not esteem the brutish statues of stone or wood that they made as much as they did these. I make mention here of the aforesaid padre, Fray Andrés de Olmos [the compiler of a (now lost) work on mythology used as the author's source], who found in Tlalmanalco one of these idols wrapped in many mantles to keep it hidden, though these were already half rotted away.

[Book II,] Chapter III. *Of how Tezcatlipuca appeared to a man who was his devotee and sent him to the house of the sun.* It is said that the men who were devotees of these dead gods, who had left them their mantles as memorials, went about with the mantles wrapped around their shoulders, sadly and pensively, looking to see if they could find their gods or if they would appear to them. It is said that the devotee of Tezcatlipuca, who was the principal idol of Mexico, persevering in his devotion, reached the sea coast, where he did appear to him, in three shapes, or forms, and called to him and said, "Come here, you! Since you are such a friend of mine, I want you to go to the house of the sun and bring back singers and instruments so you can make festivities for me, and for this purpose you must call out to the whale, the mermaid, and the turtle, so they can form a bridge that you can walk across." And so, as the bridge was made, and the sun heard him giving out with a song he happened to be singing, the sun warned the people around him and his servants not to answer the song, because whoever answered would have to go with him. And so it occurred that some of them, finding the song mellifluous, did answer him, and he took them away, together with the [skin] drum they call *vevetl* and [the log drum known as] the *tepunaztli;* and this, they say, was the beginning of the festivities and dances that they make for their gods: and the songs they sing in those *areitos* [sacred dances] they consider to be prayers, performing them in concert with a particular melody [*tono*] and choreography [*meneos*], with much concentration and gravity, without any disagreement in the voices or in the dance steps. And they preserve this same synchronization nowadays. But it is much to be advised that they not be allowed to perform the ancient songs, because all of these are filled with memories of idolatry, or be allowed to perform them with diabolical or suspicious insignias which represent the same. And it should be noted, with regard to what has been said above, that the gods killed each other by [opening] the breast, and from this, so they say, came the custom that was later practiced, of killing people as sacrifices, opening the breast with a flint knife and taking out the heart as an offering to their gods.

> —translated from the Spanish in Fray Gerónimo de Mendieta's
> *Historia eclesiástica indiana* (Mendieta 1971:79–81),
> a work completed in 1596 (ibid.: xxiii)

Appendix II

Corrections for the *Cantares* Edition

The following directions, keyed by page and line number, are for correcting errors in *Cantares Mexicanos: Songs of the Aztecs* (CMSA) and its companion volume, *A Nahuatl-English Dictionary and Concordance to the Cantares Mexicanos* (DICT). Items marked with an asterisk appeared in the errata list in the third printing of the *Dictionary* in 2002.

Cantares Mexicanos: Songs of the Aztecs

p. 30, line 2   "calling each other Huexotzincans."   read: "talking to each other as Huexotzincans."

p. 34, line 3 up   kings, as warlords . . . Bethlehem.   read: kings inspiring the return to life of deceased warriors.

p. 37, line 26   names,   read: names:

p. 38, line 7 up   omit: Enduring One(?), Maman

p. 75, line 6 up   omit: except for a "tico coto" in canto D of song 90,

p. 77, lines 6–7   by Fernando Benítez, in which . . . in the *Cantares.*   read: by Fernando Benítez, which, in full performance, *might* have been accompanied by a musical bow with a bridge separating the single string into two contrastingly tuned divisions.

p. 77, lines 14–15   in transcript by Ziehm, was obtained . . . male singer.   read: in transcript by Ziehm, has been enhanced with Ziehm's conjectural reconstruction of the two-tone cadence, using the ti-to-ki-ko notation.

p. 77, lines 1–3 up   Nayarit-Durango region, she . . . agree with mine.   read: Nayarit-Durango region, but leaving open the question of the most usual *Cantares* interval (here shown as a fourth), she conjectures a reading — developed independently, using a quite different approach — that agrees with mine.

p. 79, line 3 up   8b is wrong   read: 11b is wrong

p. 85, line 5 up   R[e]y   read: s[eño]r

p. 85, line 4 up   king   read: lord

p. 87, lines 9–10 up   getting the three . . . as revenants; then   read: getting to the Massacre of the Innocents, an occasion for weeping; then

p. 94, line 10   not convincing. Among the   read: not convincing.⁹ Among the

p. 94, lines 16–18   omit: Observe that song 85, a Chalcan . . . and a Chalcan side.⁹

p. 96, line 3   (58,   read: (56,

p. 100, table, column 1, last line   (26–26v)   read: (26–27v)

p. 119, line 2 up   completely avoided   read: translated only a few of

p. 120, line 6   still another Seler disciple, Gerdt   read: a disciple of Lehmann, Gerdt

p. 143, line 8 up   18   read: 22

p. 150, line 8 up   yan tocnihuan   read: yantocnihuan

p. 151, lines 7–9 up   glorify their . . . on the great road.   read: glorify the blood-and-shoulder toil of those who have accepted flood and blaze. O friends, in Tliliuhquitepec we rise warlike, in Hueyotlipan!

p. 165, lines 3–4   Mat is here! And princes, whirled as flowers there, are making   read: Mat's enclosed in flowers here! And princes there are making

p. 168, line 14   çanitl i   read: çanitli

p. 169, line 13   plumes — yes, a trailing cape   read: plume blouses — yes, trailing capes

p. 177, lines 21–22   we're created, we who've been   read: you're created. We've been

p. 184, line 13   çanitlan   read: çan itlan

p. 191, lines 9–10   briefly pleasured with these hearts of mine. With these I briefly live in happiness, I, Yoyontzin,   read: briefly pleasured. These hearts of mine, they briefly live in happiness, and I'm Yoyontzin,

p. 199, line 4   Tizihuatzin.   read: Tizahuatzin.

p. 217, line 14   In but a day we're gone, in but a night we're shorn   read: By day and by night we're gone, we're shorn

p. 229, line 4 up   the Enduring One,   read: become annoyed,

p. 237, line 15   "Let no one's heart flow out,   read: "Let no one be of two minds,

p. 237, lines 15–16   be below or up above,"   read: hesitate,"

p. 257, line 10 up   princes,   read: children,

p. 257, line 9 up   princes rose   read: children rose

p. 257, line 8 up   spinning *down*.   read: spinning.

p. 257, line 6 up   *princes rose in glory*   read: *children rose in glory*

p. 275, line 18   you arose   read: He was made to suffer

p. 275, line 18   O Jesucristo.   read: and He is Jesucristo.

p. 338, line 14   hual ixiptla   read: huel ixiptla

p. 349, line 13   turepaintings.   read: ture paintings.

p. 373, line 16   our flowers.   read: my flowers.

p. 387, lines 4–5   put out the fire.   read: stir up the fire.

p. 393, line 10 up   Tico etc., on one side   read: tico etc., seven times

p. 395, line 4   On the other side: tico etc.   read: another seven times: tico etc.

p. 415, line 8 up   tico coto tocoti toco toto coti,   read: tito coto tocoti toco toto coti,

p. 433, lines 1–7 up   omit: And in stanza 6 . . . DICT: tepētl.

p. 434, line 13 up   p. 62 (excerpts).   read: p. 62 (excerpts); Seler, "Einige," no. 13.

p. 434, line 5 up   GPN, 2: 88–89.   read: GPN, 2: 88–89; the paragraph that precedes the song is transcribed and translated in Seler, "Einige," p 77.

p. 436, line 23   GPN, 2: 90–93.   read: GPN, 2: 90–93; Seler, "Einige," no. 15 (excerpt).

pp. 436–502, 557   Léon   read: León

p. 446, line 16 up   *R[e]y*   read: *s[eño]r*

p. 448, last line   pp. 270–74.   read: pp. 270–74; Seler, "Einige," no. 21 (canto A).

p. 449, last line   (canto B).   read: (canto B); Seler, "Einige," no. 27 (canto C).

p. 456, line 2 up   gave their lives in battle   read: won glory

p. 457, line 1   we produce them as revenants,   read: we produce our own deceased kings as revenants,

p. 457, lines 1–3   omit: (Just as the three kings . . . with Christ in paradise.)

p. 457, line 20   *We three kings are en route to Bethlehem.*   read: *Like the three kings let us go greet the Christ child in Bethlehem.*

p. 457, line 21   omit: (war deeds)

p. 457, line 15 up   *gave their lives for Christ.*   read: *saved Christ.*

p. 457, lines 12–13 up   There they "prayed" to the virgin (made . . . sky).   read: There they prayed to the Virgin and came away praising Christ (Luke 2:20); by avoiding Herod on their way home, they saved the Christ child from the Massacre of the Innocents (Mat. 2:16, SPC 22v), who, as though killed in combat, rose in glory to the sky.

p. 457, line 11 up   With musical weeping . . . producing revenants. read: Lamentations for the Innocents (Mat. 2:18) entertain the angels.

p. 457, line 9 up   Speaking of dead kings,   read: Speaking of the dead,

p. 473, line 5   eastward   read: westward

p. 476, line 20   27–30).   read: 27–30); Seler, "Einige," no. 63.

p. 479, line 24   pp. 100–107.   read: pp. 100–107; Seler, "Einige," no. 49 (canto A and stanza 22).

p. 504, line 21   quench the flame   read: stir up the flame

p. 508, lines 29–30   omit: (This canto, expressing the thoughts . . . side of the dance floor?)

p. 509, lines 1–2   omit: (This canto, expressing the thoughts . . . side of the dance floor?)

p. 516, after line 19, column 1   add two lines: 1426–1428, Maxtla
                                          1429–1433?, "Ahquenithuiztli"

p. 525, line 14 up   see chap. 12, p. 47;   read: see chap. 12, p. 109;

p. 527, line 25   (Unfortunately . . . source.)   read: (The source is Martín de León in his *Camino del cielo* of 1611, per *Bibliografía*, p. 301.)

p. 527, lines 12–13 up   omit: Less circumspect . . . against ourselves."

p. 531, line 8 up   tzon, zanitl; and   read: tzon; and

p. 531, line 2 up   song 85, cantos C and D.   read: song 84.

p. 532, line 15   chap. 7, p. 287.   read: chap. 7, p. 294.

p. 532, line 20   chap. 64, p. 477.   read: chap. 64, p. 477. Note, however, that the term *supancuicatl* (*xopancuicatl*) appears in FC, book 9, chap. 9, p. 41.

p. 550   add entry: Seler, Eduard. "Einige der 'Cantares Mexicanos,'" *Indiana*, vol. 1 (1973), pp. 73–92.

p. 551, line 5 up   *totlaçonanantzin*   read: *totlaçonantzin*

p. 558, column 1, line 9 up 92 read: 93
p. 558, column 2, line 7 Reproach, 29f read: Reproach, 27f

A Nahuatl-English Dictionary

*cover, line 4 with an Analytical Transcription read: with an Analytic Transcription
*p. 6, line 23 such the one read: such as the one
*p. 20, line 17 up FC: `stopped read: FC: 'stopped
*p. 24, line 7 Ach in tēpillōtl read: Ach in tēcpillōtl
*p. 24, line 23 up cohorts read: companions
p. 24, line 20 up omit: by them
p. 30, after line 10 up add two entries:
AHMANA: MO, to be annoyed (see SIM). 30:3.
AHMANA:TE, to annoy s.o. (SIM). RSNE 5v:4.
p. 45, line 22 DHIST ch. 19 read: DHIST ch. 29.
p. 47, line 8 up Hern read: HERN
p. 48, line 21 up harquebus), 7:2; read: harquebus), 84v:12; āyahuitl onmantoc = the haze is spreading, 7:2;
*p. 53, line 10 3. By means . . . & 4. omit entire line
p. 57, line 17 DHIST ch. 11 p. 9 read: DHIST ch. 11 p. 99.
*p. 60, line 5 Camargo ch. 4 read: Camargo bk. 1, ch. 4
*p. 60, line 12 up techinantlan read: techinantitlan
p. 68, following line 22 add: CEMILHUITL/CENYOHUAL, day and night (MOL). Cemilhuitl on tiyahui[h] ceyohual o xīmo[hu]a = in a day oh! we're gone, in a night oh! one is shorn, 26:12, cf. 46v:4
*p. 69, lines 23-24 omit: ẓan ye qui[h]to#hu#a- . . . it to him
p. 70, line 9-10 up or up above, 32:12. read: or up above (i.e., let no one vacillate?), 32:12.
*p. 71, line 6 1,2000,000 read: 1,200,000
p. 72, lines 6-8 CEYOHUAL, a night . . . cf. 46v:4. read: CEYOHUAL, see CEMILHUITL/CENYOHUAL
*p. 72, line 15 up omit: = his principal concubine
p. 78, lines 4-5 up omit: Syn. CHICOPA.
p. 79, line 14 to one . . . on one side. read: seven times (MOLS 120v chicoppa).

p. 79, line 15   omit: Syn. **CHICO** 1.

*p. 87, line 23   **ICHPŌTZINTLI**):   read: **ICHPŌTZINTLI**); young woman(?).

*p. 87, line 24   a wench (i.e., woman of low class)   read: a young woman

p. 90, line 9   37:8.   read: 14:20, 37:8.

p. 114, line 12   omit: 71:12,

p. 115, line 13   noun, 45:10, 45v:27.   read: noun, 45:10, 45v:27; by female speaker in imitation of male usage?, 79:22.

p. 118, line 17   2. To raise s.o (from the dead). Of Jesus, 42v:28.   omit entire line

p. 118, line 18   3. Human-obj. form of   read: 2. Human-obj. form of

*p. 133, line 10   To subside(?).   read: 1. To fall down, to come falling. RSNE 32v:8. 2. To subside(?).

p. 133, line 10 up   1. Causeway   read: Causeway

p. 133, line 9 up   omit: 6v:16 (with play on 2, below?),

p. 133, lines 6–7 up   omit both lines and replace with new entry: **HUĒI OHTLIPAN**, Hueyotlipan, a Tlaxcalan town (TORQ 1:555). 6v:16.

p. 136, line 5   matrix **huītz**,   read: matrix **nemi**,

*p. 138, line 9   omit: 79v:8,

*p. 138, line 18   omit: ; s.th. wide (MOL)

p. 139, line 13 up   47v:15   read: 47v:5

*p. 146, line 8   omit: 41:2,

*p. 146, line 25   39v:18, 42:4   read: 39v:18, 41:2, 42:4

p. 147, line 16 up   & 25.   read: & 25 & 83:28 & 83v:5.

*p. 148, line 21 up   nocnīhuān, 12:7, 31v:19,   read: mocnīhuān, 12:7; nocnīhuān, 31v:19,

p. 148, line 19 up   omit: 6v:16,

p. 148, line 16 up   antocnīhuān, 6:23, 10:27,   read: antocnīhuān, 6:23, 6v:16, 10:27,

*p. 153, line 4 up   to move one   read: to move oneself

p. 162, line 27   (CAR 504:31), to spin   read: (CAR 504:31), to be twisted (of flrs, **XŌCHITL**, into a garland, **MECATL**) (FC 2:101:17–18), to spin

*p. 170, line 17 up   **ITECH TLAMIA:MO**   read: **ĪTECH TLAMIA: MO**

*p. 175, lines 18–19   omit: , var. **IUHCĀ** (?)

p. 175, line 18 up   from there, 6:12:22;   read: from there, FC 6:12:22;

p. 191, lines 21–22   **MAHMAN**, pret. . . . 30:3.   omit entire two lines.

p. 191, line 3 up   5. To extend . . . **MAHMAN**.   omit entire line.

p. 194, line 4   76:19; read 76:9;

p. 195, line 6 up   omit: , **TZĀHUA** 2

p. 197, line 17 up   **MALĪNA: MO**. 20v:7,   read: **MALĪNA: MO**. To be twisted (of flrs, **XŌCHITL**, into a garland, **MECATL**) (FC 2:101:17–18). 20v:7,

*p. 198, line 3 up   omit: & 28

p. 200, line 3 up   mani here   read: mani = here

*p. 204, line 20   Magdalen   read: Magdalene

p. 210, line 16   (6:100:22),   read: (FC 6:100:22),

p. 211, lines 5–6 up   omit: ; o[m]meya īyōllo, 32:12

p. 212, after line 13   add: **MICHI**, see **MOCHI**.

p. 215, line 1   21:17   read: 21:27

p. 217, last line   ye monamiccan).   read: ye monamiccan, MOLS antaño 'yesteryear').

*p. 222, line 19   62:10   read: 62v:10

*p. 225, lines 21–23   5. Doyenne . . . privaba).   omit all three lines

p. 225, line 24   6. Duenna.   read: 5. Duenna.

*p. 241, line 1   tlāco[h]tli   read: tlāco[h]ti

p. 247, line 15 up   on the other side,   read: another seven times,

*p. 250, line 18   73v:1;   read: 73v:1 (but cf. FC 10:172:13: tlaomepializtli = act or state of having two wives);

p. 250, after line 19 add new entry: **ŌME YŌLLŌTL**, two hearts, i.e., two minds, doubt, indecision (see MOLS dudar). Mācāc ōme-ya īyōllo = let no one be of two minds, 32:12.

*p. 252, line 19 up   + **ĪC**   read: + **²ĪC**

p. 256, line 7   **CEPPA, ĒX-**   read: **CEPPA, CHICOPA, ĒX-**

p. 259, line 15   above, 32:13; pani-*a*   read: above, see **CENTLANI**; pani-*a*

*p. 259, line 18 up   42).   read: 42),

p. 267, line 3   cf. 47v:20,   read: cf. 38:22, 47v:20,

p. 267, line 4   nopiltzin, 24v:11,   read: nopiltzin, 24v:11 (with play on 2, below),

p. 267, line 7   15; topilāhuiltil,   read: 15; tēpilhuā[n], 38:23; topilāhuiltil,

p. 267, lines 17–18   omit: pīpiltzitzinti[n] . . . Cologne), 38:22;

*p. 284, line 15 up   78:14 & 17   read: 78v:14 & 17

p. 297, line 21   78:16. See **TETĒCA**:   read: 78:16; āyahuitl moteca = the vapor (i.e., smoke) rolls (from a harquebus), 84v:12. See **TETĒCA**:

*p. 298, line 20   upon the ciy,   read: upon the city,

*p. 298, line 17 up   See -**TECH AHCI**,   read: See **ĪTECH TLAMIA: MO, -TECH AHCI**,

*p. 306, line 18 up   **TĒNTETL**, labret . . . 2.   omit entire line

p. 317, line 19 up   **TĒUHTLI?**),   read: **TEUHTLI?**),

*p. 317, line 18 up   74:17   read: 74v:17

*p. 320, line 18 up   **TLAHCĀUH**   read: **TIAHCĀUH**

*p. 325, line 5   military commander   read: high executive

*p. 325, line 4 up   6:127:2;   read: 6:127:2);

*p. 328, line 12   6: 24v:7,   read: 6; 24v:7,

*p. 330, line 15 up   FC 6:16:12   read: FC 6:19:12

p. 358, line 11   390). See **TLĪLIUHQUI TEPĒCATL**.   read: 390). 6v:16.

p. 358, lines 12–14   **TLĪLIUHQUI TEPĒCATL** . . . 6v:16.   omit all three lines

*p. 363, line 16   such Aztec cities   read: such cities

p. 367, line 25   TORQ 1:404). 54:5.   read: TORQ 1:404, called doña Marina in Diaz del Castillo ch. 36). 54:5. Cf. **DOÑA**.

p. 367,   before line 2 up   add entry: **TŌNĒHUA:TĒ**, to torment s.o. (MOL). Tōnēhualōc, 42v:28.

*p. 368, line 19 up   extinguish   read: stoke

p. 372, line 21   60:2.   read: 60:2; ontzāuhti[h]cac (error for ontzāucti[h]cac?), 10v:17.

p. 373, lines 14–18   **TZĀHUA** 1. To . . . see **MALĪNA**.   read: **TZĀHUA**, to spin (thread) (MOL). 72v:5.

*p. 377, lines 10–11   omit: **CIHUĀTZINTLI**,

p. 379, line 23 up   the life, es-   read: the life (FC 2:114:20), es-

*p. 384, line 15   **MOTĒUCZŌMAH** 1   read: **MOTĒUCZŌMAH** 2

*p. 385, line 8 up   11v:3   read: 11v:8

*p. 387, line 18 up   **XI**-   read: **XI**

*p. 387, line 4 up   Itzlolinqui   read: Itztlolinqui

*p. 389, line 21   (OLM 223)   read: (OLM 223, FC 6:228)

p. 395, line 25   (28v:24), var. comb.   read: (28v:24), **XŌCHI** (3v:7); var. comb.

p. 396, line 2 up   or flr (MOLS: read: or flr, petal (MOLS:

*p. 398, line 19 up   2:1   read: FC 9:41:14 (supancuicatl), 2:1

*p. 404, line 9   they   read: then

p. 404, lines 1–2 up   omit: Tocnīhuān . . . in tiyāōtēhua[h] = our friends with whom we rise warlike, 6v:16.

*p. 407, line 10   "ser'   read: "ser"

*p. 407, line 14   **QUETZAL:MO**   read: **QUETZA:MO**

p. 409, line 20   ahtiyécōz   read: ahticyécōz

p. 417, lines 29–30   omit: 32:12 (let no one's heart flow out),

p. 417, end of page, add: 9. See **ŌME YŌLLŌTL**.

*p. 420, line 19 up   omit: See **ZANITL**.

*p. 420, line 8 up   omit: , **ZANITL**, etc.

*p. 421, line 4   **ZANITL** . . . Ca-*n*   read: **ZANITLI**, net blouse (FC 10:181n). Ca-*n*

*p. 421, lines 5–7   ẓanitl i . . . 17:12.   read: ẓanitli quetzalli-ẏa = indeed they are plume blouses, 12:17.

p. 441, line 11 up   20   read: 26

p. 445, lines 10–12 up   ya̱n tocnīhuān tlīliuhqui tepēca[h] in tiyāōtēhua[h] huēi o[h]tlipan-a̱   read: y̱-antocnīhuān tlīliuhqui tepēc-a̱ in tiyāōtēhua[h] huēi o[h]tlipan-a̱

*p. 460, line 9   ẓanitl i   read: ẓanitli

*p. 473, last line   ẓanitl-an   read: ẓan ītlan

p. 478, line 11 up   #yc#[ye]   read: yc

p. 510, line 8 up   mahman-a̱   read: mahmana

p. 516, line 3 up   o[m]meya   read: ōme-y̱a

p. 549, line 5   tonēhualōc   read: tōnēhualōc

p. 580, after line 8   add (centered): folio 52v

*p. 704, line 5   For the arc . . . below.   omit entire line

*p. 710, line 11 up   moteyotica   read: moteyotico

p. 712, line 18   CAR 414   read: CAR 424

*p. 718, line 22 up   omit: 41:22,

p. 724, lines 22–24   omit: In describing a mirror . . . appear").

p. 725, lines 21–24   omit: For an unusual specimen . . . clause, see 6v:16.

*p. 737, before ANTIG   add: AND Andrews, *Introduction to Classical Nahuatl*

Bibliography

Source Abbreviations

ACHIM   Anderson and Schroeder, *Codex Chimalpahin*

AUB   Dibble, *Historia de la nación mexicana […] Códice de 1576 (Códice Aubin)*

CARO   Carochi, *Arte de la lengua mexicana*

CC   Codex Chimalpopoca, in Bierhorst 1992a and 1992b

CDHM   García Icazbalceta, *Colección de documentos para la historia de México*

CF   Sahagún, *Códice florentino*

CHIM   Chimalpahin, *Relaciones originales de Chalco Amaquemecan*

CM   Codex Cantares Mexicanos, in Bierhorst 1985a

CMSA   Bierhorst, *Cantares Mexicanos: Songs of the Aztecs*

CONC   Concordance to Proper Nouns (this volume)

DHIST   Durán, *Historia de las Indias*, vol. 2

DICT   Bierhorst, *A Nahuatl-English Dictionary*

FC   Sahagún, *Florentine Codex* (Anderson and Dibble ed.), 1st ed. Cited by book, page, and line nos. (e.g., FC 3:47:1–19)

FFCC   Sahagún, *Florentine Codex*, 2d ed.

GN   Grammatical Notes, in Bierhorst 1992a

GRAM   Grammatical Notes in Bierhorst 1985b

HG   Sahagún, *Historia general de las cosas de Nueva España* (Garibay ed.)

IXT   Alva Ixtlilxóchitl, *Obras históricas* (O'Gorman ed.)

KHTC   Kirchhoff et al., *Historia tolteca-chichimeca*

LASO   Sousa et al., *The Story of Guadalupe*

LASSO   Facsimile of the 1649 ed. of Lasso (or Laso) de la Vega's *Huei tlamahuiçoltica*, in Velázquez 1926

MEX   "Tezozomoc," *Crónica mexicáyotl*

MOL   The Nahuatl-Spanish section of Molina's *Vocabulario*

MOLS   The Spanish-Nahuatl section of Molina's *Vocabulario*

RSNE   "Romances de los señores de la Nueva España"

SIM   Siméon, *Dictionnaire de la langue nahuatl ou mexicaine*
SPC   Sahagún, *Psalmodia christiana* (1583)
TEZ   Tezozomoc, *Crónica mexicana*
TORQ   Torquemada, *Monarquía indiana* (1975 ed.)
TRAN   On the Translation of Aztec Poetry (this volume)
UAH   Mengin, "Unos annales históricos de la nación mexicana"
ZCHIM   Zimmermann, *Die Relationen Chimapahin's*

References

Alphonse, Ephraim S. 1956. *Guaymí Grammar and Dictionary with Some Ethnological Notes.* Bureau of American Ethnology, Bulletin 162. Washington, DC: U.S. Government Printing Office.

Alva, Bartolomé de. ca. 1640. "Comedias en mexicano" [Nahuatl adaptations of three Spanish plays: (1) Calderón's "El gran teatro del mundo"; (2) "El animal profeta," dated 1640 and attributed to Lope de Vega; and (3) Lope's "La madre de la mejor," dedicated to Horacio Carochi]. Mexican MS 462, Bancroft Library, University of California, Berkeley. See Sell, Wright, and Burkhart 2008.

Alva Ixtlilxóchitl, Fernando de. 1975–77. *Obras históricas.* Ed. Edmundo O'Gorman. 2 vols. Mexico City: Universidad Nacional Autónoma de México.

Anderson, Arthur J. O., Frances Berdan, and James Lockhart. 1976. *Beyond the Codices: The Nahua View of Colonial Mexico.* Berkeley: University of California Press.

Anderson, Arthur J. O., and Susan Schroeder. 1997. *Codex Chimalpahin.* Vols. 1 and 2. Norman: University of Oklahoma Press.

Andrews, J. Richard. 1975. *Introduction to Classical Nahuatl.* Austin: University of Texas Press.

———. 2003. *Introduction to Classical Nahuatl.* Rev. ed. Norman: University of Oklahoma Press.

Arzápalo Marín, Ramón. 1987. *El ritual de los bacabes: Edición facsimilar con transcripción rítmica, traducción, notas, índice, glosario y cómputos estadísticas.* Mexico City: Universidad Nacional Autónoma de México.

Bahr, Donald, Lloyd Paul, and Vincent Joseph. 1997. *Ants and Orioles: Showing the Art of Pima Poetry.* Salt Lake City: University of Utah Press.

Barrera Vásquez, Alfredo. 1980. *Diccionario maya Cordemex.* Mérida, Yucatán: Ediciones Cordemex.

Bierhorst, John. 1985a. *Cantares Mexicanos: Songs of the Aztecs.* Stanford, CA: Stanford University Press.

———. 1985b. *A Nahuatl-English Dictionary and Concordance to the Cantares Mexi-*

canos with an Analytic Transcription and Grammatical Notes. Stanford, CA: Stanford University Press. The third printing, 2002, has an errata list.

———. 1992a. *Codex Chimalpopoca: The Text in Nahuatl with a Glossary and Grammatical Notes.* Tucson: University of Arizona Press.

———. 1992b. *History and Mythology of the Aztecs: The Codex Chimalpopoca.* Tucson: University of Arizona Press.

———. 1994. *The Way of the Earth: Native America and the Environment.* New York: William Morrow.

———. 2001. "Cantares Mexicanos." In *The Oxford Encyclopedia of Mesoamerican Cultures,* ed. Davíd Carrasco, pp. 139–41. New York: Oxford University Press.

———. 2002. *The Mythology of Mexico and Central America.* 2d ed., rev. New York: Oxford University Press.

———. In press. "Translating an Esoteric Idiom: The Case of Aztec Poetry." In *Born in the Blood: On Native American Translation,* ed. Brian Swann. Lincoln: University of Nebraska Press.

Brinton, Daniel G. 1890. *Essays of an Americanist.* Philadelphia: Porter & Coates.

Brotherston, Gordon. 1997. Review of Louise M. Burkhart's *Holy Wednesday: A Nahuatl Drama from Early Colonial Mexico. Nahua Newsletter* 23:12–15.

Brundage, Burr Cartwright. 1972. *A Rain of Darts: The Mexica Aztecs.* Austin: University of Texas Press.

Bunzel, Ruth L. 1932. "Zuni Ritual Poetry." In *Forty-sixth Annual Report of the Bureau of American Ethnology* [...] *1928–1929,* pp. 611–835. Washington, DC: Smithsonian Institution.

Burkhart, Louise M. 1988. "The Solar Christ in Nahuatl Doctrinal Texts of Early Colonial Mexico." *Ethnohistory* 35:234–56.

———. 1989. *The Slippery Earth: Nahua-Christian Moral Dialogue in Sixteenth-Century Mexico.* Tucson: University of Arizona Press.

———. 2001. *Before Guadalupe: The Virgin Mary in Early Colonial Nahuatl Literature.* Albany and Austin: Institute for Mesoamerican Studies, State University of New York/University of Texas Press.

Cantares Mexicanos. See Bierhorst 1985a.

Carmack, Robert. 1973. *Quichean Civilization.* Berkeley: University of California Press.

———. 1988. *Harvest of Violence: The Maya Indians and the Guatemalan Crisis.* Norman: University of Oklahoma Press.

Carochi, Horacio. 1983. *Arte de la lengua mexicana* [...] *edición facsimilar de la publicada por Juan Ruyz en la ciudad de México, 1645.* Introductory study by Miguel León-Portilla. Mexico City: Universidad Nacional Autónoma de México.

———. 2001. *Grammar of the Mexican Language with an Explanation of Its Adverbs*

(*1645*). Ed. and trans. James Lockhart. Stanford, CA: Stanford University Press.

Carrasco, Davíd. 1990. *Religions of Mesoamerica: Cosmovision and Ceremonial Centers*. Prospect Heights, IL: Waveland Press.

Castillo F., Víctor M. 1972. *Nezahualcóyotl: Crónica y pinturas de su tiempo*. Texcoco: Gobierno del Estado de México.

Castro, Felipe. 1996. *La rebelión de los indios y la paz de los españoles*. Tlalpan (D.F.) and Mexico City: Centro de Investigaciones y Estudios Superiores en Antropología Social/Instituto Nacional Indigenista.

Ceely, John. 1994. *To Feed Earth and Sun: Songs of the Mexica Aztecs*. [Oakland, CA: John Ceely.]

Cervantes de Salazar, Francisco. 1985. *Crónica de la Nueva España*. Mexico City: Porrúa.

Chimalpahin Cuauhtlehuanitzin, [Domingo] Francisco de San Antón Muñón. 1965. *Relaciones originales de Chalco Amaquemecan*. Ed. S. Rendón. Mexico City: Fondo de Cultura Económica.

———. 2006. See Muñón Chimalpahin Quauhtlehuanitzin, Domingo de San Antón.

Clavijero, Francisco Javier. 1958–59. *Historia antigua de México*. Ed. Mariano Cuevas. 2d ed., rev. 4 vols. Mexico City: Porrúa.

Cobo, Bernabé. 1979. *History of the Inca Empire*. Trans. Roland Hamilton. Austin: University of Texas Press.

———. 1990. *Inca Religion and Customs*. Trans. Roland Hamilton. Austin: University of Texas Press.

Códice Ramírez, See "Relación del origen de los indios que habitan esta Nueva España según sus historias."

Códice Telleriano-Remensis. 1964. In *Antigüedades de México*, ed. José Corona Núñez, vol. 1, pp. 151–337. Mexico City: Secretaría de Hacienda y Crédito Público.

———. 1995. In Quiñones Keber 1995:3–104.

Códice Vaticano 3738 [i.e., Codex Vaticanus A = Codex Ríos]. 1964. In *Antigüedades de México*, ed. José Corona Núñez, vol. 3, pp. 7–313. Mexico City: Secretaría de Hacienda y Crédito Público.

Conquistador Anónimo. 1971. "Relación de algunas cosas de la Nueva España, y de la gran ciudad de Temistitán México." In *Colección de documentos para la historia de México*, ed. Joaquín García Icazbalceta, vol. 1, pp. 368–98. Mexico City: Porrúa.

Cortés, Hernán. 1986. *Letters from Mexico*. Trans. and ed. Anthony Pagden. New Haven: Yale University Press.

Curtis, Natalie. 1968. *The Indians' Book*. New York: Dover. Reprint of the 1923 ed.

Damrosch, David. 1993. "The Aesthetics of Conquest: Aztec Poetry before and after Cortés." In *New World Encounters,* ed. Stephen Greenblatt, pp. 139–58. Berkeley: University of California Press.

Davenport, Basil, ed. 1951. *The Portable Roman Reader.* New York: Viking Press.

Davies, Nigel. 1977. *The Toltecs until the Fall of Tula.* Norman: University of Oklahoma Press.

Densmore, Frances. 1918. *Teton Sioux Music.* Bureau of American Ethnology, Bulletin 61. Washington, DC: U.S. Government Printing Office.

————. 1929. *Pawnee Music.* Bureau of American Ethnology, Bulletin 93. Washington, DC: U.S. Government Printing Office.

Díaz del Castillo, Bernal. 1956. *The Discovery and Conquest of Mexico 1517–1521.* Ed. Genaro García. Trans. A. P. Maudslay. New York: Farrar, Straus & Giroux.

————. 1976. *Historia verdadera de la conquista de la Nueva España.* 11th ed. Mexico City: Porrúa.

Dibble, Charles E. 1963. *Historia de la nación mexicana: Reproducción a todo color del Códice de 1576 (Códice Aubin).* Madrid: José Porrúa Turanzas.

"Discursos en mexicano" [i.e., "Bancroft Dialogues" = "Huehuetlatolli documento A"]. Mexican MS 458, Bancroft Library, University of California, Berkeley.

Doctrina cristiana en lengua española y mexicana por los religiosos de la Orden de Santo Domingo. 1944. Colección de incunables americanos, siglo XVI, vol. 1. Madrid: Ediciones Cultura Hispánica. Facsimile of the 1548 ed.

Dorsey, J. Owen. 1888. "Osage Traditions." In *Sixth Annual Report of the Bureau of [American] Ethnology, 1884–85,* pp. 373–97. Washington, DC: Smithsonian Institution.

Dowling, Lee H. 1994. "The Colonial Period." In *Mexican Literature: A History,* ed. David William Foster. Austin: University of Texas Press.

Durán, Diego de. 1964. *The Aztecs: The History of the Indies of New Spain.* Ed. Doris Heyden and Fernando Horcasitas, with an introduction by Ignacio Bernal. New York: Orion Press.

————. 1967. *Historia de las Indias de Nueva España e islas de la tierra firme.* Ed. Angel M. Garibay K. Vol. 1: *Libro de los ritos y ceremonias . . . and El calendario antigua.* Vol. 2: *Historia.* Mexico City: Porrúa.

————. 1971. *Book of the Gods and Rites* and *The Ancient Calendar.* Ed. Fernando Horcasitas and Doris Heyden, with a foreword by Miguel León-Portilla. Norman: University of Oklahoma Press.

————. 1994. *The History of the Indies of New Spain.* Ed. Doris Heyden. Norman: University of Oklahoma Press.

Espinosa, Aurelio M. 1972. "Spanish Ballad." In *Standard Dictionary of Folklore, Mythology, and Legend,* ed. Maria Leach, pp. 1058–61. New York: Funk & Wagnalls.

————. 1985. *The Folklore of Spain in the American Southwest.* Ed. J. Manuel Espinosa. Norman: University of Oklahoma Press.

Foster, George M. 1945. *Sierra Popoluca Folkore and Beliefs.* University of California Publications in American Archaeology and Ethnology, vol. 42, no. 2. Berkeley: University of California Press.

García Granados, Rafael. 1952–53. *Diccionario biográfico de historia antigua de Méjico.* 3 vols. Mexico City: Instituto de Historia.

García Icazbalceta, Joaquín. 1886. *Bibliografía mexicana del siglo XVI, primera parte: Catálogo razonado de libros impresos en México de 1539 a 1600.* Mexico City: Librería Andrade y Morales.

————. 1941. *Nueva colección de documentos para la historia de México.* 3 vols. Mexico City: Salvador Chávez Hayhoe.

————. 1947. *Don fray Juan de Zumárraga.* 4 vols. Mexico City: Porrúa.

————. 1971. *Colección de documentos para la historia de México.* 2 vols. Mexico City: Porrúa. Reprint of 1858–66 ed.

————. 1981. *Bibliografía mexicana del siglo XVI: Catálogo razonado de libros impresos en México de 1539 a 1600.* 2d ed., rev. Mexico City: Fondo de Cultura Económica.

Garcilaso de la Vega, El Inca. 1966. *Royal Commentaries of the Incas and General History of Peru, Part One.* Trans. Harold V. Livermore. Austin: University of Texas Press.

Garibay K., Angel M. 1943. "Huehuetlatolli, documento A." *Tlalocan* 1:31–53.

————. 1953–54. *Historia de la literatura náhuatl.* 2 vols. Mexico City: Porrúa.

————. 1961. *Llave del náhuatl.* Rev. ed. Mexico City: Porrúa.

————. 1964. *Poesía náhuatl I: Romances de los señores de la Nueva España, manuscrito de Juan Bautista de Pomar, Tezcoco, 1582.* Mexico City: Universidad Nacional Autónoma de México.

————. 1965. *Poesía náhuatl II: Cantares mexicanos, manuscrito de la Biblioteca Nacional de México.* Part 1. Mexico City: Universidad Nacional Autónoma de México.

Gibson, Charles. 1964. *The Aztecs under Spanish Rule.* Stanford, CA: Stanford University Press.

————. 1967. *Tlaxcala in the Sixteenth Century.* Stanford, CA: Stanford University Press. Originally published 1952.

————, and John B. Glass. 1975. "A Census of Middle American Prose Manuscripts in the Native Historical Tradition." In *Handbook of Middle American Indians* (Robert Wauchope, general ed.), vol. 15, part 4, pp. 322–400. Austin: University of Texas Press.

González Peña, Carlos. 1968. *History of Mexican Literature.* Trans. Gusta Barfield Nance and Florene Johnson Dunstan. 3d ed., rev. Dallas: Southern Methodist University Press.

Graulich, Michel. 1989. "Miccailhuitl: The Aztec Festivals of the Deceased." *Numen* 36:43–71.

Guazzo, Stefano. 1993. *La civil conversazione.* Ed. Amedeo Quondam. 2 vols. Modena: Panini.

Hassig, Ross. 1988. *Aztec Warfare: Imperial Expansion and Political Control.* Norman: University of Oklahoma Press.

Hernández, Francisco. 1945. *Antigüedades de la Nueva España.* Ed. Joaquín García Pimentel. Mexico City: Pedro Robredo.

Heyden, Doris. 1985. *Mitología y simbolismo de la flora en el México prehispánico.* Mexico City: Universidad Nacional Autónoma de México.

Hill, Jane H., and Robert E. MacLaury. 1995. "The Terror of Montezuma: Aztec History, Vantage Theory, and the Category of 'Person.'" In *Language and the Cognitive Construal of the World,* ed. John R. Taylor and Robert E. MacLaury. Berlin and New York: Mouton de Gruyter.

Jonghe, Edouard de, ed. 1905. "Histoyre du Mechique: manuscrit français inédit du XVIᵉ siècle." *Journal de la Société des Américanistes de Paris,* n.s. 2:1–41.

Karttunen, Frances. 1983. *An Analytical Dictionary of Nahuatl.* Austin: University of Texas Press.

Karttunen, Frances, and James Lockhart. 1976. *Nahuatl in the Middle Years: Language Contact Phenomena in Texts of the Colonial Period.* University of California Publications in Linguistics, vol. 85. Berkeley: University of California Press.

———. 1980. "La estructura de la poesía náhuatl vista por sus variantes." *Estudios de Cultura Náhuatl* 14:15–64.

———. 1987. *The Art of Nahuatl Speech: The Bancroft Dialogues.* Los Angeles: UCLA Latin American Center, University of California.

Keats, John. 1951. *The Complete Poetry and Selected Prose.* Ed. Harold Edgar Briggs. New York: Modern Library.

Kernan, Alvin. 1990. *The Death of Literature.* New Haven: Yale University Press.

Kilpatrick, Jack Frederick, and Anna Gritts Kilpatrick. 1965. *Walk in Your Soul: Love Incantations of the Oklahoma Cherokees.* Dallas: Southern Methodist University Press.

———. 1967. *Run toward the Nightland: Magic of the Oklahoma Cherokees.* Dallas: Southern Methodist University Press.

Kirchhoff, Paul, Lina Odena Güemes, and Luis Reyes García, eds. 1976. *Historia tolteca-chichimeca* [i.e., Annals of Cuauhtinchan]. Mexico City: Instituto Nacional de Antropología e Historia.

Laughlin, Robert M. 1980. *Of Shoes and Ships and Sailing Wax: Sundries from Zinacantán.* Washington, DC: Smithsonian Institution Press.

[Law, Howard.] *Sahagún's Florentine Codex Concordance (Computerized Version).* Microfilm Collection of Manuscripts on American Indian Cultural Anthropology, series 13, nos. 80–91. 12 vols. Chicago: University of Chicago Library, 1970–72.

Lehmann, Walter. 1974. *Die Geschichte der Königreiche von Colhuacan und Mexico.* Quellenwerke zur alten Geschichte Amerikas, vol. 1. 2d printing with list of errata by Gerdt Kutscher. Stuttgart: Kohlhammer.

León, Martín de. 1611. *Camino del cielo en lengua mexicana.* Mexico City: Diego López Dávalos.

León-Portilla, Miguel. 1967. *Trece poetas del mundo azteca.* Mexico City: Universidad Nacional Autónoma de México.

———. 1992. *Fifteen Poets of the Aztec World.* Norman: University of Oklahoma Press. Re-edition of León-Portilla 1967, in English, with revisions.

Lockhart, James. 1991. *Nahuas and Spaniards: Postconquest Central Mexican History and Philology.* Stanford, CA: Stanford University Press.

———. 1992. *The Nahuas after the Conquest: A Social and Cultural History of the Indians of Central Mexico, Sixteenth through Eighteenth Centuries.* Stanford, CA: Stanford University Press.

López de Gómara, Francisco. 1964. *Cortés: The Life of the Conqueror [Historia de la conquista de México].* Trans. Lesley Byrd Simpson. Berkeley: University of California Press.

———. 1988. *Historia de la conquista de México.* Mexico City: Porrúa.

Lowie, Robert H. 1933. "Crow Prayers." *American Anthropologist,* n.s. 35:433–42.

———. 1939. "Ethnographic Notes on the Washo." In *University of California Publications in American Archaeology and Ethnology,* vol. 36, pp. 301–52. Berkeley: University of California Press.

———. 1956. *The Crow Indians.* New York: Holt, Rinehart & Winston. Reissue of 1935 ed.

Matthews, Washington. 1969. *Navaho Legends.* New York: Kraus. Reprint of 1897 ed.

Méndez Plancarte, Alfonso, ed. 1964. *Poetas novohispanos, primer siglo (1521–1621).* 2d ed. Mexico City: Universidad Nacional Autónoma de México.

Mendieta, Gerónimo de. 1971. *Historia eclesiástica indiana.* Mexico City: Porrúa.

Mengin, Ernst. 1939. "Unos annales históricos de la nación mexicana: Die Manuscrits mexicains nr. 22 und 22 bis der Bibliothèque Nationale de Paris" [i.e., Anales de Tlatelolco]. *Baessler-Archiv* (Berlin) 22, nos. 2–3.

Molina, Alonso de. 1970. *Vocabulario en lengua castellana y mexicana y mexicana y castellana.* Mexico City: Porrúa.

Mooney, James. 1891. "The Sacred Formulas of the Cherokees." In *Seventh Annual Report of the Bureau of [American] Ethnology [...] 1885–1886,* pp. 301–97. Washington, DC: Smithsonian Institution.

————. 1932. *The Swimmer Manuscript: Cherokee Sacred Formulas and Medicinal Prescriptions.* Ed. Frans M. Olbrechts. Bureau of American Ethnology, Bulletin 99. Washington, DC: Smithsonian Institution.

Motolinía [Fray Toribio de Benavente]. 1971a. "Historia de los indios de la Nueva España." In *Colección de documentos para la historia de México,* ed. Joaquín García Icazbalceta, vol. 1, pp. 1–249. Mexico City: Porrúa. Reprint of 1858 ed.

————. 1971b. *Memoriales o libro de las cosas de la Nueva España y de los naturales de ella.* Ed. Edmundo O'Gorman. Mexico City: Universidad Nacional Autónoma de México.

MS 1628-bis. Biblioteca Nacional, Mexico City.

Muñón Chimalpahin Quauhtlehuanitzin, Domingo de San Antón. 2006. *Annals of His Time: Don Domingo de San Antón Muñón Chimalpahin Quauhtlehuanitzin.* Ed. James Lockhart, Susan Schroeder, and Doris Namala. Stanford, CA: Stanford University Press.

Muñoz Camargo, Diego. 1892. *Historia de Tlaxcala.* Mexico City: Secretaría de Fomento.

Nicholson, H. B. 1971. "Religion in Pre-Hispanic Central Mexico." In *Handbook of Middle American Indians* (Robert Wauchope, general ed.), vol. 10, pt. 1, pp. 395–446. Austin: University of Texas Press.

Olmos, Andrés de. 1972. *Arte para aprender la lengua mexicana.* Ed. Rémi Siméon. Guadalajara: Edmundo Aviña Levy. Reprint of 1875 ed.

Osorio Romero, Ignacio. 1980. *Floresta de gramática, poética y retórica en Nueva España (1521–1767).* Mexico City: Universidad Nacional Autónoma de México.

Padden, R. C. 1970. *The Hummingbird and the Hawk.* New York: Harper & Row.

Parmentier, Richard J. 1979. "The Mythological Triangle: Poseyemu, Montezuma, and Jesus in the Pueblos." In *Handbook of North American Indians* (William C. Sturtevant, general ed.), vol. 9 (*Southwest,* volume ed. Alfonso Ortiz), pp. 609–22. Washington, DC: Smithsonian Institution Press.

Paso y Troncoso, Francisco del, ed. 1953. *Tratado de las idolatrías, supersticiones, dioses, ritos, hechicerías y otras costumbres gentílicas de las razas aborígenes de México.* 2 vols. 2d ed., enlarged. Mexico City: Ediciones Fuente Cultural (Librería Navarro).

Pasztory, Esther. 1998. *Aztec Art.* Norman: University of Oklahoma Press.

Patch, Robert W. 1998. "Culture, Community, and 'Rebellion' in the Yucatec Maya Uprising of 1761." In *Native Resistance and the Pax Colonial in New Spain,* ed. Susan Schroeder, pp. 67–83. Lincoln: University of Nebraska Press.

Peña, Margarita, ed. 2004. *Flores de baria poesía: Cancionero novohispano del siglo XVI.* 3rd ed., rev. Mexico City: Fondo de Cultura Económica.

Pérez de Ribas, Andrés. 1944. *Historia de los triunfos de nuestra santa fe entre gentes las más bárbaras.* . . . 3 vols. Mexico City: Editorial Layac. Originally published 1645.

Ponce, Don Pedro. 1984. "Brief Relation of the Gods and Rites of Heathenism." Trans. J. Richard Andrews and Ross Hassig. In Ruiz de Alarcón 1984:211–18.

Pope, Alexander. 1956. *Collected Poems.* Ed. Bonamy Dobrée. London and New York: J. M. Dent/E. P. Dutton.

Procesos de residencia, instruídos contra Pedro de Alvarado y Nuño de Guzmán. 1847. Ed. J. F. Ramírez. Mexico City: n.p.

Quiñones Keber, Eloise. 1995. *Codex Telleriano-Remensis: Ritual, Divination, and History in a Pictorial Aztec Manuscript.* Austin: University of Texas Press.

"Relación del origen de los indios que habitan esta Nueva España según sus historias" [Códice Ramírez]. 1975. In Hernando Alvarado Tezozomoc, *Crónica mexicana,* ed. Manuel Orozco y Berra, pp. 17–92. Mexico City: Porrúa. Reprint of 1878 ed.

Rhodes, Willard. n.d. "Music of the American Indian: Kiowa." Booklet accompanying Library of Congress phonograph album AFS-L35. Washington, DC: Library of Congress, Archive of Folk Song.

Ricard, Robert. 1966. *The Spiritual Conquest of Mexico.* Trans. Lesley Byrd Simpson. Berkeley: University of California Press. Originally published as *Conquête spirituelle de Mexique,* 1933.

"Romances de los señores de la Nueva España." MS CDG-980 (G-59), Nettie Lee Benson Latin American Collection, University of Texas Library, Austin.

Ross, John, and Frank Bardacke, eds. 1995. *Shadows of Tender Fury: The Letters and Communiqués of Subcomandante Marcos and the Zapatista Army of National Liberation.* New York: Monthly Review Press.

Roys, Ralph L. 1965. *Ritual of the Bacabs.* Norman: University of Oklahoma Press.

Ruiz de Alarcón, Hernando. 1953. "Tratado de las supersticiones y costumbres gentílicas que oy viven entre los indios naturales desta Nueva España." In Paso y Troncoso 1953 2:17–180.

———. 1982. *Aztec Sorcerers in Seventeenth-Century Mexico: The Treatise on Superstitions.* Ed. Michael D. Coe and Gordon Whittaker. Albany and Austin: Institute for Mesoamerican Studies, State University of New York at Albany/University of Texas Press.

———. 1984. *Treatise on the Heathen Superstitions That Today Live among the Indians* [. . .] Ed. J. Richard Andrews and Ross Hassig. Norman: University of Oklahoma Press.

Sahagún, Bernardino de. 1583. *Psalmodia christiana, y sermonario de los sanctos del año, en lengua mexicana.* Mexico City: Pedro Ocharte.

———. 1950–83. *Florentine Codex: General History of the Things of New Spain.* Ed.

Arthur J. O. Anderson and Charles E. Dibble. Parts 1–13 (introductory volume and books 1–12). Books 1–3 and 12. 2d ed., rev., 1970–81. Santa Fe and Salt Lake City: School of American Research/University of Utah Press.

————. 1969. *Historia general de las cosas de Nueva España.* Ed. Angel M. Garibay K. 4 vols. 2d ed. Mexico City: Porrúa.

————. 1971. *A History of Ancient Mexico.* Trans. Fanny R. Bandelier. Detroit: Blaine Ethridge. Reprint of 1932 ed.

————. 1979. *Códice florentino.* 3 vols. Mexico City: Secretaría de Gobernación.

————. 1993. *Psalmodia christiana.* Trans. Arthur J. O. Anderson. Salt Lake City: University of Utah Press.

————. 1997. *Primeros Memoriales: Paleography of Nahuatl Text and English Translation.* Ed. Thelma Sullivan et al. Norman: University of Oklahoma Press.

Sandstrom, Alan R. 1991. *Corn Is Our Blood: Culture and Ethnic Identity in a Contemporary Aztec Village.* Norman: University of Oklahoma Press.

Sarmiento de Gamboa, Pedro. 1965. "Historia de los incas" [Historia índica]. In *Biblioteca de autores españoles,* ed. Carmelo Sáenz de Santa María, vol. 4. Madrid: Atlas.

Schoolcraft, H. R. 1845. *Oneóta, or Characteristics of the Red Race of America.* New York: Wiley & Putnam.

Schultze-Jena, Leonhard. 1957. *Alt-Aztekische Gesänge.* Stuttgart: W. Kohlhammer Verlag.

Seler, Eduard. 1973. "Einige der 'Cantares Mexicanos.'" *Indiana: Beiträge zur Völker und Sprachenkunde, Archäologie und Anthropologie des Indianischen Amerika* 1:73–92.

Sell, Barry D., Louise M. Burkhart, and Stafford Poole, eds. 2006. *Nahuatl Theater Volume 2: Our Lady of Guadalupe.* Norman: University of Oklahoma Press.

Sell, Barry D., Elizabeth R. Wright, and Louise M. Burkhart, eds. 2008. *Nahuatl Theater Volume 3: Spanish Golden Age Drama in Mexican Translation* [Comedias en mexicano]. Norman: University of Oklahoma Press. See Alva ca. 1640.

Shaw, Mary, ed. 1971. *According to Our Ancestors: Folk Texts from Guatemala and Honduras.* Norman: Summer Institute of Linguistics of the University of Oklahoma.

Siméon, Rémi. 1963. *Dictionnaire de la langue nahuatl ou mexicaine.* Graz, Austria: Akademische Druck- & Verlagsanstalt. Reprint of 1885 ed.

Smith, C. C. 1972. "On the Ethos of the 'Romancero viejo.'" In *Studies of the Spanish and Portuguese Ballad,* ed. N. D. Shergold, pp. 5–24. London: Tamesis Books.

Sousa, Lisa, Stafford Poole, and James Lockhart, eds. 1998. *The Story of Guadalupe: Luis Laso de la Vega's* Huei tlamahuiçoltica *of 1649.* Stanford and Los Angeles: Stanford University Press/UCLA Latin American Center.

Sullivan, Thelma D. 1974. "The Rhetorical Orations, or *Huehuetlatolli*, Collected by Sahagún." In *Sixteenth-Century Mexico: The Work of Sahagún*, ed. Munro S. Edmonson, pp. 79–109. Albuquerque: School of American Research/University of New Mexico Press.

Taggart, James M. 1983. *Nahuat Myth and Social Structure*. Austin: University of Texas Press.

Telleriano-Remensis. See *Códice Telleriano-Remensis*.

Tezozomoc, Fernando Alvarado. 1949. *Crónica mexicáyotl*. Trans. Adrián León. Mexico City: Universidad Nacional Autónoma de México. Note: The *Crónica mexicáyotl* is now attributed to Chimalpahin: see ACHIM vol. 1.

———. 1975. *Crónica mexicana*. Ed. Manuel Orozco y Berra. Mexico City: Porrúa. Reprint of 1878 ed.

Thomas, Hugh. 1993. *Conquest: Montezuma, Cortés, and the Fall of Old Mexico*. New York: Simon & Schuster.

Torquemada, Juan de. 1975. *Monarquía indiana*. 3 vols. Mexico City: Porrúa. Reprint of 1723 ed.

Trigger, Bruce G. 1991. "Distinguished Lecture in Archeology." *American Anthropologist* 93:551–69.

Velázquez, Primo Feliciano. 1926. *Huei tlamahuiçoltica [omonexiti in ilhvicac tlatocacihvapilli Santa Maria totlaçonantzin Gvadalvpe in nican hvei altepenahvac Mexico itocayocan Tepeyacac]: Libro en lengua mexicana que el Br. Luis Lasso de la Vega hizo imprimir en México el año de 1649*. Mexico City: Carreño & Hijo. Includes facsimile of the 1649 ed.

Verrill, A. Hyatt. 1929. *Old Civilizations of the New World*. Indianapolis: Bobbs-Merrill.

Wood, Stephanie. 2003. *Transcending Conquest: Nahua Views of Spanish Colonial Mexico*. Norman: University of Oklahoma Press.

Wright, Elizabeth R. 2008. "From the Mexican Mission to the Madrid Stage: A History of Spain's Popular Theater as Told from across the Atlantic." In Sell, Wright, and Burkhart 2008.

Zimmermann, Günter. 1965. *Die Relationen Chimalpahin's zur Geschichte México's*. 2 parts (Universität Hamburg, Abhandlungen aus dem Gebiet der Auslandskunde, vols. 68–69; series B, vols. 38–39). Part 1: *Die Zeit bis zur Conquista 1521*. Part 2: *Das Jahrhundert nach der Conquista (1522–1615)*. Hamburg: Cram, De Gruyter & Co.

Index

All proper nouns in song texts are entered in the Concordance to Proper Nouns, p. 189; and most common nouns in song texts, with locations, are in the Guide to Vocabulary, p. 71.

www.ingramcontent.com/pod-product-compliance
Ingram Content Group UK Ltd.
Pitfield, Milton Keynes, MK11 3LW, UK
UKHW032055180225
455276UK00001B/73